PRAISE FOR SYD FIELD

"[Syd Field is] the most sought-after screenwriting teacher in the world."—*Hollywood Reporter*

"Syd Field is the preeminent analyzer in the study of American screenplays."
—JAMES L. BROOKS, Academy Award–winning writer, director, producer

"I based *Like Water for Chocolate* on what I learned in Syd's books. Before, I always felt structure imprisoned me, but what I learned was structure really freed me to focus on the story."
—LAURA ESQUIVEL, writer, *Like Water for Chocolate*

"If I were writing screenplays ... I would carry Syd Field around in my back pocket wherever I went."
—STEVEN BOCHCO, writer/producer/director, *NYPD Blue*

"Syd Field's book[s] have been the Bible and Talmud for a generation of budding screenwriters."—Salon.com

SCREENPLAY:
The Foundations of Screenwriting

"*Screenplay* is one of the bibles of the film trade and has launched many a would-be screenwriter on the road to Hollywood."—*Library Journal*

"[Syd Field is the] guru of would-be screenwriters.... *Screenplay* is their bestselling bible."—*Los Angeles Herald Examiner*

"Full of common sense, an uncommon commodity."—*Esquire*

"Quite simply the *only* manual to be taken seriously by aspiring screenwriters."—TONY BILL, Academy Award–winning producer, director

"Impressive because of its rare combinations: a technical book, apparently mechanically sound, that's quite personable and lively and also seems to care about us, about our doing things right and making good. His easy-to-follow, step-by-step approaches are comforting and his emphasis on right attitude and motivation is uplifting."
—*Los Angeles Times Book Review*

"A much-needed book."
> —FRANK PIERSON, Academy Award–winning screenwriter;
> president, Writers Guild of America, West

"The basics of the craft in terms simple enough to enable any beginner to develop an idea into a submittable script."—*American Cinematographer*

"A much-needed book ... straightforward and informed ... accurate and clear, and should be enormously helpful to novices."—*Fade-In*

"The complete primer, a step-by-step guide from the first glimmer of an idea to marketing the finished script."—*New West*

"Experienced advice on story development, creation and definition of characters, structure of action, and direction of participants. Easy-to-follow guidelines and a commonsense approach mark this highly useful manual."—*Video*

"Great advice for screenwriters. I always tell young writers to pick up *Screenplay* and read it right away—then either embrace it or rebel against it, but it'll certainly get your mind turning in the right ways."
> —DAVID KOEPP, award-winning writer, director,
> *Spider-Man, Secret Window, War of the Worlds*

THE SCREENWRITER'S WORKBOOK:
Exercises and Step-by-Step Instruction for Creating
a Successful Screenplay

"One of the standards in the industry."—Amazon.com

SELLING A SCREENPLAY:
The Screenwriter's Guide to Hollywood

"A wonderful book that should be in every filmmaker's library."
> —HOWARD KAZANJIAN, producer, *Raiders of the Lost Ark,*
> *Return of the Jedi, Demolition Man*

"An informative, engaging look at the inside of the dream factory. This is a terrific aid for screenwriters who are trying to gain insight into the Hollywood system."
> —DAVID KIRKPATRICK, producer, former head of Paramount Pictures

FOUR SCREENPLAYS:
Studies in American Screenplay

"A book that writers will stand in line for and studio executives will Xerox."
  —JAMES L. BROOKS, Academy Award–winning writer, director, producer

"What does it take to write a great script? You'll find the answer here. . . . This is Field's masterpiece and a required purchase for all film collections."—*Library Journal*

"A first-rate analysis of why good screenplays work: a virtual must for aspiring screenwriters."
                    —LINDA OBST, producer, *How to Lose a Guy in Ten Days,*
                                                    Sleepless in Seattle

"A fascinating view into the most overlooked process of filmmaking."
                    —MICHAEL BESMAN, producer, *About Schmidt*

"Theory comes alive with this hands-on approach to what makes four great screenplays tick."
                    —DEBORAH JELIN NEWMYER, producer, executive vice president,
                                                    Amblin Entertainment

"*Four Screenplays* is not only Syd Field's most instructive book . . . it's the most fun to read."
                    —ANNA HAMILTON PHELAN, screenwriter, *Girl, Interrupted*

"One of the very best books I have read on movies or screenplays. Syd writes both with passion and an astute understanding."
                    —HANS ZIMMER, film composer, *Gladiator,*
                                        The Last Samurai, Thelma & Louise

THE SCREENWRITER'S PROBLEM SOLVER:
How to Recognize, Identify, and Define Screenwriting Problems

"Whatever your problem, screenwriting guru Syd Field can help."
                                                    —Amazon.com

GOING TO THE MOVIES:
A Personal Journey Through Four Decades of Modern Film

"The master teacher of screenplay writing ... reveals himself to be a true Hollywood character. No one sees films quite the way Field does.... An original thinker worth appreciating."—*Kirkus Reviews*

"Although cloaked in modesty, his illuminating, consistently entertaining memoir displays enough wit, intelligence and empathy to inspire a host of great films."—*Publishers Weekly*

"Syd Field knows movies inside and out, and this, his most personal book yet, is charming, warmhearted, and very wise. Grab some popcorn, sit back and share some big-screen magic with the master."
—TED TALLY, Academy Award–winning screenwriter,
The Silence of the Lambs

"What really makes this book is how well he conducts us on his journey ... [and] his true love for the movies."—*Booklist*

"Those of us who've wondered why Syd would devote himself to raising the bar for screenwriting now learn why—a lifelong and passionate love for movies and filmmaking."
—MARC NORMAN, Academy Award–winning screenwriter,
Shakespeare in Love

"A fascinating journey through thirty years of moviegoing—asking the question we all ask: 'What makes a movie work?' and finding the answers."
—FAY KANIN, former president,
Academy of Motion Picture Arts and Sciences

"Field forges new pathways into understanding the transforming powers of the screenplay. In this insightful testament to film craft, Field's influence on generations of film devotees represents a climate of opinion, respected and imitated. Nothing is more rare."
—JAMES RAGAN, director, Professional Writing Program,
University of Southern California

"Field's passion for cinema shines throughout."—*Library Journal*

"Syd Field has spent a lifetime seeking answers to what makes a great movie. Now he shares his own remarkable story about the movies and the legendary filmmakers who inspired his extraordinary career."—*Variety*

SYD FIELD

NPLAY

THE FOUNDATIONS OF SCREENWRITING

REVISED EDITION

Delta
Trade Paperbacks

SCREENPLAY
A Delta Book

PUBLISHING HISTORY
Dell Trade Paperback edition published July 1984
Delta trade paperback revised edition / December 2005

Published by Bantam Dell
A Division of Random House, Inc.
New York, New York

Book design by Sabrina Bowers

LIBRARY OF CONGRESS CATALOGING-IN-PUBLICATION DATA
Field, Syd.
Screenplay : the foundations of screenwriting / by Syd Field.
p.   cm.
ISBN-13: 978-0-385-33903-2
ISBN-10: 0-385-33903-8
1. Motion picture authorship.   I. Title.
PN1996 .F43 2005
808.2'3 22   2005048491

*To all those who went before
and to all those who follow . . .
and
To the great Siddha Saints and Masters
who lit the flame and keep the fire burning . . .*

A SPECIAL THANKS

To the extraordinarily gifted screenwriters Robert Towne, James Cameron, David Koepp, and Stuart Beattie; to Marc Heims at DreamWorks; to Sterling Lord and Shannon Jamieson Vazquez, who ran the rapids with me on this; and to all the people in Landmark Education who gave me the space, the opportunity, and the support to grow and expand enough to write this book.

And of course, to Aviva, who shares the light of this path with me.

Contents

Introduction

"The book says that we may be through with
the past, but the past may not be through
with us."

—*Magnolia*
Paul Thomas Anderson

In 1979, when I first wrote *Screenplay: The Foundations of Screenwriting,* there were only a few books on the market that dealt with the art and craft of screenwriting. The most popular was Lagos Egri's *The Art of Dramatic Writing,* first published in the 1940s. Though it was not really a book about screenwriting, but playwriting, the principles laid out were precise and clear. At that time, there was no real distinction made between the crafts of writing for the stage and writing for the screen.

Screenplay changed all that. It laid out the principles of dramatic structure to establish the foundations of screenwriting. It was also the first book to use well-known and popular movies of the time to illustrate the craft of writing for the screen. And, as we all know, screenwriting is a craft that occasionally rises to the level of art.

When it was first published, it became an immediate best seller, or "an instant sensation," as my publisher labeled it. Within the first few months of publication it went through several printings and became a "hot" topic of discussion. Everyone, it seemed, was surprised by its meteoric success.

Except me. During my teaching and lecturing on screenwriting in the 1970s at Sherwood Oaks Experimental College in Hollywood, I saw people from all walks of life burning with an incredible desire to write screenplays. Hundreds of people flowed thorough my course on screenwriting, and it soon became clear that everyone had a story to tell. They just didn't know how to tell it.

Since that day in the early spring of 1979 when *Screenplay* first arrived on bookstore shelves, there has been a tremendous upsurge in the evolution of writing for the screen. Today, the popularity of screenwriting and filmmaking is an integral part of our culture and cannot be ignored. Walk into any bookstore and you'll see shelves and shelves devoted to all aspects of filmmaking. In fact, the two most popular majors on college campuses are business and film. And with the dramatic rise of computer technology and computer graphic imagery, the expanded influence of MTV, reality TV, Xbox, PlayStation, and new wireless LAN technology, and the enormous increase in film festivals both here and abroad, we're in the middle of a cinematic revolution. It won't be too long before we make a short film on our telephones, e-mail them to our friends, and project them on our TV. Clearly, we have evolved in the way we *see* things.

Take a look at the epic adventure *Lord of the Rings* (all three parts), or the portrait of the modern family illustrated in *American Beauty,* or the emotional and visual impact of *Seabiscuit,* or the literary presentations of *The Bourne Supremacy, Cold Mountain, Memento, Rushmore, Magnolia, The Royal Tenenbaums,* or *Eternal Sunshine of the Spotless Mind,* compare them to any films of the '70s or '80s, and you'll see the distinctions of this revolution: the images are fast; the information conveyed is visual, rapid; the use of silence is exaggerated; and the special effects and music are heightened and more pronounced. The concept of time is often more subjective and nonlinear, more novelistic in tone and execution. Yet, while the tools and technique of storytelling have evolved and progressed based on the needs and technologies of the time, the art of story-telling has remained the same.

Movies are a combination of art and science; the technological revolution has literally changed the way we *see* movies and there-fore, by necessity, has changed the way we *write* movies. But no mat-ter what changes are made in the execution of the material, the nature of the screenplay is the same as it has always been: A screen-play is *a story told with pictures, in dialogue and description, and placed within the context of dramatic structure.* That's what it is; that is its nature. It is the art of visual storytelling.

The craft of screenwriting is a creative process that can be learned. To tell a story, you have to *set up* your characters, introduce the *dramatic premise* (what the story is about) and the *dramatic situation* (the circumstances surrounding the action), create obstacles for your characters to *confront* and overcome, then *resolve* the story. You know, boy meets girl, boy gets girl, boy loses girl. All stories, from Aristotle through all the constellations of civilization, embody the same dramatic principles.

In *Lord of the Rings: The Fellowship of the Ring,* Frodo becomes the ring bearer to return the ring to its place of origin, Mount Doom, so he can destroy it. That is his dramatic need. How he gets there and completes the task is the story. *Lord of the Rings: The Fellowship of the Ring* sets up the characters and situation and narrative through line; it establishes Frodo and the Shire, as well as the Fellowship, who set off on their mission to Mount Doom. Part II, *The Two Towers,* dramatizes the obstacles Frodo, Sam, and the Fellowship confront on their journey to destroy the ring. They are confronted with obstacle after obstacle that hinder their mission. At the same time, Aragorn and the others must overcome many challenges to defeat the Orcs at Helms Deep. And Part III, *The Return of the King,* resolves the story: Frodo and Sam reach Mount Doom and watch as the ring and the Gollum fall into the fires and are destroyed. Aragorn is crowned king, and the hobbits return to the Shire and their life plays out.

Set-up, confrontation, and resolution.

It is the stuff of drama. I learned this when I was a kid sitting in a darkened theater, popcorn in hand, gazing in awe and wonder at the images projected on the white river of light reflected on that monster screen.

A native of Los Angeles (my grandfather arrived here from Poland in 1907), I grew up surrounded by the film industry. When I was about ten, as a member of the Sheriff's Boys' Band, I was cast in Frank Capra's *The State of the Union,* starring Spencer Tracy and Katharine Hepburn. I don't remember much about the experience except that Van Johnson taught me how to play checkers.

On Saturday afternoons, my friends and I used to sneak into the neighborhood theater and watch the serials of *Flash Gordon* and *Buck Rogers*. During my teens, going to the movies became a passion, a form of entertainment, a distraction, and a topic of discussion, as well as a place to make out and have fun. Occasionally, there would be unforgettable moments—like watching Bogart and Bacall in *To Have and Have Not*, or Walter Huston's mad dance as he discovered gold in the mountains in *The Treasure of the Sierra Madre*, or watching Brando stagger up the gangplank at the end of *On the Waterfront*.

I attended Hollywood High School and was invited to join the Athenians, one of the many clubs whose members hung out together during high school. A short time after graduation, one of my best friends, Frank Mazzola, also a member of the Athenians, met James Dean and formed a strong relationship with him. Frank introduced Dean to what a high school "club" was like during this period (by today's standards it would probably be referred to as a gang). Director Nicholas Ray and James Dean chose Frank to be the "gang" consultant in *Rebel Without a Cause* and to play the part of Crunch in the movie, so the Athenians became the model of the club/gang in *Rebel Without a Cause*. Occasionally Dean would come with us when we strolled down Hollywood Boulevard on a Saturday night looking for trouble. We were the so-called tough kids, never backing down from anything, whether it was a dare or a fight. We managed to get into a lot of trouble.

Dean loved hearing about our "adventures" and would continually pump us for details. When we pulled some wild stunt, whatever it was, he wanted to know how it started, what we were thinking, how it felt. Actors' questions.

It was only after *Rebel Without a Cause* was released and stormed the world that I became aware of how significant our contribution to the movie had been. The irony of Dean's having hung out with us during that period had no real effect on me until after he died; only then, when he became an icon of our generation, did I begin to grasp the significance of what we had contributed.

It was Mazzola who convinced me to take an acting class, which ultimately transformed my life; it was one of those moments that impact a series of other moments and led me to the path I'm still following to this day. My family—aunts and uncles (my parents had died several years earlier)—wanted me to be a "professional person," meaning a doctor, lawyer, or dentist. I had been working part-time at Mount Sinai Hospital and I liked the drama and pace of emergency room medicine, so I entertained thoughts about becoming a doctor. I enrolled at the University of California, packed up the few belongings I had, and drove to Berkeley. It was August 1959.

Berkeley at the dawn of the '60s was an active crucible of revolt and unrest; banners, slogans, and leaflets were everywhere. Castro's rebel force had just overthrown Batista, and signs were everywhere, ranging from "Cuba Libre" and "Time for the Revolution" to "Free Speech," "Abolish ROTC," "Equal Rights for Everyone," and "Socialism for All, & All for Socialism." Telegraph Avenue, the main street leading onto campus, was always lined with a colorful display of banners and leaflets. Protest rallies were held almost every day, and when I'd stop to listen, FBI agents, trying to be inconspicuous in their shirts and ties, would be taking pictures of everyone. It was a joke.

It didn't take long for me to be swept up in the activities personifying the fervid issues of the time. Like so many others of my generation, I was influenced and inspired by the "beats"—Kerouac, Ginsberg, Gregory Corso: the poet/saints who were blazing a trail of rebellion and revolution. Inspired by their voices and their lives, I, too, wanted to ride the waves of change. It wasn't too long before the campus exploded into a political frenzy initiated by Mario Savio and the Free Speech Movement.

It was during my second semester at Berkeley that I auditioned for, and was cast as, Woyzeck in the German Expressionist drama *Woyzeck*, by Georg Büchner. It was while I was performing *Woyzeck* that I met the great French film director Jean Renoir.

My relationship with Renoir literally changed my life. I've learned there are two or three times during a lifetime when something happens that alters the course of that life. We meet someone, go somewhere, or do something we've never done before, and those moments are the possibilities that guide us to where we're supposed to go and what we're supposed to do with our lives.

People say I was extremely fortunate to be working with Renoir, that it was a chance and fortuitous accident of being in the right place at the right time. That's true. But over the years, I've learned not to believe too much in luck or accidents; I think everything happens for a reason. There's something to be learned from every moment, every experience we encounter during the brief time we spend on this planet. Call it fate, call it destiny, call it what you will; it really doesn't matter.

I auditioned for the world premiere of Renoir's play *Carola*, and was cast in the third lead, playing the part of Campan, the stage manager of a theater in Paris during the Nazi occupation in the last days of World War II. For almost a year, I sat at Renoir's feet, watching and learning about movies through his eyes. He was always commenting on film, his opinions vocal and fervent about everything he saw or wrote, either as an artist, a person, or a humanitarian. And he was all of these. Being in his presence was an inspiration, a major life lesson, a joy, a privilege, as well as a great learning experience. Though movies had always been a major part of my life, it was only during the time I spent with Renoir that I turned my focus to film, the same way a plant turns toward the sun. Suddenly, I saw movies in a whole new light, as an art form to study and learn, seeking in the story and images an expression and understanding of life. My love for the movies has fed and nourished me ever since.

"*Qu'est-ce que le cinéma?*" is the question Renoir always used to ask before he showed us one of his films. "*What is film?*" He used to say movies are more than mere flashing images on the screen: "They are an art form that becomes larger than life." What can I say about Jean Renoir? He was a man like any other, but what separated him, at least in my mind, was his great heart; he was open, friendly, a man of great intelligence, wisdom, and wit who seemed to influence the lives of everyone he touched. The son of the great Impressionistic painter Pierre-Auguste Renoir, Jean, too, had the great gift of sight. Renoir taught me about film, mentored me in the art of visually telling a story, and imparted the gift of insight. He showed me the door, then held it open as I walked through. I've never looked back.

Renoir hated the cliché. He would quote his father about bringing an idea into existence. "If you paint the leaf on a tree without using a model," Renoir told us the great Impressionistic painter once said, "your imagination will only supply you with a few leaves; but Nature offers you millions, all on the same tree. No two leaves are exactly the same. The artist who paints only what is in his mind must very soon repeat himself." If you look at Renoir's great paintings, you'll see what he meant. No two leaves, no two flowers, no two people are ever painted in the same way. It's the same with his son's films: *Grand Illusion*, *Rules of the Game* (considered two of the greatest films ever made), *The Golden Coach*, *Picnic on the Grass*, and many more. Renoir told me he "painted with light," the same way his father painted with oils. Jean Renoir was an artist who discovered the cinema in the same way his father "discovered" Impressionism. "Art," he said, "should offer the viewer the chance of merging with the creator."

Sitting in a movie theater watching those flickering images flutter across the screen is like witnessing the vast range of human experience: from the opening sequence of *The Lord of the Rings: The Fellowship of the Ring* to *The Royal Tenenbaums;* from *The Matrix* to *Close Encounters of the Third Kind;* from the first few shots of *Bridge on the River Kwai* to capturing the scope of human history as a wooden club thrown into the air merges into a spacecraft in Stanley Kubrick's *2001*. Thousands of years and the evolution of humankind condensed into the poetry of two pieces of film; it is a moment of magic and wonder, mystery and awe. Such is the power of film.

For the past few decades, as I've traveled and lectured around the world on the art and craft of screenwriting, I have watched the style of screenwriting evolve into a more visual medium. As I mentioned, we're seeing certain techniques of the novel, like stream of consciousness and chapter headings, beginning to seep into the modern screenplay. (*Kill Bill I* and *II, The Hours, The Royal Tenenbaums, American Beauty, The Bourne Supremacy, The Manchurian Candidate,* and *Cold Mountain* are just a few examples.) It's clear that a whole new computer-savvy generation, who grew up with interactive software, digital storytelling, and editing applications sees things in a more visual way and is thus able to express it in a more cinematic style.

But when all is said and done, the principles of screenwriting don't change; they are the same no matter in what time or place or era we live. Great films are timeless—they embody and capture the times in which they were made; the human condition is the same now as it was then.

My purpose in writing *Screenplay* was to explore the craft of screenwriting and illustrate the foundations of dramatic structure. When you want to write a screenplay, there are two aspects you have to deal with. One is the preparation required to write it: the research, thinking time, character work, and laying out of the structural dynamic. The other is the execution, the actual writing of it, laying out the visual images and capturing the dialogue. *The hardest thing about writing is knowing what to write.* That was true when I first wrote the book, and it is now.

This is not a "how-to" book; I can't teach anybody *how to write* a screenplay. People teach themselves the craft of screenwriting. All I can do is show them *what* they have to do to write a successful screenplay. So, I call this a *what-to* book, meaning if you have an idea for a screenplay, and you don't know what to do or how to do it, I can show you.

As a writer-producer for David L. Wolper Productions, a freelance screenwriter, and head of the story department at Cinemobile Systems, I have spent years writing and reading screenplays. At Cinemobile alone, I read and synopsized more than two thousand screenplays in a little over two years. And of all those two thousand screenplays, I only found forty to submit to our financial partners for possible film production.

Why so few? Because ninety-nine out of a hundred screenplays I read weren't good enough to invest millions of dollars in. Put another way, only one out of a hundred screenplays I read was good enough to consider for film production. And at Cinemobile, our job was making movies. In one year alone, we were directly involved in the production of some 119 motion pictures, ranging from *The Godfather* to *Jeremiah Johnson* to *Deliverance* to *Alice Doesn't Live Here Anymore* to *American Graffiti*.

At that time, in the early '70s, Cinemobile was a portable location facility that literally revolutionized film production. Filmmakers no longer had to rely on a supply caravan to carry cast, crew, and equipment to whatever location they were using. Basically, the Cinemobile was a Greyhound bus with an eight-wheel-drive, so we could store equipment in the luggage area, then transport cast and crew to the top of a mountain, shoot three to eight pages of script each day, and return home. My boss, Fouad Said, the creator of the Cinemobile, became so successful that he decided to make his own movies, so he went out and raised several million dollars in a few weeks, with a revolving fund of many million more, if needed. Pretty soon everybody in Hollywood was sending him screenplays. Thousands of scripts came in, from stars and directors, from studios and producers, from the known and the unknown.

That's when I was given the opportunity to read the submitted screenplays and evaluate them in terms of cost, quality, and probable budget. My job, as I was constantly reminded, was to "find material" for our three financial partners: the United Artists Theatre Group; the Hemdale Film Distribution Company, headquartered in London; and the Taft Broadcasting Company, parent company of Cinemobile.

So I began reading screenplays. As a screenwriter taking a much-needed break from more than seven years of freelance writing (I had written nine screenplays: two were produced, four were optioned, and three nothing ever happened with), my job at Cinemobile gave me a totally new perspective on writing a screenplay. It was a tremendous opportunity, a formidable challenge, and a dynamic learning experience.

I kept asking myself what made the screenplays I recommended better than the others. At first I didn't have any answers, but I held it in my consciousness and thought about it a long time.

Every morning, when I arrived at work, there would be a stack of screenplays on my desk, waiting. No matter what I did, no matter how fast I read or how many scripts I skimmed, skipped, or tossed, one solid fact always remained: The size of the pile never changed. I knew I could never get through the pile.

Reading a screenplay is a unique experience. It's not like reading a novel, play, or article in the Sunday paper. When I first started reading, I read the words on the page slowly, drinking in all the visual descriptions, character nuances, and dramatic situations. But that didn't work for me. I found it too easy to get caught up in the writer's words and style. I learned that most of the scripts that read well—meaning they featured lovely sentences, stylish and literate prose, and beautiful dialogue—usually didn't work. While they might read like liquid honey flowing across the page, the overall feeling was that of reading a short story or a strong journalistic piece in a magazine like *Vanity Fair* or *Esquire*. But that's not what makes a good screenplay.

I started out wanting to read and "do coverage" on—synopsize—three screenplays a day. I found I could read two scripts without a problem, but when I got to the third, the words, characters, and actions all seemed to congeal into some kind of amorphous goo of plotlines concerning the FBI and CIA, punctuated with bank heists, murders, and car chases, with a lot of wet kisses and naked flesh thrown in for local color. At two or three in the afternoon, after a heavy lunch and maybe a little too much wine, it was difficult to keep my attention focused on the action or nuances of character and story. So, after a few months on the job, I usually found myself closing my office door, propping my feet up on the desk, turning off the phones, leaning back in the chair with a script on my chest, and taking a catnap.

I must have read more than a hundred screenplays before I realized that I didn't know what I was doing. What was I looking for? What made a screenplay good or bad? I could tell whether I liked it or not, yes, but what were the elements that made it a good screenplay? It had to be more than a string of clever bits and smart dialogue laced together in a series of beautiful pictures. Was it the plot, the characters, or the visual arena where the action took place that made it a good screenplay? Was it the visual style of writing or the cleverness of the dialogue? If I didn't know the answers to that, then how could I answer the question I was repeatedly being asked by agents, writers, producers, and directors: What was I looking for? That's when I understood that the real question for me was, How do I read a screenplay? I knew how to write a screenplay, and I certainly knew what I liked or disliked when I went to the movies, but how did I apply that to the reading of a screenplay?

The more I thought about it, the clearer I became. What I was looking for, I soon realized, was a style that exploded off the page, exhibiting the kind of raw energy found in scripts like *Chinatown, Taxi Driver, The Godfather,* and *American Graffiti.* As the stack of scripts on my desk grew higher and higher, I felt very much like Jay Gatsby at the end of *The Great Gatsby,* F. Scott Fitzgerald's classic novel. At the end of the book, Nick, the narrator, recalls how Gatsby used to stand looking out over the water at the image of the green light, beckoning him to past memories of unrequited love. Gatsby was a man who believed in the past, a man who believed that if he had enough wealth and power, he could turn back time and re-create it. It was that dream that spurred him as a young man to cross over the tracks, searching for love and wealth, searching for the expectations and desires of the past that he hoped would become the future.

The green light.

I thought a lot about Gatsby and the green light as I struggled through those piles of screenplays searching for "the good read," that special and unique screenplay that would be "the one" to make it through the gauntlet of studios, executives, stars, financial wizards, and egos and finally end up on that monster screen in a darkened theater.

It was just about that time that I was given the opportunity to teach a screenwriting class at the Sherwood Oaks Experimental College in Hollywood. At that time in the '70s, Sherwood Oaks was a professional school taught by professionals. It was the kind of school where Paul Newman, Dustin Hoffman, and Lucille Ball gave acting seminars; where Tony Bill taught a producing seminar; where Martin Scorsese, Robert Altman, and Alan Pakula gave directing seminars; where John Alonzo and Vilmos Zsigmond, two of the finest cinematographers in the world, taught classes in cinematography. It was a school where producers, professional production managers, cameramen, film editors, writers, directors, and script supervisors all came to teach their craft. It was the most unique film school in the country.

I had never taught a screenwriting class before, so I had to delve into my own writing and reading experience to evolve my basic material.

What is a good screenplay? I kept asking myself. And pretty soon I started getting some answers. When you read a good screenplay, you know it—it's evident from page one, word one. The style, the way the words are laid out on the page, the way the story is set up, the grasp of dramatic situation, the introduction of the main character, the basic premise or problem of the screenplay—it's all set up in the first few pages of the script: *Chinatown, Five Easy Pieces, The Godfather, The French Connection, Shampoo,* and *All the President's Men* are all perfect examples.

A screenplay, I soon realized, is a story told with pictures. It's like a *noun;* it has a subject, and is usually about a *person,* or persons, in a *place,* or places, doing his, or her, or their *"thing."* The *person* is the main character and *doing his/her thing* is the action. Out of that understanding, I saw that any good screenplay has certain conceptual components common to the screenplay form.

These elements are expressed dramatically within a structure that has a definite beginning, middle, and end, though not necessarily in that order. When I reexamined the forty screenplays submitted to our financial partners—including *The Godfather, American Graffiti, The Wind and the Lion, Alice Doesn't Live Here Anymore,* and others—I realized they all contained these basic concepts, regardless of how they were cinematically executed.

I began teaching this conceptual approach to writing the screenplay. If the aspiring writer knows what a screenplay is, *what it looks like,* I reasoned, it can be used as a guide or blueprint to point out the path through the forest.

I've now been teaching this approach to screenwriting for over twenty-five years. It's an effective and comprehensive approach to the writing of a screenplay and the art of visual storytelling. My material has evolved and been applied by thousands and thousands of students all over the world. The principles in this book have been totally embraced by the film industry. It's not uncommon for major film studios and production companies to contractually stipulate that a delivered screenplay must have a definite three-act structure and be no longer than 2 hours and 8 minutes, or 128 pages, in length. (There are always exceptions, of course.)

Many of my students have been very successful: Anna Hamilton

Phelan wrote *Mask* in my workshop, then went on to write *Gorillas in the Mist;* Laura Esquivel wrote *Like Water for Chocolate;* Carmen Culver wrote *The Thorn Birds;* Janus Cercone wrote *Leap of Faith;* Linda Elstad won the prestigious Humanitas Award for *Divorce Wars;* and such prestigious filmmakers as James Cameron *(Terminator* and *Terminator 2: Judgment Day, Titanic),* Ted Tally *(The Silence of the Lambs, The Juror),* Alfonso and Carlos Cuarón *(Y Tu Mamá También, Harry Potter and the Prisoner of Azkaban),* Ken Nolan *(Black Hawk Down),* David O. Russell *(Three Kings, I Heart Huckabees),* and Tina Fey *(Mean Girls),* to name just a few, used the material when they began their screenwriting careers.

At this writing, *Screenplay* has been reprinted nearly 40 times, gone through several editions, and been translated into some 22 languages, along with several black market editions: first in Iran, then in China, then Russia.

When I began thinking about revising this book, I quickly realized that most of the films I had written about were from the '70s and that I wanted to use more contemporary examples, movies people might be more familiar with. But as I went back into the book and saw the film examples I had originally used, I realized that most of them are now considered classics of the American cinema—films like *Chinatown, Harold and Maude, Network, Three Days of the Condor,* and others. These films still hold up, on both an entertainment and a teaching level. In most cases, the films are as valid today as they were when they were made. Despite having some dated attitudes, they continue to capture a particular moment in time, a time of unrest, social revolution, and violence that mirrors some of the antiwar sentiments prevalent today. The nightmare in Iraq is very similar to the nightmare in Vietnam. What I see and understand now, in hindsight, is that the principles of screenwriting that I delineated at the dawn of the '80s are just as relevant now as they were then. Only the expression has changed.

This material is designed for everyone. Novelists, playwrights, magazine editors, housewives, businessmen, doctors, actors, film editors, commercial directors, secretaries, advertising executives, and university professors—all have benefited from it.

My intention in this book is to enable you to sit down and write a screenplay from the position of choice, confidence, and security that you know what you're doing. As I said earlier, *the hardest thing about writing is knowing what to write.* When you complete this book, you will know exactly *what* to do to write a professional screenplay. Whether you do it or not is up to you.

Talent is God's gift; either you've got it or you don't. But writing is a personal responsibility; either you do it or you don't.

What Is a Screenplay?

"Suppose you're in your office.... A pretty stenographer you've seen before comes into the room and you watch her.... She takes off her gloves, opens her purse and dumps it out on the table.... She has two dimes and a nickel—and a cardboard match box. She leaves the nickel on the desk, puts the two dimes back into her purse and takes her black gloves to the stove.... Just then your telephone rings. The girl picks it up, says hello—listens—and says deliberately into the phone, "I've never owned a pair of black gloves in my life." She hangs up ... and you glance around very suddenly and see another man in the office, watching every move the girl makes...."

"Go on," said Boxley smiling. "What happens?"

"I don't know," said Stahr. "I was just making pictures."

> —*The Last Tycoon*
> F. Scott Fitzgerald

In the summer of 1937, F. Scott Fitzgerald, drinking far too much, deeply in debt, and drowning in the suffocating well of despair, moved to Hollywood seeking new beginnings, hoping to reinvent himself by writing for the movies. The author of *The Great Gatsby, Tender Is the Night, This Side of Paradise,* and the uncompleted *The Last Tycoon,* perhaps America's greatest novelist, was, as one friend put it, seeking redemption.

During the two and a half years he spent in Hollywood, he took the craft of screenwriting "very seriously," says one noted Fitzgerald authority: "It's heartbreaking to see how much effort he put into it." Fitzgerald approached every screenplay as if it were a novel and often wrote long backstories for each of the main characters before putting one word of dialogue down on paper.

Despite all the preparation he put into each assignment, he was obsessed with finding the answer to a question that haunted him continuously: *What makes a good screenplay?* Billy Wilder once compared Fitzgerald to "a great sculptor who is hired to do a plumbing job. He did not know how to connect the pipes so the water could flow."

Throughout his Hollywood years, he was always trying to find the "balance" between the words spoken and the pictures seen. During this time, he received only one screen credit, adapting the novel *Three Comrades* by Erich Maria Remarque (starring Robert Taylor and Margaret Sullavan), but Joseph L. Mankiewicz eventually rewrote his script. He worked on rewrites for several other movies, including a disastrous week on *Gone With the Wind* (he was forbidden to use any words that did not appear in Margaret Mitchell's novel), but after *Three Comrades*, all of his projects ended in failure. One, a script for Joan Crawford called *Infidelity*, was left uncompleted, canceled because it dealt with the theme of adultery. Fitzgerald died in 1941, working on his last, unfinished novel, *The Last Tycoon*.

He died believing himself to be a failure.

I've always been intrigued by the journey of F. Scott Fitzgerald. What resonates with me the most is that he was constantly searching for *the answer* to what made a good screenplay. His overwhelming external circumstances—his wife Zelda's institutionalization, his unmanageable debts and lifestyle, his excessive drinking—all fed into his insecurities about the craft of screenwriting. And make no mistake: Screenwriting is a craft, a craft that can be learned. Even though he worked excessively hard, and was disciplined and responsible, he failed to achieve the results he was so desperately striving for.

Why?

I don't think there's any one answer. But reading his books and writings and letters from this period, it seems clear that he was never exactly sure what a screenplay *was;* he always wondered whether he was "doing it right," whether there were certain rules he had to follow in order to write a successful screenplay.

When I was studying at the University of California, Berkeley, as an English lit major, I read the first and second editions of *Tender Is the Night* for one of my classes. It is the story of a psychiatrist who marries one of his patients, who, as she slowly recovers, exhausts his vitality until he is "a man used up." The book, the last one Fitzgerald completed, was considered technically faulty and was commercially unsuccessful.

In the first edition of the novel, Book I is written from the point of view of Rosemary Hoyt, a young actress who shares her observations about meeting the circle that surrounds Dick and Nicole Diver. Rosemary is on the beach at Cap d'Antibes on the French Riviera, watching the Divers enjoying an outing on the sand. As she watches, she sees them as a beautiful couple who appear, at least from her point of view, to have everything going for them. They are, she thinks, the ideal couple. Rich, beautiful, intelligent, they look to be the embodiment of what everyone wants for himself or herself. But the second book of the novel focuses on the life of Dick and Nicole, and we learn that what we saw through Rosemary's eyes was only the relationship they showed to the world; it was not really true. The Divers have major problems, which drain them emotionally and spiritually, and ultimately destroy them.

When the first edition of *Tender Is the Night* was published, sales were poor, and Fitzgerald thought he had probably been drinking too much and might have compromised his vision. But from his Hollywood experience, he came to believe he did not introduce his main characters early enough. "Its great fault," Fitzgerald wrote of *Tender Is the Night* to his editor, Maxwell Perkins, "is that the *true* beginning—the young psychiatrist in Switzerland—is tucked away in the middle of the book." He decided that when the second edition was printed, he would interchange the first section with the second and open the novel with Dick Diver in wartime Switzerland in order to explain the mystery about the Divers' courtship and marriage. So he opened the book focusing on the main character, Dick Diver. But that didn't work either, and Fitzgerald was crushed. The book was financially unsuccessful until many years later, when Fitzgerald's genius was finally acknowledged.

What strikes me so vividly is what Fitzgerald *didn't* see; his opening section focusing on how Rosemary saw the Divers was more cinematic than novelistic. It's a great cinematic opening, setting up the characters as others see them, like an establishing shot; in this first edition, Fitzgerald was *showing* us how this model couple looked to the world, beautiful and rich, seeming to have everything. How we look to the outside world, of course, is a lot different from who we really are behind closed doors. My personal feeling is that it was Fitzgerald's insecurity about the craft of screenwriting that drove him to change that great opening.

F. Scott Fitzgerald was an artist literally caught between two worlds, caught between his genius as a writer and his self-doubt and inability to express that genius in screenplay form.

Screenwriting is a definite craft, a definite art. Over the years, I've read thousands upon thousands of screenplays, and I always look for certain things. First, how does it look on the page? Is there plenty of white space, or are the paragraphs dense, too thick, the dialogue too long? Or is the reverse true: Is the scene description too thin, the dialogue too sparse? And this is before I read one word; this is just what it "looks" like on the page. You'd be surprised how many decisions are made in Hollywood by the way a screenplay looks—you can tell whether it's been written by a professional or by someone who's still aspiring to be a professional.

Everybody is writing screenplays, from the waiter at your favorite bar or restaurant to the limo driver, the doctor, the lawyer, or the barista serving up the White Chocolate Dream Latte at the local Coffee Bean. Last year, more than seventy-five thousand screenplays were registered at the Writers Guild of America, West and East, and out of that number maybe four or five hundred scripts were actually produced.

What makes one screenplay better than another? There are many answers, of course, because each screenplay is unique. But if you want to sit down and spend six months to a year writing a screenplay, you first have to know what a screenplay *is—what its nature is.*

What is a screenplay? Is it a guide, or an outline, for a movie? A blueprint, or a diagram? Or maybe it's a series of images, scenes, and sequences strung together with dialogue and description, like pearls on a strand? Perhaps it's simply the landscape of a dream?

Well, for one thing, a screenplay is not a novel, and it's most certainly not a play. If you look at a novel and try to define its fundamental nature, you'll see that the dramatic action, the story line, usually takes place inside the head of the main character. We see the story line unfold through the eyes of the character, through his/her point of view. We are privy to the character's thoughts, feelings, emotions, words, actions, memories, dreams, hopes, ambitions, opinions, and more. The character and reader go through the action together, sharing in the drama and emotion of the story. We know how they act, feel, react, and figure things out. If other characters appear and are brought into the narrative line of action, then the story embraces their point of view, but the main thrust of the story line always returns to the main character. The main character is who the story is about. In a novel the action takes place inside the character's head, within the *mindscape* of dramatic action.

A play is different. The action, or story line, occurs onstage, under the proscenium arch, and the audience becomes the fourth wall, eavesdropping on the lives of the characters, what they think and feel and say. They talk about their hopes and dreams, past and future plans, discuss their needs and desires, fears and conflicts. In this case, the action of the play occurs within the *language* of dramatic action; it is spoken in words that describe feelings, actions, and emotions.

A screenplay is different. Movies are different. Film is a visual medium that dramatizes a basic story line; it deals in pictures, images, bits and pieces of film: We *see* a clock ticking, a window opening, a person in the distance leaning over a balcony, smoking; in the background we hear a phone ringing, a baby crying, a dog barking as we see two people laughing as their car pulls away from the curb. "Just making pictures." The nature of the screenplay deals in pictures, and if we wanted to define it, we could say that a screenplay is a *story told with pictures, in dialogue and description, and placed within the context of dramatic structure.*

That is its essential nature, just like a rock is hard and water's wet.

Because a screenplay is a story told with pictures, we can ask ourselves, what do all stories have in common? They have a beginning, middle, and an end, not necessarily in that order, as Jean-Luc Godard says. Screenplays have a basic linear structure that creates the *form* of the screenplay because it holds all the individual elements, or pieces, of the story line in place.

To understand the principle of structure, it's important to start with the word itself. The root of structure, *struct,* has two definitions that are relevant. The first definition means "to build" or "to put something together," like a building or car. The second definition is "the relationship between the parts and the whole."

The parts and the whole. This is an important distinction. What is the relationship between the parts and the whole? How do you separate one from the other? If you take the game of chess, for example, the game itself is a whole composed of four parts: (1) *the pieces*—the queen, king, bishop, pawns, knights, etc.; (2) *the player(s),* because someone has to play the game of chess, either against another person or a computer; (3) *the board,* because you can't play chess without a board, and (4) *the rules,* because you can't play a chess game unless you play by the rules. Those four parts—the pieces, the player(s), the board, and the rules—are integrated into the whole, and the result is a game of chess. It is the relationship between these parts and the whole that determines the game.

The same relationship holds true in a story. A story is the whole, and the elements that make up the story—the action, characters, conflicts, scenes, sequences, dialogue, action, Acts I, II, and III, incidents, episodes, events, music, locations, etc.—are the parts, and this relationship between the parts and the whole make up the story.

Good structure is like the relationship between an ice cube and water. An ice cube has a definite crystalline structure, and water has a definite molecular structure. But when the ice cube melts into water, how can you separate the molecules of ice from the molecules of water? Structure is like gravity: It is the glue that holds the story in place; it is the base, the foundation, the spine, the skeleton of the story. And it is this relationship between the parts and the whole that holds the screenplay together. It's what makes it what it is.

It is the *paradigm* of dramatic structure.

A *paradigm* is a model, example, or conceptual scheme. The paradigm of a table, for example, is a top with four legs. Within the paradigm, we can have a low table, high table, narrow table, or wide table; we can have a round table, square table, rectangular table, or octagonal table; we can have a glass table, wood table, plastic table, wrought-iron table, or whatever, and the paradigm doesn't change— it remains what it is, a top with four legs. Just the way a suitcase remains a suitcase; it doesn't matter how big or small, or what the shape is; it is what it is.

If we wanted to take a screenplay and hang it on the wall like a painting, this is what it would look like:

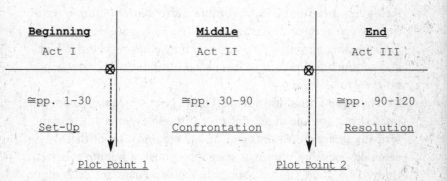

This is the *paradigm* of a screenplay. Here's how it's broken down:

ACT I IS THE SET-UP

If a screenplay is a story told with pictures, then what do all stories have in common? A beginning, middle, and end, though not necessarily, as mentioned, in that order; it is a story told in pictures, in dialogue and description, and placed within the context of dramatic structure.

Aristotle talked about the three unities of dramatic action: time, place, and action. The normal Hollywood film is approximately two hours long, or 120 minutes; foreign films tend to be a little shorter, though that's changing as we bridge the language of international film. But in most cases, films are approximately two hours in length, give or take a few minutes. This is a standard length, and today, when a contract is written in Hollywood between the filmmaker and production company, it states that when the movie is delivered, it will be no longer than 2 hours and 8 minutes. That's approximately 128 pages of screenplay. Why? Because it's an economic decision that has evolved over the years. At this writing, it costs approximately $10,000 to $12,000 per minute (and getting higher and higher every year) to shoot a Hollywood studio film. Second, a two-hour movie has a definite advantage in the theaters simply because you can get in more viewings of the movie per day. More screenings mean more money; more theaters mean more screenings, which means more money will be made. Movies are show *business,* after all, and with the cost of moviemaking being so high, and getting higher as our technology evolves, today it's really more business than show.

The way it breaks down is this: One page of screenplay is approximately one minute of screen time. It doesn't matter whether the script is all action, all dialogue, or any combination of the two—generally speaking, a page of screenplay equals a minute of screen time. It's a good rule of thumb to follow. There are exceptions to this, of course. The script of *Lord of the Rings: The Fellowship of the Ring* is only 118 pages, but the movie is more than three hours long.

Act I, the beginning, is a unit of dramatic action that is approximately twenty or thirty pages long and is held together with the dramatic context known as the *Set-Up.* Context is the space that *holds* something in place—in this case, the content. For example, the space inside a glass is the *context*; it holds the *content* in place—whether it's water, beer, milk, coffee, tea, or juice. If we want to get creative, a glass can also hold raisins, trail mix, nuts, grapes, etc.—

but the space inside doesn't change The *context* is what *holds* the *content* in place.

In this unit of dramatic action, Act I, the screenwriter *sets up* the story, establishes character, launches the dramatic premise (what the story is about), illustrates the situation (the circumstances surrounding the action), and creates the relationships between the main character and the other characters who inhabit the landscape of his or her world. As a writer you've only got about ten minutes to establish this, because the audience members can usually determine, either consciously or unconsciously, whether they do or don't like the movie by that time. If they don't know what's going on and the opening is vague or boring, their concentration and focus will falter and start wandering.

Check it out. The next time you go to a movie, do a little exercise: Find out how long it takes you to make a decision about whether you like the film or not. A good indication is if you start thinking about getting something from the refreshment stand or find yourself shifting in your seat; if that happens, the chances are the filmmaker has lost you as a viewer. Ten minutes is ten pages of screenplay. I cannot emphasize enough that this first ten-page unit of dramatic action is the most important part of the screenplay.

In *American Beauty* (Alan Ball), after the brief opening video scene of the daughter Jane (Thora Birch) and her boyfriend, Ricky (Wes Bentley), we see the street where Lester Burnham (Kevin Spacey) lives, and hear his first words in voice-over: "My name is Lester Burnham. I'm forty-two years old. In less than a year, I'll be dead.... In a way, I'm dead already." Then we see Lester as he begins his day. He wakes up and jerks off (the high point of his day, he adds), and then we see his relationship with his family. All this is set up and established within the first few pages, and we learn that: "My wife and daughter think I'm this gigantic loser, and they're right.... I have lost something. I don't know what it was, but I have lost something.... I feel sedated.... But you know, it's never too late to get it back." And that lets us know what the story is all about: Lester regaining the life he has lost or given up, and becoming whole and complete again as a person. Within the first few pages of the screenplay we know the main character, the dramatic premise, and the situation.

In *Chinatown* (Robert Towne), we learn on page one that Jake Gittes (Jack Nicholson), the main character, is a sleazy private detective specializing in "discreet investigation." We *see* this when he shows Curly (Burt Young) pictures of his wife having sex in the park. We also see that Gittes has a certain flair for this type of investigation. A few pages later, we are introduced to a certain Mrs. Mulwray (Diane Ladd), who wants to hire Jake Gittes to find out "who my husband is having an affair with." That is the dramatic premise of the film, because the answer to that question is what leads us into the story. The dramatic premise is what the screenplay is about; it provides the dramatic thrust that drives the story to its conclusion.

In *Lord of the Rings: The Fellowship of the Ring* (Fran Walsh, Philippa Boyens, and Peter Jackson, based on the book by J. R. R. Tolkien), we learn in the first six pages of the screenplay the history of the ring and its magnetic attraction. It's a beautiful opening that sets up all three stories. It also sets up the story as Gandalf arrives in the Shire. We meet Frodo (Elijah Wood), Bilbo Baggins (Ian Holm), Sam (Sean Astin), and the others, see how they live, and are introduced to the ring. We also get an overview of Middle Earth. This opening sets up the rest of the *Fellowship,* including the two sequels, *The Two Towers* and *Return of the King.*

In *Witness* (Earl Wallace and William Kelley), the first ten pages reveal the world of the Amish in Lancaster County, Pennsylvania. The script opens with the funeral of Rachel's (Kelly McGillis's) husband, then we follow her to Philadelphia, where her child witnesses the murder of an undercover cop, and that in turn leads to her relationship with the main character, John Book (Harrison Ford), another cop. The entire first act is designed to reveal the dramatic premise and situation and to set up the relationship between an Amish woman and a tough Philadelphia cop.

ACT II IS CONFRONTATION

Act II is a unit of dramatic action approximately sixty pages long, and goes from the end of Act I, anywhere from pages 20 to 30, to the end of Act II, approximately pages 85 to 90, and is held together with the dramatic context known as *Confrontation*. During this second act the main character encounters obstacle after obstacle that keeps him/her from achieving his/her dramatic need, which is defined as *what the character wants to win, gain, get, or achieve during the course of the screenplay.* If you know your character's dramatic need, you can create obstacles to it and then your story becomes your character, overcoming obstacle after obstacle to achieve his/her dramatic need.

In *Cold Mountain,* Inman (Jude Law) struggles over two hundred miles to return home to Cold Mountain. This dramatic need is both internal and external: It is Inman's longing to return to a place in his heart that existed prior to the war, and Cold Mountain is also the place where he lived and grew up, as well as where his loved one, Ada (Nicole Kidman), resides. His desire, his dramatic need to return home, is fraught with obstacle after obstacle, and still he persists, only to fail at the end. Literally, the entire movie is overcoming the obstacles of war and the internal will to survive.

In *Chinatown,* a detective story, Act II deals with Jake Gittes's collisions with people who try to keep him from finding out who's responsible for the murder of Hollis Mulwray and who's behind the water scandal. The obstacles that Gittes encounters and overcomes dictate the dramatic action of the story. Look at *The Fugitive.* The entire story is driven by the main character's dramatic need to bring his wife's killer to justice. Act II is where your character has to deal with surviving the obstacles that you put in front of him or her. What is it that drives him or her forward through the action? What does your main character want? What is his or her dramatic need? In *Lord of the Rings: The Two Towers,* the entire film involves Frodo, Sam, and the Fellowship's confronting and managing to overcome obstacle after obstacle, leading to the climactic battle at Helms Deep.

All drama is conflict. Without conflict, you have no action; without action, you have no character; without character, you have no story; and without story, you have no screenplay.

ACT III IS RESOLUTION

Act III is a unit of dramatic action approximately twenty to thirty pages long and goes from the end of Act II, approximately pages 85 to 90, to the end of the screenplay. It is held together with the dramatic context known as *Resolution*. I think it's important to remember that resolution does not mean ending; *resolution means solution.* What is the solution of your screenplay? Does your main character live or die? Succeed or fail? Get married or not? Win the race or not? Win the election or not? Escape safely or not? Leave her husband or not? Return home safely or not? Act III is that unit of action that *resolves* the story. It is not the ending; the ending is that specific scene or shot or sequence that ends the script.

Beginning, middle, and end; Act I, Act II, Act III. *Set-Up, Confrontation, Resolution*—these parts make up the whole. It is the relationship between these parts that determines the whole.

But this brings up another question: If these parts make up the whole, the screenplay, how do you get from Act I, the *Set-Up*, to Act II, the *Confrontation*? And how do you get from Act II to Act III, the *Resolution*? The answer is to create a *Plot Point* at the end of both Act I and Act II.

A *Plot Point* is defined as *any incident, episode, or event that hooks into the action and spins it around in another direction*—in this case, Plot Point I moves the action forward into Act II and Plot Point II moves the action into Act III. Plot Point I occurs at the end of Act I, anywhere from pages 20 to 25 or 30.

A *Plot Point* is always a function of the main character. In *Lord of the Rings: The Fellowship of the Ring,* Plot Point I is the beginning of the journey, that moment when Frodo and Sam leave the Shire and set out on their adventure through Middle Earth. Plot Point II is when the Fellowship reaches Lothlorien, and Galadriel (Cate Blanchett) reveals to Frodo the fate of Middle Earth should the ring not reach Mount Doom. Frodo becomes the reluctant hero, in much the same way that Neo (Keanu Reeves) in *The Matrix* (Larry and Andy Wachowski), accepts his mantle of responsibility at Plot Point I: his journey as "The One" begins at Plot Point I. It is the true beginning of that story.

If we take a look at *The Matrix,* we can see Plot Points I and II clearly delineated. In Plot Point I, Neo chooses the Red Pill, and Act II begins when he is literally reborn; at Plot Point II, Neo and Trinity (Carrie-Anne Moss) rescue Morpheus (Laurence Fishburne), and only then does Neo accept the truth that he is "The One."

Plot Points serve an essential purpose in the screenplay; they are a major story progression and keep the story line anchored in place. In *Chinatown,* Jake Gittes is hired by the wife of a prominent man to find out if her husband is having an affair. Gittes follows him and sees him with a young girl. That's the Set-Up. Plot Point I occurs after the newspaper story is released claiming Mr. Mulwray has been caught in a "love nest." That's when the *real* Mrs. Mulwray shows up with her attorney and threatens to sue Jake Gittes and have his license revoked. If *she* is the real Mrs. Mulwray, who was the woman who hired Jake Gittes? And *why* did she hire him? And *who* hired the phony Mrs. Mulwray? And *why*? The arrival of the real Mrs. Mulwray is what hooks into the action and spins it around in another direction—in this case, Act II. It is story progression; Jake Gittes must find out who set him up, and why. The answer is the rest of the movie.

In *Cold Mountain,* as Inman recovers from his wounds he receives a letter from Ada. We hear her say, in voice-over, "Come back to me. Come back to me is my request." Inman nods; his decision is made: He will desert the Confederate Army and return home to Ada and Cold Mountain, return to the place in his heart.

Plot Points do not have to be big, dynamic scenes or sequences; they can be quiet scenes in which a decision is made, such as Inman's, or when Frodo and Sam leave the Shire. Take the sequence in *American Beauty* where Lester Burnham and his wife are at the high school basketball game and see their daughter's friend Angela (Mena Suvari) performing at halftime. It moves the story forward and sets Lester's emotional journey of liberation in motion. In *The Matrix,* Plot Point I is where Neo is offered the choice of the Red Pill or the Blue Pill. He chooses the Red Pill, and this truly is the beginning of the story. All of Act I has set up the elements and led Neo to this moment.

Remember, the paradigm is the *form* of a screenplay, what it looks like. Any page numbers I reference are only a guideline to indicate approximately *where* the story progresses to the next level, not *how* it progresses. How you do that is up to you. It is the form of the screenplay that is important, not the page numbers where Plot Points occur. There may be many Plot Points during the course of the story line; I only focus on Plot Points I and II because these two events are the anchoring moments that become the foundation of the dramatic structure in the screenplay.

Plot Point II is really the same as Plot Point I; it is the way to move the story forward, from Act II to Act III. It is a story progression. As mentioned, it usually occurs anywhere between pages 80 or 90 of the screenplay. In *Chinatown,* Plot Point II occurs when Jake Gittes finds a pair of horn-rim glasses in the pond where Hollis Mulwray was murdered, and knows the glasses belonged either to Mulwray or to the person who killed him. This leads us to the *Resolution* of the story.

In *Cold Mountain,* Plot Point II is a quiet moment; after Inman meets the woman Sara (Natalie Portman) and rescues her and her baby from the Northerners, he reaches a point where he can see the Blue Ridge Mountains. The script reads: "Somewhere in there is home, is Ada. He goes on." That's all; such a small scene, but loaded with such emotion: He's home. That leads us into Act III, the *Resolution.*

Do all good screenplays fit the paradigm? Yes. But just because a screenplay is well structured and fits the paradigm doesn't make it a good screenplay, or a good movie. The paradigm is a form, not a formula. Structure is what holds the story together.

What's the distinction between form and formula? The form of a coat or jacket, for example, is two arms, a front, and a back. And within that form of arms, front, and back you can have any variation of style, fabric, color, and size—but the form remains intact.

A formula, however, is totally different. A formula never varies; certain elements are put together so they come out *exactly the same* each and every time. If you put that coat on an assembly line, every coat will be exactly the same, with the same pattern, the same fabric, the same color, the same cut, the same material. The coat does not change, except for the size. A screenplay, on the other hand, is unique, a totally individual presentation.

The paradigm is a form, not a formula; it's what holds the story together. It is the spine, the skeleton. Story determines structure; structure doesn't determine story.

The dramatic structure of the screenplay may be defined as *a linear arrangement of related incidents, episodes, or events leading to a dramatic resolution.*

How you utilize these structural components determines the form of your screenplay. *The Hours* (David Hare, adapted from the novel by Michael Cunningham) is told in three different time periods and has a definite structure. It's the same with *American Beauty:* The whole story is told in flashback, just like Woody Allen's *Annie Hall. Cold Mountain* is also told in flashback, but has a definite beginning, middle, and end. *Citizen Kane* is also told in flashback, but this does not detract from its form.

The *paradigm* is a model, an example, or a conceptual scheme; it is what a well-structured screenplay looks like, an overview of the story line as it unfolds from beginning to end.

Screenplays that work follow the paradigm. But don't take my word for it. Go to a movie and see whether you can determine its structure for yourself.

Some of you may not believe that. You may not believe in beginnings, middles, and ends, either. You may say that art, like life, is nothing more than several individual "moments" suspended in some giant middle, with no beginning and no end, what Kurt Vonnegut calls "a series of random moments" strung together in a haphazard fashion.

I disagree.

Birth? Life? Death? Isn't that a beginning, middle, and end? Spring, summer, fall, and winter—isn't that a beginning, middle, and end? Morning, afternoon, evening—it's always the same, but different. Think about the rise and fall of great ancient civilizations— Egyptian, Greek, and Roman, each rising from the seed of a small community to the apex of power, then disintegrating and dying.

Think about the birth and death of a star, or the beginning of the universe. If there's a beginning, like the Big Bang, is there going to be an end?

Think about the cells in our bodies. How often are they replenished, restored, and re-created? Every seven years—within a seven-year cycle all the cells in our bodies are born, function, die, and are reborn again.

Think about the first day of a new job, or a new school, or a new house or apartment; you'll meet new people, assume new responsibilities, create new friendships.

Screenplays are no different. They have a definite beginning, middle, and end, but not necessarily in that order.

If you don't believe the paradigm, or in the three-act structure first laid down by Aristotle, go check it out. Go to a movie—go see several movies—and see whether they fit the paradigm or not.

If you're interested in writing screenplays, you should be doing this all the time. Every movie you see is a learning process, expanding your awareness and comprehension of what a movie is: a story told with pictures.

You should also read as many screenplays as possible in order to expand your awareness of the form and structure. Many screenplays have been reprinted in book form and most bookstores have them, or can order them. You can also go online and do a Google search under "screenplays" and find a number of sites that allow you to download screenplays. Some are free, some you pay for.

I have my students read and study scripts like *Chinatown*, *Network* (Paddy Chayefsky), *American Beauty*, *The Shawshank Redemption* (Frank Darabont), *Sideways* (Alexander Payne and Jim Taylor), *The Matrix*, *Annie Hall*, and *Lord of the Rings*. These scripts are excellent teaching aids. If they aren't available, read any screenplay you can find. The more the better.

The paradigm works. It is the *foundation* of every good screenplay, the foundation of *dramatic structure*.

2

The Subject

> "Rosebud...Maybe that was something he lost.... You see, Mr. Kane was a man who lost almost everything he had."
>
> —Everett Sloane speculating on the meaning of "Rosebud"
> *Citizen Kane*
> Herman Mankiewicz and Orson Welles

Orsen Welles's *Citizen Kane* has been universally acclaimed as the greatest film ever made. From the very first frame, the full portrait of Kane's character is set up visually; the film opens shrouded in fog and the first thing we see is a high wired chain-link fence bolstered with the initial K. Deep in the background, a huge, isolated mansion stands high on the hill. Moving closer, we see boxes and crates of antiques, artworks, and ancient artifacts stacked everywhere. Huge pens house exotic animals, and then we're inside the enormous castle, so full, yet so empty of life. Then we cut to an extreme close-up of the man known as Citizen Kane as he whispers his last word: "Rosebud." A glass paperweight falls from his fingers and breaks open, and we see snow, the first glimpse of a lost childhood.

Like a classic mystery, the story begins. Who is Charles Foster Kane? What is he? Who or what is Rosebud? As if in answer, we cut to a darkened screening room filled with chain-smoking reporters and watch newsreel footage of Charles Foster Kane, a man larger than life, filled with an insatiable appetite, a man of total excess.

The great director Robert Wise (*West Side Story, The Sound of Music, The Sand Pebbles,* to name just a few) edited the film, and he shared with me in one of our conversations that Welles first shot all the simulated newsreel footage, and then, to make it appear more "real," he had Wise crinkle it up and drag it across the cutting room floor. It lent an authentic, credible look to the film. Kane's entire life is visually set up in less than a minute—through pictures, not words.

Citizen Kane is truly a story told with pictures, a search for the hidden meaning of Kane's life, which revolves around the last words he utters on his deathbed. I call it "an emotional detective story," because the search for who and what Rosebud is leads us to uncover the life of Charles Foster Kane. It's the answer to this question that tells us what the movie is about. It is the subject of the screenplay.

What do you need to write a screenplay? An idea, of course, but you can't sit down to write a script with just an idea in mind. An idea, while essential, is nothing more than a vague notion. It has no detail, no depth, no dimension. No, you need more than just an idea to start writing a screenplay.

You need a subject to embody and dramatize the idea. A subject is defined as an action and a character. An *action* is what the story is about, and a *character* is who the story is about.

Every screenplay has a subject—it is what the story is about.

If we remember that a screenplay is like a noun, about a person in a place, doing his/her "thing," we can see that the person is the *main character* and doing his/her "thing" is the *action*. So, when we talk about the subject of a screenplay, we're talking about an *action* and a *character* or *characters*.

Every screenplay dramatizes an action and a character. You, as the screenwriter, must know *who* your movie is about and *what* happens to him or her. It is a primary principle in writing, not only in screenplays but in all forms of writing.

Only at the end of *Citizen Kane*, after his death (which is where the story really begins), when the warehouse is being cleared of what seems to be endless piles of junk, curios, furniture, and unpacked crates, do we understand the significance of Rosebud. As the camera moves into a darkened corner, we see a huge collection of toys, paintings, and statues. Slowly, the camera pans Kane's possessions, until it reaches the blazing furnace. Workmen are tossing various items into the flames. One of the items is a sled, the very one Kane had as a boy in Colorado. When it's thrown into the fire the camera moves in tight on the sled, and as it catches fire, the name "Rosebud" is revealed.

Only then do we recall that when Mr. Thatcher, the executor of Kane's estate, first describes his meeting with Kane as a boy of ten or so, young Charles is sledding down the hill in the snow. It is an emotionally riveting moment, emblematic of the lost youth Kane would spend his life searching for, but never find. We cut outside the huge mansion as the smoke from Kane's lost youth curls upward into the night sky. The film ends with the same shot of the iron fence that opened the film. "I was with him from the very beginning," Mr. Bernstein says during the film, adding, "Mr. Kane was a man who lost everything he had." It is one of the great moments in movie history.

If you want to write a screenplay, *what* is it about? And *who* is it about? *Citizen Kane* begins with a search based on a dying man's last words and ends up revealing the secret of his entire life. Seeking the answer provides the narrative thrust, the emotional through line of the film.

Do you know the subject of your screenplay? What it's about? And who is it about? Can you express it in a few sentences? Do you, for example, want to tell the story of two women going on a crime spree? If you do, do you know who these two women are? Where they came from? What their background is? And then, what crimes did they commit? And why? Do you know what happens to them at the end? Defining the answers to these questions allows you to gather enough information to write your screenplay from the position of choice, confidence, and security. If you know what you're doing, then you can figure out the best way of doing it.

Knowing your subject is the starting point of writing the screenplay. And make no mistake: Every screenplay has a subject. *The Last Samurai* (John Logan) is about an embittered Civil War mercenary (Tom Cruise) who travels to Japan and is ultimately transformed by the people who were originally his enemy, a band of samurai warriors. The *character* is the Civil War mercenary, and the *action* is how he is transformed in thought, word, and action, allowing him to regain a sense of self he had lost after the war ended. But that's only what the film is about on the surface. On a deeper level, what it's really about is how the American military adviser learns to embody the virtues of honor and loyalty.

Cold Mountain is about Inman's returning home to the town he lived in prior to the war and returning to his loved one, Ada. But on a deeper, more emotional level, the story is about a place in the heart, a place filled with love and meaning, a place that was sacred before hostilities began and before people started killing in the name of political "correctness," a place that took this great gift of life for granted, before our sensibilities and moral standards began to crumble in the chasm of war.

Bonnie and Clyde (David Newman and Robert Benton) is a story about Clyde Barrow and his gang holding up banks in the Midwest during the Depression and the robbers' eventual downfall. Action and character. It's essential to isolate your generalized idea into a specific dramatic premise. And that becomes the starting point of your screenplay.

Again, every story has a definite beginning, middle, and end. In *Bonnie and Clyde*, the beginning dramatizes the meeting of Bonnie (Faye Dunaway) and Clyde (Warren Beatty) and the forming of their gang. In the middle, they hold up several banks and the law goes after them. In the end, they are caught by the forces of society and killed. Set-Up, Confrontation, and Resolution.

When you can articulate your subject in a few sentences, in terms of action and character, you're ready to begin expanding the elements of structure and story. It may take several pages of free-association writing about your story before you can begin to grasp the essentials and reduce a complex story line to a simple sentence or two. Don't worry about it. Just keep doing it, and you will be able to articulate your story idea clearly and concisely.

Knowing what you are writing about is absolutely essential as you delve deeper into the action and characters. Because if *you* don't know what your story is about, who does? The reader? The viewer? If you don't know what you're writing about, how do you expect someone else to know? The writer must always exercise *choice* and *responsibility* in determining the dramatic execution of the story. Choice and responsibility—these words will be a familiar refrain throughout this book. Every creative decision must be made by *choice*, not necessity. If your character *walks* out of a bank, that's one story. If he *runs* out of a bank, that's another story.

Many times you may feel the urge to sit down and start writing a screenplay but you don't really know what to write about. So you go looking for a subject. Just know that when you're looking for your subject, your subject is really looking for you. You'll find it someplace, at some time, probably when you're least expecting it. It will be yours to follow through on or not, as you choose.

What or whom do you want to write about? A character? A particular emotional situation? An experience that you or one of your family members or friends has gone through? Many people already have ideas they want to turn into a screenplay. Others don't. How do you go about finding a subject?

An idea in a newspaper or on the TV news or an incident that might have happened to a friend or relative can be the subject of a movie. *The Pianist* (Ron Harwood, from the memoir by Wladyslaw Szpilman) is a film about survival, based on the writings of a survivor of the Holocaust, but it also reflects the childhood of director Roman Polanski. *Saving Private Ryan* (Robert Rodat) is based on an actual incident that occurred during World War II. In *The Royal Tenenbaums* (Wes Anderson and Owen Wilson), the subject is a dysfunctional family dealing with failure and forgiveness. *Dog Day Afternoon* (Frank Pierson) was a newspaper article before it became a movie.

Before Robert Towne wrote *Chinatown*, he once told me, he wanted to write a Raymond Chandler–type detective story. He found the material for *Chinatown* in a Los Angeles water scandal he read about in an old newspaper of that period, and used the backdrop of the Owens Valley scandal for his detective story. *Shampoo* (Robert Towne and Warren Beatty) grew out of several incidents involving a celebrated Hollywood hairstylist. *Collateral* (Stuart Beattie) emerged during the writer's conversation with a taxi driver. *Taxi Driver* (Paul Schrader) is a story about the loneliness of driving a cab in New York City. *Bonnie and Clyde, Butch Cassidy and the Sundance Kid* (William Goldman), and *All the President's Men* (William Goldman) grew out of real people in real situations. Your subject will find you, given the opportunity. It's very simple. Trust yourself. Just start looking for an action and a character.

When you can express your idea succinctly in terms of action and character—my story is about this person, in this place, doing his/her "thing"—you're beginning the preparation of your screenplay.

The next step is expanding your subject. Fleshing out the action and focusing on the character broadens the story line and accentuates the details. Gather your material any way you can. It will always be to your advantage.

Over the years, I talked to a lot of people who wondered about the value, or necessity, of doing research. I began my career in film by making documentaries for David L. Wolper, working on such shows as the *Biography* series with Mike Wallace, winner of the Peabody Award; *Hollywood and the Stars;* the *National Geographic* shows; *Men in Crisis;* some of the Jacques Cousteau specials; and many more. It was while I was at Wolper that I learned the value of research. It became an indispensable part of my writing and teaching experience.

On every show I've ever been associated with, as writer, director, producer, or researcher, I've begun the process by finding out as much as I can about the subject. As far as I'm concerned, research is absolutely essential. All writing entails research, and research means gathering information. Remember, the hardest part of writing is knowing what to write.

By doing research—whether in written sources such as books, magazines, or newspapers or through personal interviews—you acquire information. The information you collect allows you to operate from the position of choice, confidence, and responsibility. You can choose to use some, or all, or none of the material you've gathered; that's your choice, dictated by the terms of the story. Not using it because you don't have it offers you no choice at all, and will always work against you and your story.

Too many people start writing their material with only a vague, half-formed idea in their heads. This works for about thirty pages, then falls apart. You don't know what happens next, or what to do next, or where to go, and you end up getting angry, confused, and frustrated. Then, in most cases, you give up.

There are two kinds of research. One I call *text* research. That means going to the library and pulling out books and newspaper and magazine articles and reading about a period, people, a profession, or whatever. If you're writing a period piece or a historical piece, you need to gather information about the time and the events that happened during it and then weave your emotional through line into your characters. I get most of my information from reading about the period and any first-person writings I can find. If you're writing about a subject that you don't know much about, you need to get information to make your story line real, believable, and true. Edward Zwick, who directed *The Last Samurai,* worked extensively with John Logan, the writer. Zwick spent more than a year reading about the Japanese culture and the samurai tradition.

The second form of research I call *live* research. It means going to the source—doing live interviews, talking to people, getting a "feel" for the subject. If it is necessary or possible to conduct personal interviews, you'll be surprised to find that most people are willing to help you in any way they can, and will often go out of their way to assist you in your search for accurate information. Personal interviews offer another advantage: They can give you a more immediate and spontaneous slant than a book, newspaper, or magazine story. It's the next best thing to having experienced something yourself. Remember: The more you know, the more you can communicate. And be in a position of choice and responsibility when making creative decisions.

At present, I'm writing a sci-fi epic space adventure, about a cosmic phenomenon that drastically impacts Earth. Since I know nothing about cosmic events of this magnitude, I made contact with the media relations person at the Jet Propulsion Laboratory in Pasadena, California, and she gave me a lot of information, along with the names of some scientists. I then spent almost three months learning about the phenomenon known as a "gamma ray burst." With this information, even though I'm stretching the bounds of reality to "fit" my creative purpose, the subject is still based on reality, what *could* happen if this event actually came to pass.

A while ago I had the opportunity of working on a story with Craig Breedlove, onetime holder of the World Land Speed Record, and the first man to go 400, 500, and 600 miles per hour on land and live. Craig created a jet-propelled car that traveled at a speed of 400 miles per hour for a quarter mile. The rocket system was the same system used to land a man on the moon. I spent several days hanging out with him and reading the history of the Land Speed Record.

The story is about a man breaking the World Water Speed Record in a rocket boat. But a rocket boat doesn't exist, at least at this writing. I had to do all kinds of research to find out about my subject matter. What is the Water Speed Record? Where do you go to break the record? Is it possible for a rocket boat to beat the record? How do the officials time the boats? Is a speed of over 400 miles per hour on water possible? From my conversations with Craig, I learned about rocket systems, the Water Speed Record, and designing and building a racing boat. And out of those conversations came an action and a character. And a way to fuse fact and fiction into a dramatic story line.

The principle rule of storytelling bears repetition: The more you know, the more you can communicate.

Research is essential in writing a screenplay. Once you choose your subject, and can state it briefly in a sentence or two, you can begin preliminary research. Determine where you can go to increase your knowledge of the subject. Paul Schrader, who wrote *Taxi Driver,* once wanted to write a movie that took place on a train. So he took a train from Los Angeles to New York, and when he stepped off the train he realized he didn't have a story; he hadn't found one. That's okay. Choose another subject. Schrader went on to write *Obsession,* and Colin Higgins, who wrote *Harold and Maude,* went on to write a train story, *Silver Streak.* Richard Brooks spent eight months researching *Bite the Bullet* before he put one word on paper. He did the same thing with *The Professionals* and *In Cold Blood,* even though he based the latter on Truman Capote's exhaustively researched book. Waldo Salt, who wrote *Midnight Cowboy,* researched *Coming Home* by speaking to and recording some twenty-six paralyzed Vietnam veterans, which resulted in two hundred hours of taped interviews.

Waldo Salt believed in capturing "the truth" of the characters in a story. I had the good fortune of having several conversations with Waldo, and he was not only an extraordinary writer, but an extraordinary person. We talked about the craft of screenwriting a lot, and Waldo told me that he believed the character's need (the *dramatic need*—what the character wants to win, gain, or achieve) determines the dramatic structure. His words resonated with me immediately, and I shared with him that I had recently come to the same understanding while I was analyzing Woody Allen's *Annie Hall:* The character's need determines the creative choices he/she makes during the screenplay, and gaining clarity about that need allows you to be more complex, more dimensional, in your character portrayal.

It was a powerful moment for both of us as we sat in an unspoken glow of communication that was more powerful than words, and it led to a long and passionate discussion about capturing "the truth of the human condition" in a screenplay. The key to a successful screenplay, Waldo emphasized, was preparing the material. Dialogue, he said, is "perishable," because the actor can always improvise lines to make something work. But, he added forcefully, the character's dramatic need is sacrosanct. That cannot be changed, because it holds the entire story in place. Putting words down on paper, he said, is the easiest part of the screenwriting process; it is the visual conception of the story that takes so long. And he quoted Picasso: "Art is the elimination of the unnecessary."

If you're writing a story about a bicycle racer like Lance Armstrong, for example, what kind of racer is he? A sprinter or a long-distance racer? Where do the bicycle races take place? Where do you want to set your story? In what city? Are there different types of races, or racing circuits? Associations and clubs? How many races are held throughout the year? What about international competition? Does it affect your story? The character? What kind of bikes are used? How do you become a bicycle racer? These questions must be answered before you start putting words on paper.

Research gives you ideas, a sense of people, situation, and locale. It allows you to gain a degree of confidence so you are always on top of your subject, operating from choice, not necessity or ignorance.

Start with your subject. When you think *subject*, think *action* and *character*. This is what subject looks like in a diagram.

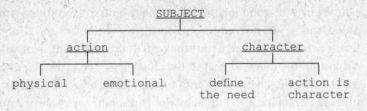

There are two kinds of action—*physical* action and *emotional* action. Physical action can be a battle sequence, like the opening of *Cold Mountain;* or a car chase, as in *Bullitt* or *The French Connection;* or a race, or competition, or fight, fed by revenge, as in *Kill Bill I* and *II* (Quentin Tarantino); or the shoot-out on a farm that makes up the last act of *Witness*. Emotional action is what happens inside your characters during the story. Emotional action is the center of the drama in *Cold Mountain, Love Story, The Royal Tenenbaums, American Beauty,* and *Lost in Translation* (Sofia Coppola). The emotional context of the great Italian director Michelangelo Antonioni's films makes up the internal action in masterpieces like *Blow-Up, L'Avventura, L'Eclisse,* and *La Notte*. The search for the correct way to live in our times is the centerpiece of the maestro's oeuvre. As you can see, most films contain both kinds of action, physical and emotional.

Ask yourself what kind of story you are writing. Is it an outdoor action-adventure movie, or is it a story about a relationship, an emotional story? Once you determine what kind of action you're dealing with, you can move into the life of your character.

First, *define the dramatic need* of your character. What does your character want? What is his/her need? What drives him to the resolution of your story? In *Chinatown,* Jake Gittes's need is to find out who set him up, and why. In *The Bourne Supremacy* (Tony Gilroy), Jason Bourne (Matt Damon) needs to know *who* wants to kill him, and *why*. You must define the need of your character. What does he/she want?

Sonny (Al Pacino) holds up the bank in *Dog Day Afternoon* to get money for a sex-change operation for his male lover. That is his need. If your character creates a system to beat the tables in Las Vegas, how much does he need to win before he knows if the system works or doesn't? The need of your character gives you a goal, a destination, an ending to your story. How your character achieves or does not achieve that goal becomes the action of your story.

As I said before, and will say again, all drama is conflict. If you know the *need* of your character, you can create obstacles to fulfill that need. How he/she overcomes those obstacles is your story. Conflict, struggle, overcoming obstacles, both inside and outside, are the primary ingredients in all drama—in comedy, too. It is the writer's responsibility to generate enough conflict to keep the reader, or the audience, interested. The job of the screenwriter is to keep the reader turning pages. The story always has to move forward, toward its resolution.

And it all comes down to knowing your subject. If you know the action and character of your screenplay, you can define the need of the character and then create obstacles to that need. The dramatic need of The Bride (Uma Thurman) in *Kill Bill* is simply revenge. It is the fuel that feeds the story engine.

In *Midnight Cowboy*, Joe Buck (Jon Voight) comes to New York to hustle women. That is his need. It is also his dream. And, as far as he's concerned, he's going to make a lot of money and satisfy a lot of women in the process.

What are the obstacles he immediately confronts? He gets hustled by Ratso (Dustin Hoffman), loses his money, doesn't have any friends or a job, and the women of New York don't even acknowledge his existence. Some dream! His need collides head-on with the harsh reality of New York City. That's conflict.

Without conflict, there is no action. Without action, there is no character. Action is Character. What a person does is what he *is*, not what he *says*!

When you begin to explore your subject, you will see that all things are related in your screenplay. Nothing is thrown in by chance, or because it's cute or clever. "There's a special Providence in the fall of a sparrow," Shakespeare observed. "For every action there is an equal and opposite reaction" is Newton's Third Law of Motion, a natural law of the universe. The same principle applies to your story. It is the subject of your screenplay.

KNOW YOUR SUBJECT!

As an exercise, find a subject you want to explore in screenplay form. If need be, look through the daily newspaper to see if a person, or incident, or situation grabs your attention. Think about how you might want to structure your story, then reduce it to a few sentences in terms of action and character, then write it out. Remember, it may take you a few pages to find out what you want to do, and another page or two to clarify it, but then you'll be able to eliminate the unnecessary and focus on your subject.

3

The Creation of Character

> "What is character but the determination of incident? And what is incident but the illumination of character?"
>
> —*The Art of Fiction*
> Henry James

What is Character?

That's a question that has haunted literary theorists from the beginning of the written word. The challenge of creating real people in real situations is so varied, so multifaceted, so unique, so individually challenging, that trying to define *how* you do it is like trying to hold a bundle of water in your hands. Generation after generation of noted writers, from Aristotle to Aeschylus, from Ibsen to Ionesco, from Eugene O'Neill to Arthur Miller, have struggled to capture the art and the craft of creating good characters.

One of the most articulate literary theorists of the nineteenth century was the great American novelist Henry James, author of *Portrait of a Lady, Wings of the Dove, Turn of the Screw,* and *Daisy Miller,* among other masterworks. James was fascinated with the art of fiction writing, and approached it like a scientist, the same way his brother, William James, the famous psychologist, studied the dynamics of the human mind. Henry James wrote several essays trying to document and define the intricacies of creating character. In one of those essays, *The Art of Fiction,* James poses a literary question: *What is character but the determination of incident? And what is incident but the illumination of character?*

It's a profound statement.

The key word, of course, is *incident.* According to the dictionary, an incident is "a specific occurrence or event that occurs in connection or relationship to something else." Screenplays are usually about a key incident, and the story is the character acting and reacting to it. It is the major source of all action and all character. After twenty-five years of reading and analyzing screenplays and movies, I have only recently begun to understand the importance of the incident. All good movies, it seems, focus on the unfolding of a specific incident or event; and it is this incident that becomes the engine that powers the story to its completion.

Frodo's assuming the mantle of ring bearer in *Lord of the Rings* is the key incident in that film; as is Lester Burnham's seeing the young girl Angela in *American Beauty;* as is Jake Gittes's being confronted by the real Mrs. Mulwray in *Chinatown.* Sometimes incidents and events in our lives bring out the best in us, or the worst. Sometimes we recover from these events and sometimes we don't— but they always impact us. At other times how we act and react, or deal with a particular situation, reveals our "true" nature and tells us who we really are. Miles in *Sideways* is a good illustration of that. When he is saving his special bottle of wine for a "special occasion," he sees he doesn't have a special time or place for opening it. So he sits alone, in a fast-food joint, hiding his bottle of wine.

Events in a screenplay are specifically designed to bring out the truth about the characters so that we, the reader and audience, can transcend our ordinary lives and achieve a connection, or bond, between "them and us." We see ourselves in them and enjoy a moment, perhaps, of recognition and understanding.

In *The Art of Fiction,* Henry James says that the incidents you create for your characters are the best ways to *illuminate* who they are—that is, reveal their true nature, their essential character. How they respond to a particular incident or event, how they act and react, what they say and do is what really defines the essence of their character.

How can we relate this concept to the process of creating character?

Thelma & Louise (Callie Khouri) is a story about two women who kill a man, then attempt to flee the law and escape to Mexico, but get caught at the Grand Canyon and, rather than go to prison, choose to take their own lives. If you take a look at these two characters, they are two distinct, individual people who have the same dramatic need: to escape safely to Mexico. They are different aspects of each other, and they share everything, their life as well as their death. And during the course of their journey, we get to know them, love them, and wish that things might have been different.

The reason why Henry James's statement is so relevant is because the elements *within* the character really determine the incident; how the character reacts to that incident is what illuminates and truly defines his/her character. In *Thelma & Louise,* it's set up immediately, at the beginning of Act I. Thelma (Geena Davis) and Louise (Susan Sarandon) set out for a weekend holiday in the mountains, stop at a bar, and meet a guy named Harlan, who takes a liking to Thelma. He plies her with drinks, then attempts to rape her in the parking lot. It turns ugly, until Louise comes along, threatens Harlan with Thelma's gun, and, when he mouths off to her, loses it, pulls the trigger, and kills him. Plot Point I. It is the key incident in the movie. Now the "real" story is about their attempt to escape to Mexico.

As mentioned, Plot Point I is the true beginning of the screenplay and swings the story around into Act II. For the rest of the story, Thelma and Louise are on the run. As they race down the highway of their life, like so many other characters in so many other movies, they are forced to come to grips with themselves, find out who they really are, and ultimately take responsibility for their lives and actions. *Thelma & Louise* is a road movie, yes, but it's really a journey of enlightenment, a journey of self-discovery. And it begins with the incident, the hub of the wheel of action.

It is the character that determines the incident, in this case Louise's killing Harlan, then fleeing in fear and uncertainty. What's important for me, and you, as writers, is to ask what it was within Louise's character that caused her to pull the trigger—because this incident is what ultimately reveals and *illuminates* the character. In Louise's case, it is an incident that happened to her when she was a young woman; it's only mentioned briefly, but it's implied that she was raped in Texas and then brought charges against her attackers, but could get no satisfaction, no revenge, no justice. Indeed, instead of being seen as the victim, she was considered by many to have been the instigator. At that moment, she made a promise to herself: She would never take one step inside the state of Texas ever again. This decision ultimately brings about her death.

Joseph Campbell reflects in *The Power of Myth* that in mythic terms, the first part of any journey of initiation must deal with the death of the old self and the resurrection of the new. Campbell says that the hero, or heroic figure, "moves not into outer space but into inward space, to the place from which all being comes, into the consciousness that is the source of all things, the kingdom of heaven within. The images are outward, but their reflection is inward."

It seems to me that the Louise in Act I who pulled the trigger, killing Harlan, is not the Louise who really killed him; rather, it was the young Louise, caught in the web of female justice, Texas style, who actually pulled that trigger. She never recovered from her experience, and it simmered in her consciousness below the thin veneer of time and memory, just waiting for a chance to erupt.

Writers create characters in a variety of different ways. I once asked Waldo Salt how he went about creating characters, and he replied that the first thing he did was to choose a simple dramatic need; then he would add to it, coloring it until it became a universal chord common to Everyman. For Waldo, that became the essence of his character. And he was a master screenwriter, a major artist.

What's the best way to go about creating character? And how do you establish a relationship between your character, his or her dramatic choices, and the story you're telling? How do you determine whether your character will drive a car, or ride a bicycle, or take the bus or subway, and what kind of paintings or posters hang in his/her house or apartment?

Character is the essential internal foundation of your screenplay. The cornerstone. It is the heart and soul and nervous system of your screenplay. Before you can put one word down on paper, you must know your character.

In a screenplay, the story always moves forward, from beginning to end, whether in a linear or nonlinear fashion. It doesn't matter if it's a story like *Titanic* or *The Hours; Lord of the Rings* or *The English Patient* (Anthony Minghella); *The Shawshank Redemption* or *Memento* (Christopher Nolan). The way you drive your story forward is by focusing on the *actions* of the *character* and the dramatic choices he or she makes during the narrative story line.

So what is character? Action is character; a person is what he *does*, not what he *says*. Film is behavior. Because we're telling a story in pictures, we must show how the character acts and reacts to the incidents and events that he/she confronts and overcomes (or doesn't overcome) during the story line. If you're writing your script and sense your characters are not as sharp or defined as you think they should be, and feel they should be stronger, more dimensional, and more universal in terms of thoughts, feelings, and emotions, the first thing you must determine is whether they're an active force in the screenplay—whether they cause things to happen, or whether things happen to them.

But first, who is your main character? Who is your story about? If your story is about three guys preparing to steal moon rocks, which one of the three is the *main character*? You have to know that. In *Lord of the Rings,* do you know who the main character is? Is it Frodo, Sam, Gandalf (Ian McKellen), or Aragorn (Viggo Mortensen)? Or is it all of them? If you aren't sure, just ask yourself: Who is this story about? In *Lord of the Rings,* you could say, with good cause, that Aragorn is the main character because he leads the Fellowship, makes the decisions, and becomes the king. But take away all the trappings and the story is really about returning the ring to its place of origin, Mount Doom, so it can be destroyed. That's what this story is about; therefore, Frodo is the main character. You can have more than one main character, of course, but it certainly clarifies things if you identify a single hero or heroine.

Frequently a story is about what distinguishes the main character from the other characters. Who is the main character in *The Shawshank Redemption*? Red, the Morgan Freeman character, has the largest part of the movie, and he is the character telling us about Andy Dufrense (Tim Robbins). But the story is really about Andy, so even though his part is not as large as Red's, he is the main character because the story is about *him*. What about *Butch Cassidy and the Sundance Kid*? Butch (Paul Newman) is the main character. He is the man making the decisions. Butch has a great line where he broaches one of his usual wild schemes to Sundance (Robert Redford), and Sundance just looks at him, doesn't say a word, and turns away. And

Butch mutters to himself: "I got vision and the rest of the world wears bifocals." And it's true. Within the context of that screenplay, Butch Cassidy *is* the main character—he is the character who *plans* things, who *acts*. Butch leads and Sundance follows. It is Butch's idea to leave for South America; he knows their outlaw days are numbered, and to escape the law, death, or both, they must leave. He convinces Sundance and Etta Place to go with him. Sundance is a *major* character, not the *main* character. Once you establish the main character, you can explore ways to create a full-bodied, dimensional character portrait.

There are several ways to approach creating your characters and all of them are valid, but you must choose the best way for you. The method outlined below gives you the opportunity of choosing what you want to use, or not use, in developing your characters.

First, establish your main character. Who is your story about? Separate the components of his/her life into two basic categories: *interior* and *exterior*. The interior life of your character takes place from birth up until the time your story begins. It is a process that *forms* character. The exterior life of your character takes place from the moment your film begins to the conclusion of the story. It is a process that *reveals* character.

Film is a visual medium. You must find ways to reveal your character's conflicts *visually*. You cannot reveal what you don't know. Thus, it's important to make the distinction between *knowing* your character as a thought, notion, or idea in your head and revealing him or her on paper.

Diagrammed, it looks like this:

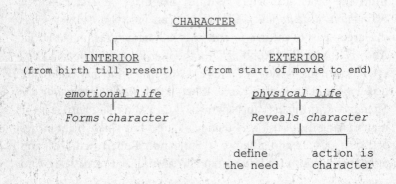

The *Character Biography* is an exercise that reveals your character's *interior* life, the emotional forces working on your character from birth. Is your character male or female? If male, how old is he when the story begins? Where does he live, what city or country? Where was he born? Was he an only child, or did he have brothers and sisters? What kind of childhood did he have? Happy? Sad? Physically or medically challenging? What was his relationship to his parents? Did he get into a lot of trouble as a kid? Was he mischievous? What kind of a child was he? Outgoing, an extrovert; or studious, an introvert?

When you begin formulating your character from birth, you begin to see your character build. Pursue his/her life through the first ten years; include his/her preschool and school years, relationships with friends and family and teachers. Did a single parent raise your character? Mother or father? Aunt or uncle? How did they get along? Is your character streetwise or sheltered? What kind of jobs did the parent(s) have to make ends meet?

Move into the second ten years of your character's life, ages ten to twenty. That means middle and high school. What kind of influences did your character have while growing up? Friends? What kind of interests? School, athletics, social, political? Did your character take an interest in extracurricular or after-school activities, like a debating club? What about sexual experiences? Relationships with peers? Did your character have to work part-time during high school? What about any sibling relationships? Any envy or hostility present? In other words, you want as much information as you can get about your character as he/she is growing up. What about relationships with teachers? What kind of relationship did your character have with his/her parents during these years? Did any major traumatic event happen that may have emotionally influenced your character? In high school, what kind of experience did he/she have? Did he/she have many friends or just a few friends? Did he/she feel like an outsider? Take a look at *Mean Girls* (Tina Fey). The whole film is built around feeling unpopular.

Paul Thomas Anderson's *Magnolia* deals with the themes of reconciliation and forgiveness, revealing how parents' actions shape and influence their children. (Ibsen's great play *Ghosts* deals with the same themes, with how the sins of the father are passed on to the son.) In *Magnolia*, Earl (Jason Robards) is on his deathbed and confesses his sins, attempting to forgive himself for walking out on his dying wife and son, thus leaving the then fourteen-year-old Frank (Tom Cruise) to care for his dying mother alone. That incident has affected Frank's entire life and led him to develop a lifestyle where he seeks to convince men that sex is a weapon that can be used to "destroy the opposite sex." By confronting Earl on his deathbed, Frank is able to complete his relationship with his father before he dies.

Move into the college years. Did your character go to college, or even consider college? What college or university did he or she go to? What was his or her major? Was your character active politically? Did he or she join clubs or student body organizations? Did your character have a significant relationship while in college? What happened in this relationship? How long were they together? Did they get married? When the story begins, is your character married, widowed, single, separated, or divorced? If married, for how long and to whom?

Continue to trace your character's life until the story begins. Examine his/her career, relationships, dreams, hopes, and aspirations. Many times reality collides with dreams and fantasies and generates a sense of conflict within the character's life. Ask yourself questions; be observant; notice your own friends, family, and acquaintances. Sometimes you can use the information you observe in a slightly different form.

Remember, you are not your character. You do not have the same name, same situation, or same birth date. The time frame of events you want to write about may have to be modified to gain greater insight into the character. You may share certain similarities with the character, but if you think you're going to use yourself as the model, it's not going to work. Writing is the ability to ask yourself questions and wait for the answers. As a side note, it's important to phrase your creative questions to begin with the word *what*, not *why*. *What* implies a specific response; if you ask yourself a question beginning with the word *why*, you can get many different answers, and they may all be correct. So try to phrase any questions using the word *what*: *What* causes my character to react in this manner? (Not: *Why* does my character do this?) *What* is the purpose of this scene? It may take a while to phrase the question, and the answer may not appear as soon as you would like it to, but trust the process; it's bigger than you are. That's why I call writing a character biography creative research. You're asking questions and getting answers. You're building the interior life of your character, the emotional life, on a firm foundation so that your character can move and evolve in a definite *character arc* through the story, can change and grow through certain emotional stages of the action. It's not very often that characters will be the same at the beginning of a story as they are at the end; their thoughts and feelings will probably change during the emotional through line of the action.

Once you've established the interior aspect of your character in a character biography, you can move into the *exterior* portion of your story.

The *exterior* aspect of your character takes place during the actual time of the screenplay, from the first fade-in to the final fade-out. It is important to examine the relationships in the lives of your characters, as they have the potential of becoming a resource for greater depth of character, including subplots, secondary actions, and any possible intercutting you may want to do to build the relationship between characters and story.

How do you make your characters real, believable, and multi-dimensional people during your story? From fade-in to fade-out?

The best way to do this is to separate your characters' lives into three basic components—their *professional life,* their *personal life,* and their *private life.* These areas of your characters' lives can be dramatized over the course of the screenplay.

Professional: What does your main character do for a living? You need to know this. As mentioned, if *you* don't know your character, who does? Where does he or she work? Is she the vice president of a bank? A construction worker? A doctor? A sound technician? A scientist? A professor? The clearer you are, the more believable your characters become. Are they sad or happy with their lives? Do they wish their lives were different—another job, or another wife, or possibly another self? In Michelangelo Antonioni's *The Passenger,* David Locke (Jack Nicholson) finds a dead man and decides to take his identity, not knowing what his destiny will be. Sometimes we wish for what the other person has.

Go into your character's workplace and start defining the people that he or she interacts with on a daily basis; his/her boss, the various assistants, secretaries, salesmen, corporate heads, and so on. Define the relationships with coworkers. Are the relationships good, bad, supportive, happy, or sad; are there any conflicts in the relationships? If so, what are they about? Professional jealousy, anger, different personality types? How does your character deal with it? With argument and discussion? Or by silence and withdrawal? By launching personal attacks?

If your character works in an office environment, what is his/her job description? Who is his/her strongest supporter? How well do the two of them get along? Do they confide in each other? Socialize with each other during off hours? How does she get along with her boss? Is it a good relationship, or is there some resentment because of the way things are going in the office, or pending mergers or buyouts, or possible looming salary cutbacks and layoffs?

In a free-association essay of about a page or two, define your character's professional life. Don't try to censor yourself; just throw it all down on the page. When you can describe and explore the relationships of your main character with the other people in his/her professional life, you're creating a personality and a point of view. And that's the starting point of building and broadening and enhancing the richness of your character's life.

Personal: Is your main character married, single, widowed, divorced, or separated? Is your character in a relationship when the story begins? If so, who is he/she with and how long have they been together? If your character is married, whom did he or she marry? Someone he met at school, or dated, or was fixed up with? Is the person your character is with when the story begins from the same background as she or do they come from "different sides of the tracks"? Above or below him/her in terms of education or profession? Childhood sweethearts? College lovers? How long have they been married? What does the marriage look like? Here's where the length of the marriage comes in. If they have recently married, their relationship is different from that of a couple who have been married for several years. Do they go places, do things together? Or do they take each other for granted? Do they have many friends and participate in social functions, or do they have only a few friends? Is the marriage strong, or is your character thinking about, or participating in, extramarital affairs?

Finding ways to illustrate and reveal your character's relationships are challenging, but rewarding. Think about conflicts; he may want one thing, she another. It may be as important as whether or not to have children, or simply that he likes sporting events and she likes the theater. Go into this marriage and write it out. You can do this as it applies to your individual screenplay, either as a background relationship or in the foreground, as part of the action.

My favorite film marriage is seen in *Citizen Kane*. Kane's marriage is revealed in one incredible sequence, which begins with the marriage and honeymoon of Kane and his first wife. In the next cut, we see them at breakfast having an intimate conversation. There is a *swish pan* (the camera swishes quickly out of the frame) and we see them in different clothes talking and reading the paper at breakfast. *Swish pan* and we see them at a slightly larger table having a very heated discussion. *Swish pan* to them having a more vocal argument about his spending so much time at his newspaper. *Swish pan* to them at a much larger table, both silent, both reading the paper, he reading the *Inquirer,* she reading the *Post,* his primary competitor. She asks him something and he simply grunts in reply. *Swish pan* to them at a very long table eating in total silence. A significant period of time covered in about a minute. The sequence tells us so much about their relationship, and it's all done in brief shots, using pictures instead of words. A screenplay, remember, is a story told with pictures.

If your character is single, what is his/her single life like? Dating many people, or getting somewhat serious about someone? If he or she is alone when the story begins, when was his/her last relationship? Was it serious or just a three-month fling? What are his/her likes or dislikes? If your character is seeing someone when the story begins, how long have they been together? Any conflicts in the relationship? What do they disagree about? What do they have in common? Any ex-girlfriends or ex-boyfriends in the equation? How do they work it out? Any other areas they have conflicts in? In terms of a relationship, is she/he ready to move into some kind of commitment?

Is she divorced? If yes, how long was she married? To whom? What really happened that caused the breakup? How long were they together? Any children? If yes, how often does she see the kids? And how do the children feel about the divorce or someone new that one of their parents might be seeing?

All these aspects of your character's relationships should be explored, thought about, written about. When you have doubts about your character, go into your own life. Ask yourself—if you were in that situation, what would you do in your character's place? This is not to say that you are your character. You may have certain things in common with your character, but I'll say it again: You are *not* your character.

Define the personal relationships of your character in a page or two. In free-association or automatic writing, just throw down all your thoughts, words, and feelings on the page, and don't worry what it looks like or reads like. No one is going to see this but you.

Private: What does your character do when he or she is alone? Watch a lot of TV? Exercise—training for a triathlon competition? Is he into sports, and goes to the gym three times a week? Does she jog, do yoga, or take spinning classes? Take a creative writing class one night a week? Does she have any pets? What kind? What hobbies does your character have? Does he/she collect stamps, garden, or take cooking classes? The *private* aspect covers the area of your character's life when he/she is alone.

What's so beneficial about knowing your characters' professional, personal, and private lives is that you have something to cut away to; if you are writing your screenplay and don't know what happens next, you can go into the professional, personal, or private aspects of your character's life and find something to show to move the story forward.

Aristotle says in the *Poetics:* "Life consists in action and its end is a mode of action, not a quality." That means your character has to be active, has to be doing things, causing things to happen, not just reacting all the time. Sometimes it's necessary for your character to react to a situation, but you can't have your main character constantly reacting only to things that happen to him. If that happens, he disappears off the page, and your story appears soft, without an edge. Your character is what he/she does. Film is a visual medium, and the writer's responsibility is to choose an image, or picture, that cinematically dramatizes his or her character. You can create a dialogue scene in a small and stuffy hotel room, or have the scene occur at the beach or under the stars. One is visually closed; the others visually open and dynamic. It's your story, your choice.

If we wanted to diagram the concept of character, it would look like this:

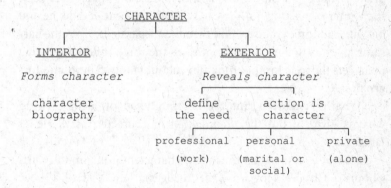

ACTION IS CHARACTER.

Film is behavior. We can know a lot about characters by how they react, or behave, in certain situations. Pictures, or images, reveal different aspects of character. Whereas character reveals the deep-seated nature of who people are, in terms of values, actions, and beliefs, *characterization* is expressed in the way people live, the cars they drive, the pictures they hang on the wall, their likes and dislikes, what they eat, and other forms of individual character expression. Character is expressed in who they are, by their actions and reactions, by their creative choices. Characterization, on the other hand, is expressed in their taste and how they look to the world, what they wear, the cars they drive.

Form your characters by creating a character biography, then *reveal* them by showing who they are in the professional, personal, and private aspects of their lives.

How powerful and effective can the character biography be? It is a tremendous tool, revealing insights about the main character and the source of possible conflict. The character biography can be used effectively within the body of the screenplay. Occasionally things happen while you're writing your character biography in free association and events leap off the page at you. Sometimes you can include these incidents or events in the screenplay. In *The Royal Tenenbaums,* the first few pages of the screenplay set up the characters; the Narrator tells us the family history in a very novelistic approach: "Royal Tenenbaum bought the house on Archer Avenue in the winter of his thirty-fifth year.... Over the next decade, he and his wife had three children, and then they separated...." As the narrator gives us this information, we see the three children growing up. It sets the tone for the entire film, about family, failure, and forgiveness.

"What is character but the *determination* of incident? And what is incident but the *illumination* of character?" says Henry James.

In *Seabiscuit,* there are four main characters: Tom Smith (Chris Cooper), Charles Howard (Jeff Bridges), Red Pollard (Tobey Maguire), and the horse, Seabiscuit. All of them have lost something: Tom Smith lost his freedom; Charles Howard lost his young son; Red Pollard lost his parents when he was "given away" during the Depression; Seabiscuit was deemed unworthy and given away when he was six months old. The film traces the journey of these four characters and their search for belonging, not only for themselves, but for the country at large. During America's Depression in the 1930s, these three men and this horse inspired the entire country and gave people something to cheer about, to feel good about.

What's the value of creating a character biography? Look at *Seabiscuit:* The Narrator tells us that Seabiscuit "was the son of Hard Tack, sired by the mighty horse Man o' War ... but the breeding did little to impress anyone.... At six months he was shipped off to train with the legendary trainer Sunny Fitzsimmons.... Fitzsimmons decided the horse was lazy and felt sure he could train the obstinance out of him.... When he didn't improve, they decided the colt was incorrigible.... They made him a training partner to 'better' horses, forcing him to lose head-to-head duels to boost the confidence of the other animal.... When they finally did race him, he did just what they had trained him to do: He lost.... By the time he was a three-year-old, Seabiscuit was running in two cheap claiming races a week. Soon he grew as bitter and angry as his sire Hard Tack had been.... He was sold for the rock-bottom price of two thousand dollars.... And, of course, it all made sense....Champions were large. They were sleek. They were without imperfection.... This horse ran as they had always expected him to...."

It took all four of them—Tom Smith, Charles Howard, Red Pollard, and Seabiscuit—to join forces as a team, each member an essential part of the whole, and become the pride and joy of America. "You know," Red Pollard says in a voice-over at the end of the film, "everybody thinks we found this broken-down horse and fixed him...but we didn't.... He fixed us. Every one of us. And, I guess in a way, we kind of fixed each other, too."

———————

If you want to write a screenplay, decide who you are writing about. As an exercise, choose a character and write a character biography. Free-associate. Just throw down thoughts, words, or ideas. Don't worry about grammar and punctuation. Write in fragments. You may want to start from birth but you don't have to follow your character's life in a linear form. Skip around if you have to; let your creative consciousness dictate the flow of character. Break your character's life down into the first ten years, the second ten years, the third ten years, and beyond. Write about five to seven pages in free association, and if you choose, write more. When I write a character biography, I'll write more than twenty pages, starting with my character's parents and grandparents on both sides, and then

I'll even use past lives and astrology to get further insight into my character.

After you've completed the character biography, think about your character's professional life, personal life, and private life. Focus on the relationships that occur during the screenplay.

KNOW YOUR CHARACTER.

4

Building a Character

"Amos Charles Dundee is a tall, broad-shouldered, rawboned man in his late thirties. Opinionated, strong-willed, quick-tempered, he is a realist who sees the world exactly as it is and can't get enough of it. An artist, perhaps a sculptor of battle, who knows that for him death is as close as the owl perched upon the thigh of night. It is a very personal world to Amos Charles Dundee and win, lose, or draw, he will play it according to his needs and wants. Dundee is a *soldier*. He gives orders well and takes them badly. . . . A wise man who can be a fool . . . who will go his own way come hell or high water and so far has yet to look back or regret . . . who so far has yet to fail."

—*Major Dundee*
Sam Peckinpah, Oscar Saul

When I first began writing screenplays, I had the good fortune of hanging out with Sam Peckinpah during the time he was writing *The Wild Bunch*. His niece, Deneen Peckinpah, and I had both worked with Jean Renoir on the world premiere of his play *Carola* when we were students at UC Berkeley. When she came to L.A. seeking an acting career, she stayed with Sam at the beach.

Since I was just starting out writing screenplays, I was like a sponge, absorbing as much as I could about the art and craft. It was during those summer months that I was blessed to be around the man who literally changed the style and impact of the Western film.

I write a lot about this period and my relationship with Peckinpah in *Going to the Movies*.

Sam was amazing—brilliant in his visual awareness, talkative when he felt comfortable, and, of course, moody and self-destructive when he was drinking too much or thought someone had gone behind his back or broken their word to him.

Most of Sam's films deal with characters who are dedicated or obsessed—take your pick—and caught in the maelstrom of changing times. He explored this theme, *unchanged men in a changing time,* in most of his films: *Ride the High Country* (N. B. Stone), *Major Dundee* (Oscar Saul), *The Wild Bunch* (Walon Green), *The Ballad of Cable Hogue* (John Crawford and Edmund Penny), *Straw Dogs* (David Zelag Goodman), *The Getaway* (Walter Hill), *Junior Bonner* (Jeb Rosebrook), *Pat Garrett and Billy the Kid* (Rudy Wurlitzer), and others.

When I first met him, I'd heard stories about his drunken antics, the difficulties he had on the set with his crew, his sense of "perfectionism," the conflicts he had with the studios and producers, so I didn't really know what to expect. I found him to be tough and honest, with a keen sensibility and understanding. He wasn't drinking the "hard stuff," he said, only two beers a day, and during our conversations I learned he had not made a film since *Major Dundee*, four years earlier.

Cowritten with Oscar Saul, *Dundee* had been a traumatic experience for him. The studio had reneged on the contract and taken it away from him, recut it, and butchered it, even though he had "final cut" built into his contract. The title music, by Mitch Miller's sing-along gang, was absolutely ridiculous. In his words, it had been a "personal disaster," and it was while working on *Dundee* that he got the reputation of being "difficult"—meaning "unemployable" in Hollywood vernacular. Charlton Heston, Deneen told me, had returned his salary, and Peckinpah demanded that his name be taken off the credits, but the studio refused. He wanted to reshoot the opening sequence the way he had written it, but the studio said no. In effect, he was fired from his own film. He couldn't get any work after that and was only now being given a chance to rewrite and direct *The Wild Bunch* by producer Phil Feldman.

There were so many questions I wanted to ask him about writing a screenplay: I wanted to find out how he created and built his characters; what he looked for when he searched for a subject, or story, to write about; if he artificially created the story's conflict, or if it was inherent in the story. The list went on and on, but I wanted to be cool, so I asked him only a few questions at a time. Sam was open and receptive and seemed to enjoy our conversations.

He always found great visual metaphors that reflected the indicators of change and their impact upon the characters. I think that's one of the ingredients Peckinpah brought to the contemporary Western: He showed us bits and pieces of character that reflected this theme of not belonging, of being "outside" and behind the times, and then wove these concepts into moments of visual action. *Ride the High Country* opens with a lone rider, Joel McCrea, riding into a town where a carnival is in full swing. Suddenly an antique Model T turns the corner and the driver, dressed in a long coat and goggles, starts honking angrily for McCrea to move out of the way. Then a camel bursts into view, followed by a horse, and the two race neck and neck to the finish line of a horse-and-camel race, the camel winning by almost a full length. In the opening sequence of *The Wild Bunch*, William Holden offers his arm to an elderly lady and helps her cross the street just before he and his gang rob the bank as a Temperance Parade gets under way.

Late one afternoon, after Sam had finished his day's writing on *The Wild Bunch*, we were enjoying a beer and watching the sun set when I asked how he structured his stories. He paused for a moment, then told me that he liked to "hang" his stories around a centerpiece. Typically, he said, he would build the action up to a certain event, about midway through the story, then let everything else be the result of that event. In *The Wild Bunch* it is the train robbery, done almost in total silence. It's a magnificent sequence; once he sets up the story and characters, everything leads to the train robbery and the rest of the movie unfolds as a result of that sequence.

We discussed it for a while, then he left the room and returned a few minutes later holding a script. It was the screenplay for *Major Dundee*. "Take a look at it," he urged.

The story takes place right after the Civil War and traces

Dundee's (Charlton Heston's) relentless quest to track down the band of renegade Apaches and rescue the homesteader children who had been taken hostage during the massacre that opens the story. Dundee doesn't care how he does it, or the price he inflicts upon others to achieve his goal. It's Dundee's obsession that drives his character through the narrative story line. That, I discovered, was his dramatic need. That's what his purpose was, his mission, the engine that drove the story line.

I read *Major Dundee* over and over again, taking notes, literally studying it as if I were preparing for a final exam. It was an incredible education. I began to *see* things: how Peckinpah structured and set up the story in the opening sequence, how he established the characters visually, then built the story to highlight the centerpiece—the ambush by the Apaches.

When I was making documentaries for David Wolper, I understood the importance of having a strong opening scene or sequence, something that will immediately grab the attention of the reader or audience. *Major Dundee* opens with a Halloween party at an isolated ranch on the Western frontier just before the end of the Civil War; the music's playing, the people are dancing, laughing, and having a good time, while costumed children run around outside, playing games. Then Sam cuts from the painted face of a child playing cowboys and Indians to the face of an Apache brave painted for war. Amid the music and dance, as children giggle and scream in joy and mock fright, the Apaches launch their attack, killing everyone and everything except the male children and the horses.

It's a remarkable opening, something I call "pure Peckinpah." The contradiction between the images of the children in their Halloween costumes and the painted faces of the Apaches killing and scalping was horrifying. I marveled, too, at how Peckinpah introduces Major Dundee. The way he's described in the stage directions tells us everything we need to know: "*Opinionated, strong-willed, quick-tempered.... An artist, perhaps a sculptor of battle, who knows that for him death is as close as the owl perched upon the thigh of night.... He gives orders well and takes them badly.... A wise man who can be a fool... who will go his own way come hell or high water... who so far has yet to fail.*"

I wanted to write characters like that. I wanted to enrich the characters in my screenplays so that they were fully formed and realized, multidimensional, real people in real situations. So I started asking myself questions: How do you take the *idea* of a person that exists in a scrambled, fragmented form and make him or her into a living, flesh-and-blood person, a person you can relate to and identify with? How do you go about putting life into your characters? How do you build character?

As soon as I phrased the questions I knew there was no definitive answer—because building character is part of the mystery and magic of the creative process. It is an ongoing, never-ending, continuing practice. In order to really solve the problem of *character,* it's essential to go into your characters and build the foundations and fabric of their lives, then add ingredients that will heighten and expand the portrait of who they are.

So, I kept asking myself: What makes a good character? What *is* character? To find the answer, I needed to figure out what qualities we all have in common.

When you think about it, underneath this skin of ours we're really the same, you and I; certain things unite us. We share the same needs, the same wants, the same fears and insecurities; we want to be loved, have people like us, be successful, happy, and healthy.

When I went back to reread *Major Dundee* with this in mind, I started analyzing the characters in terms of their individual needs and wants.

Reading it from this perspective, I saw four things, four essential qualities that seemed to go into the making of good characters: (1), the characters have a strong and defined *dramatic need;* (2), they have an individual *point of view;* (3), they personify an *attitude;* and (4), they go through some kind of *change,* or *transformation.*

Those four elements, those four qualities, make up good character. Using that as a starting point, I saw that every main, or major, character has a strong dramatic need. *Dramatic need* is defined as *what your main characters want to win, gain, get, or achieve during the course of your screenplay.* The *dramatic need* is what drives your characters through the story line. It is their purpose, their mission, their motivation, driving them through the narrative action of the story line.

In most cases you can express the dramatic need in a sentence or two. It is usually simple and can be stated through a line of dialogue, if you choose; or it does not have to be expressed at all. But you, as writer, *must know* your character's dramatic need.

In *Thelma & Louise,* the dramatic need is to *escape safely* to Mexico; that's what drives these two characters through the entire story line. In *Cold Mountain,* Inman's dramatic need is to *return home,* and Ada's is to survive and adapt to the conditions around her. In *Lord of the Rings,* as mentioned, it's to *carry* the ring to Mount Doom and *destroy* it in the fire that created it.

In *Apollo 13* (William Broyles Jr. and Al Reinert), the dramatic need is to return the astronauts safely to earth. But it didn't start out that way. When the story began, the dramatic need of *Apollo 13,* the astronaut's mission, was to walk on the moon; but that changed when the oxygen tank blew. The dramatic question then became not whether they were going to land on the moon but whether they would be able to survive and return safely to Earth.

There are times that the dramatic need will change during the course of the story. If your character's dramatic need does change, it will usually occur at Plot Point I, the true beginning of your story. In *Thelma & Louise,* Louise's killing Harlan at Plot Point I forces the action into a new direction; instead of spending a weekend in the mountains, Thelma and Louise have now become fugitives from the law. Their dramatic need is to escape. In *Dances With Wolves* (Michael Blake), John Dunbar's (Kevin Costner's) dramatic need is to escape from the lunacy of the Civil War and go to the farthermost point of the frontier. But when he finally reaches his goal, Fort Sedgewick—Plot Point I—his dramatic need changes, and now he must learn how to adapt to the land and establish a relationship with the Sioux.

What is your main character's dramatic need? Can you define it in a few words? Articulate it? If *you* don't know your character's dramatic need, who does? You must know it. If you like, you can establish dramatic needs for other characters in the screenplay. The dramatic need is the engine that powers the character through the story line.

The second thing that makes good character is *point of view.* Point of view is defined as *the way a person sees, or views, the world.* Every person has an individual point of view. Point of view is a belief system, and as we know, what we believe to be true *is* true. There's an ancient Hindu scripture titled the *Yoga Vasistha* that states, *"The World is as you see it."* That means that what's inside our head—our thoughts, feelings, emotions, memories—is reflected outside, in our everyday experience. It is our mind, how we *see* the world, that determines our experience. As one Great Being puts it: "You are the baker of the bread you eat."

Point of view shades and colors the way we see the world. Have you ever heard phrases like: "Life is unfair," "You can't fight City Hall," "All life is a game of chance," "You can't teach an old dog new tricks," "Life is unlimited opportunity," "You make your own luck," or "Success is based on who you know"? These are all points of view. We all have points of view, singular and unique, individual to the personal experience and expression of each person. It should be mentioned that a point of view is acquired through *personal experience.*

If your character is a parent, she/he could reflect a "parent's" point of view. Or he/she could be a student and view the world from a "student's" point of view. A housewife has a specific point of view. So does a criminal, terrorist, cop, doctor, lawyer, rich man, poor man—all present individual and unique *points of view.*

Do you know what your character's point of view is?

Is your character an environmentalist? A humanist? A racist? Someone who believes in fate, destiny, and astrology? Does your character believe in voodoo or witchcraft, or that the future can be revealed through a medium or psychic? Does your character believe that the limitations we confront are self-imposed, like Neo in *The Matrix*? Does your character put his faith in doctors, lawyers, *The Wall Street Journal, The New York Times*? His/her belief in *Time, People, Newsweek,* and the evening news?

Point of view is an individual and independent belief system. I believe in God. That's a point of view. Or, I don't believe in God. That's also a point of view. Or, I don't know whether there is a God or not; that's also a point of view. All three statements are true within the individual fabric of the character. There is no right or wrong here, no good or bad, no judgment, justification, or evaluation. Point of view is neither right nor wrong; it is as singular and distinctive as a rose on a rosebush. No two leaves, no two flowers, no two people are ever the same.

The Native Americans believe the Earth is a living being. Therefore, all living things on this planet are part of Mother Earth, whether a human, tree, rock, animal, stream, or flower. All life is sacred. That's a point of view.

Your character's point of view may be that the indiscriminate slaughtering of dolphins and whales is morally wrong because they are two of the most intelligent species on the planet, maybe smarter than man. Your character supports that point of view by participating in demonstrations and wearing T-shirts with *Save the Whales and Dolphins* on it.

Look for ways your characters can support and dramatize their points of view. Knowing your characters' points of view becomes a good way to generate conflict. If your characters believe in luck, they believe that there's a chance they can win the lottery. But anyone who believes that it's "fixed" is not going to waste a dollar on a pick.

In *The Shawshank Redemption,* there's a short scene between Andy and Red that reveals the difference in their points of view. After almost twenty years in Shawshank Prison, Red is cynical because, in his eyes, the concept of *hope* is simply a four-letter word. His spirit has been so crushed by the prison system that he angrily declares to Andy, "Hope is a dangerous thing. Drives a man insane. It's got no place here. Better get used to the idea." And it is Red's emotional journey that leads him to the understanding that "hope is a good thing." The film ends on a note of hope, with Red breaking his parole and riding the bus to meet Andy in Mexico: "I hope I can make it across the border. I hope to see my friend and shake his hand. I hope the Pacific is as blue as it has been in my dreams.... I *hope.*"

Andy has a different point of view; he believes that "there are things in this world not carved out of gray stone, that there's a small place inside of us they can never lock away. Hope." And that's what keeps Andy going in prison, that's what makes him sacrifice a week of his life in solitary, "the hole," just so he can listen to an aria from a Mozart opera.

The third thing that makes good character is *attitude. Attitude* is defined as a *manner* or *opinion,* and is a way of acting or feeling that reveals a person's personal opinion. An attitude, differentiated from a point of view, is an *intellectual decision,* so it can, and probably will, be classified by a judgment: right or wrong, good or bad, positive or negative, angry or happy, cynical or naive, superior or inferior, liberal or conservative, optimistic or pessimistic. Being "right" all the time is an attitude; so is being "macho." Voicing a political opinion is also an attitude; just look at the many opinions about the war in Iraq. In the same way, have you ever gone into a store to buy something and found yourself dealing with a salesperson who does not want to be there, has negative energy and thinks he/she is superior to you? That's an attitude. Have you ever walked into a fancy restaurant not wearing the "right" clothes? It's that kind of judgment, where someone is convinced he's right and you're wrong; judgments, opinions, evaluations all stem from attitude. It's an *intellectual decision* one makes. Understanding your character's attitude allows him/her to reach out and touch his/her humanity in an individual way. Is he/she enthusiastic about his/her life and job, or unhappy? We all know people who express different parts of themselves through their attitude; someone who feels the world owes them a living, or blames their lack of success on "who you know."

The Truth About Cats and Dogs (Audrey Wells) is a delightful romantic comedy that is entirely based on the characters' attitudes. Abby (Janeane Garofalo) is a woman who lives by her attitude; her opinion is that all men want in a woman is a pretty face and a great body. This attitude governs her behavior throughout the entire film. And Nora (Uma Thurman) takes it for granted that she's not very bright. She thinks of herself as the "dumb blonde" with the heart of gold. Both Abby and Nora have to learn that their attitudes are not their real selves. Their journey through the film is to accept themselves as they truly are.

Sometimes it's difficult to separate *point of view* from *attitude*. Many of my students struggle to define these two qualities, but I tell them it really doesn't matter; when you're creating the basic core of your character, you're taking one large ball of wax and, in this case, pulling it apart into four separate pieces. The parts and the whole, right? Who cares whether one part is the point of view and another the attitude? It doesn't make any difference; the parts and the whole are really the same thing. So if you're unsure about whether a particular character trait is a point of view or an attitude, don't worry about it. Just separate the concepts in your own mind.

The fourth element that makes up good character is *change*, or *transformation*. Does your character change during the course of your screenplay? If so, what is the change? Can you define it? Articulate it? Can you trace the emotional arc of the character from the beginning to the end? In *The Truth About Cats and Dogs*, both characters undergo a change that brings about a new awareness of who they are. Abby's final acceptance that she is really loved *for who she is* completes the character arc of the change.

In *The Shawshank Redemption*, Andy has endured prison life for some nineteen years when he learns who actually murdered his wife and her lover. When the warden refuses to help him get a new trial and Tommy, the witness, is killed, he realizes the warden will never let him out. Andy had entered prison considering himself guilty, even though he hadn't killed his wife and her lover; he was guilty, yes, as Red tells him, not of pulling the trigger, but of being a bad husband. Now that he has served "his time," he realizes the moment has come for him to be free once again. It is his redemption. As we learn later, he's been preparing to escape for years.

Having a character change during the course of the screenplay is not a requirement if it doesn't fit your character. But transformation, change, seems to be an essential aspect of our humanity, especially at this time in our culture. I think we're all a little like Melvin (Jack Nicholson) in *As Good as It Gets* (Mark Andrus and James L.

Brooks). Melvin may be complex and fastidious as a person, but his dramatic need is expressed toward the end of the film when he says, "When I'm with you I want to be a better person." I think we all want that. Change, transformation, is a constant of life, and if you can impel some kind of emotional change within your character, it creates an arc of behavior and adds another dimension to who he/she is. If you're unclear about the character's change, take the time to write an essay in a page or so, charting his or her emotional arc.

Again, it's important to remember that when you're writing a screenplay, the main character must be active; she must *cause things to happen,* not let things happen to her. It's okay if she reacts to incidents or events some of the time, but if she is always reacting, she becomes passive, weak, and that's when the character seems to disappear off the page. Minor characters appear more interesting than the main character and seem to have more life and flamboyance.

Film is behavior; action is character and character, action; what a person does is who he is, not what he says.

Thelma & Louise is a good example. The script sets up the two women by showing who they are. Louise is unmarried, a waitress, and has a boyfriend, Jimmy, a musician, who's playing a gig on the road and hasn't called her once in three weeks. She's upset and resolves that she's not going to be home when he returns. So she decides to go to a friend's cabin in the mountains without telling him where she's gone. When he does arrive home, she just won't be there. He'll get a taste of how it feels. That's the backstory.

Thelma, on the other hand, appears to be a "ditzy" housewife. Her kitchen is a mess, and her "breakfast" consists of little nibbles from a frozen candy bar, which she puts back in the freezer only to whip out again for another bite. What she does and how her kitchen looks reveal an aspect of her character; we *see* who she is by what she does, her actions.

Her husband, Darryl (Christopher McDonald), an arrogant, egotistical fool, is a high school hero whose best years are behind him. He treats Thelma with so little respect that she has to lie to him so she can go away for the weekend with her friend. Even then, her guilt influences her to leave something in the microwave for him

when he comes home from work. You get what you settle for in a relationship, Louise tells her. That's the life and relationship that
Thelma has chosen for herself.

Act I sets up their relationship. When they pull into the parking
lot of the Silver Bullet bar, during the first ten pages, we learn more
about them in terms of their relationship with the men in their
lives. By the time Harlan tries to rape Thelma, at the end of Act I,
their characters have already been established. When Louise pulls
the trigger, killing Harlan, their lives and destiny change. That's Plot
Point I. This *incident* makes them two fugitives on the run and alters
and defines their characters.

Killing Harlan is the incident that really determines their characters. Their flight to Mexico becomes a journey of insight and self-
discovery that eventually leads to their deaths. Their destiny has
been determined by their actions, and their actions have illuminated who they really are. They have burned their bridges and literally "run out of world," as writer Callie Khouri says. There is no way
back. You can't step into the same river twice.

The essence of character is action—what a person does is who
he is. A friend of mine had the opportunity of flying to New York
for a business interview. She had mixed feelings about going. The
interview was for a prestigious and high-salaried job she wanted;
but she didn't know whether she was willing to move to New York.
She wrestled with the problem for more than a week, then finally
decided to go, packed her bags, and drove to the airport. But when
she parked her car at the airport, she "accidentally" locked her keys
inside the car—with the motor running. It's a perfect example of
action revealing character; it told her what she knew all along—she
didn't want to go to New York!

A scene like that can illustrate a lot about your character.

Is your character late, or early, or right on time for appointments? Does your character react to authority the way Woody Allen
does in *Annie Hall* when he tears up his driver's license in front of a
policeman? Every action, every word of dialogue, every individual
character trait expands our knowledge and comprehension of the
character.

One of Henry James's theories is termed the *Theory of Illumination.* James said that if your character occupies the center of a circle and all the other characters he interacts with surround him, then each time a character interacts with the main character, the other characters can reveal, or illuminate, different aspects of the main character. The analogy he used was walking into a darkened room and turning on the floor lamps located in each corner. Each lamp illuminates a different part of the room. In the same way, different aspects of your main character can be illuminated by what other people say about him or her. This is how we know that Bob Harris, the Bill Murray character in *Lost in Translation,* is a movie star: He's sitting at the bar, alone, when two guys start telling him how much they loved his movies, and wonder whether he did all his own stunts. In that one exchange, we learn he is an action star, one whose career seems to be on the decline.

Sometimes during the writing process you'll find that what doesn't work often shows you what does. Once one of my students was writing a drama, complete with unhappy, or "tragic," ending. But suddenly, at the beginning of the third act, his characters started acting "funny." Gag lines started coming out, and the resolution became funny, not serious. Every time he sat down to write, the humor just poured out; he couldn't stop it. He became frustrated, finally giving up in despair.

He was almost apologetic when he came to me. In all honesty, he explained, he didn't know what to do. I suggested that he sit down and start writing, that he let the words and dialogue come out as they wanted to. If it's funny, let it be funny, I told him; just write and complete the third act. Then he could see what he had. If it was funny all the way through and he didn't like it, all he had to do was put it in a drawer somewhere, file it away, and then go back and write the third act the way he'd wanted to in the first place.

He did it, and it worked. He threw out the comedy version of the third act, then wrote it serious, the way he wanted to. The comedy was something he *had* to do, something he *had* to get out. It was his way of avoiding completing the screenplay. Phil Alden Robinson, writer-director of *Field of Dreams* (and many other films), told me that the same thing had happened to him, and that the exercise of writing it out, even though it might be totally wrong for the screenplay, was one of the most important things he learned from reading this book.

Many times, writers on the verge of completing a project want to hold on to it and not finish it. After all, what are you going to do after it's complete? Have you ever read a book and hated to finish it? You postpone reading the last few chapters or pages because you want to hang on to the pleasure it has given you. We all do it. Just recognize it as a natural phenomenon, and don't worry about it.

If this happens to you, simply write the material the way it comes out. See what happens. Writing is always an adventure; you never really *know* what's going to come out.

When you're writing you'll find it may take you about sixty pages before you make contact with your characters, before they start talking to you, tell you what *they* want to *do* and *say*. Once you've made contact and established a connection with them, they'll take over. Let them do what they want. Trust your ability to exercise the choice of action and direction during the "words on paper" stage.

Just don't expect your characters to start talking to you from page one. It doesn't work that way. Even if you've done your creative research and know your characters, you might have to experience some resistance before you break through and get in touch with them.

Dialogue is really a function of character. If you know your character, your dialogue may very well flow easily with the unfolding of your story. Many people worry about their dialogue: It's awkward, or stilted; all the characters sound alike; they're constantly explaining things. Writing dialogue is a learning process, an act of coordination. The more you do it, the easier it gets.

Dialogue serves two main purposes: Either it moves the story forward, or it reveals information about the main character. If the dialogue does not serve either one of these functions, then take it out. It's okay for the first sixty pages of your first draft to be filled with awkward dialogue. Don't worry about it—the last sixty pages will be smooth and functional because, again, the more you do it, the easier it gets. And afterward you can go back and smooth out the dialogue in the first part of the screenplay.

The end result of all your work and research and preparation and thinking time will be characters who are authentic and believable, real people in real situations.

And that's what it's all about.

5

Story and Character

"You don't throw a whole life away just
'cause it's banged up a little."

—*Seabiscuit*
Gary Ross

One of my favorite screenwriting exercises when I was teaching at Sherwood Oaks Experimental College was "creating a character." The entire class joined in creating a character, and out of that character came the idea for a story. Everyone participated, throwing out ideas and suggestions, and gradually a character began forming and we started shaping a story. It took a couple of hours, and we usually ended up with a solid character, and sometimes a pretty good idea for a movie.

We had a good time, and it began a process that seemingly managed to parallel the symmetrical chaos of the creative experience. Creating a character *is* a process, and until you've done it, until you've experienced it, you're more than likely to stumble around awkwardly like a blind man in a fog complaining about how things aren't where they used to be.

There are really only two ways to approach writing a screenplay. One is to get an idea, then create your characters to fit that idea. Three people stealing moon rocks from NASA in Houston is an example of this. You take the idea, then "pour" your characters into it: a down-and-out jockey getting an opportunity to ride in the Santa Anita Handicap, as in *Seabiscuit;* or a boxer getting the opportunity to fight the Heavyweight Champion of the World, as in *Rocky;* or a man holding up a bank to get money for a sex-change operation, as in *Dog Day Afternoon;* or an embittered Civil War mercenary captured by his enemies and transformed by their way of life, as in *The Last Samurai;* or a man setting out to break the Water Speed Record, as in *The Run.* In this scenario, you create the characters to fit the idea.

Another way to approach a screenplay is by creating a character, then letting a need, an action, and, ultimately, a story emerge out of that character. Virginia Woolf in *The Hours* is a perfect example of this: a woman seeking a creative outlet in a stifling life. So is Alice, in *Alice Doesn't Live Here Anymore.* Roman Polanski had an idea about a survivor during the Holocaust, and out of this idea emerged *The Pianist.* He found the memoirs of a survivor, and together with Ron Harwood forged a screenplay that was close to his own personal experience. Jane Fonda had an idea about a Vietnam veteran coming home, expressed it to her associates, and *Coming Home* was created. Sofia Coppola wanted to write a screenplay about loneliness, so she created a situation, then developed her characters, and *Lost in Translation* came into being. Create a character and you'll create a story.

How do we go about creating a character? We start from scratch. I ask a series of questions and the class responds with answers. I take the answers and shape them into a character. And, out of that character, a story emerges.

Sometimes it works beautifully; we come up with an interesting character and a good dramatic premise for a movie. Other times it doesn't work at all. But considering the limited time we have and the circumstances of the class, we don't do too badly.

The following is an edited and abridged version of a class that happened to work well. The questions I asked went from general to specific, from *context* to *content.* When you read it, you might want to substitute your own answers for the ones we selected and make the story your own.

"Let's create a character," I tell the class. "I'll ask questions, you supply the answers."

They agree to that, amid some laughter.

"Okay," I say, "how are we going to start?"

"Boston," a guy booms out from the back of the room.

"Boston?"

"Yeah," he says. "He's from Boston!"

"No," several women yell. "*She's* from Boston!"

"That's okay with me," I say, then ask if it's okay with everyone else. They agree.

"Okay." Our subject is a woman from Boston. That's our starting point.

"How old is she?" I ask.

"Twenty-four." Several people agree.

"No," I say. Late twenties or early thirties. Why? someone asks. I reply that when you're writing a screenplay, you're writing it *for* someone, for a *star*, someone who is "bankable." Right now, I would think of Julia Roberts, Cameron Diaz, Charlize Theron, Nicole Kidman, Halle Berry, Renee Zellweger. We move on.

"What's her name?" I ask.

The name Sarah comes into my head, and we go with it.

"Sarah what?"

Sarah Townsend, I decide. A name is a name.

Our starting point becomes Sarah Townsend, late twenties or early thirties, from Boston. She is our subject.

Then we create the *context*.

Let's get her personal history. For the sake of simplicity, I'm going to give one answer to each question I ask. In class there are several answers given and I select only one. Feel free to disagree with them if you want; or make up your own answers, create your own character, your own story.

"What about her parents?" I ask. "Who's her father?"

A doctor, we decide.

Her mother?

A doctor's wife.

"What's her father's name?"

Lionel Townsend.

What's his background?

We toss a lot of ideas around and finally end up with this: Lionel Townsend belongs to the upper strata of Boston society. Wealthy, smart, conservative, he attended medical school at Boston University, then went to St. Louis to do his internship at Washington University.

What about Sarah's mother? What was she before she became a doctor's wife?

A teacher. "Elizabeth's her name," someone remarks. Good. Elizabeth might have been teaching in St. Louis when she met Lionel, and she continues teaching grade school during the time he's completing his medical school education. When he begins his medical practice back in Boston, she gets pregnant and gives up her teaching.

"When did Sarah's parents get married?" I ask.

If Sarah's in her late twenties, early thirties, her parents must have married in the early '70s, either during or after the Vietnam War. They've been married more than thirty years. "How'd you figure that out?" someone asks.

"Subtraction," I reply.

What's the relationship between mother and father?

Consistent, and possibly routine. For what it's worth, I add, Sarah's mother's a Capricorn, her father's a Libra.

When was Sarah born?

Early or mid '70s. April, an Aries. Does she have any brothers or sisters? No, she's an only child.

Remember, this is a process. For every question asked there are many answers. If you don't agree with them, change them to create your own character.

What kind of childhood did she have?

A lonely one. She wanted brothers and sisters. She was alone most of the time. She probably had a good relationship with her mother until she was in her teens. Then, as always between parent and child, things went haywire.

What's the relationship between Sarah and her father?

Good, but strained. Possibly he wanted a son instead of a daughter, and to please her father, Sarah became a tomboy. Possibly Sarah is *always* trying to find a way to please her father, to earn his love and affection. Becoming a tomboy helps with this problem, but creates another one by antagonizing her mother. This will figure later in her relationships with men.

Sarah's family is like all other families, but we're sketching in as much detailed conflict as we can for dramatic purposes.

We're beginning to grasp the dynamics of the Townsend family. So far, there's not been too much disagreement, so we continue to explore the *context* of Sarah Townsend.

I remark that many young women search for their father or for father figures throughout their lives, much in the way that many men search for their mothers in the women they meet. It's interesting to use this as a foundation of character. Not that it happens all the time, but it *does* happen; therefore let's be aware of it so that we can possibly use it to our advantage.

There's a lot of discussion about this. I explain that when you're creating a character, you have to compile nuances that you can either use or not. I tell the class this exercise is based on trial and error: We're going to use what works and discard what doesn't.

Her mother probably educates Sarah in the ways of the world and, no doubt, cautions her about men. She might tell her daughter, "You can never trust a man. They're only after one thing—your body." Or, "They don't like a woman who's too smart." And so on and so on. What Sarah's mother tells her may be true for some of you, or it may not be, I tell the class; use your own experience in creating a character.

Perhaps at an early age Sarah expressed the desire to become a doctor, like her father, and her mother cautioned her against that, saying, "It's a long, tough grind." Maybe her mother is a person who wants to be right all the time, or a person for whom looking good, appearance, is everything, like Mary Tyler Moore's character in *Ordinary People* (Alvin Sargent). Let's move on. What kind of high school experience did Sarah have?

Active, social, the beginnings of rebellion. She made good grades without having to work very hard for them. She had many friends, and was a leader in rebelling against many of the school's restrictive policies. Her music tastes became eclectic and her parents endured these years with patience but not too much understanding.

Most young people rebel, and Sarah's no exception. She graduates and goes to Vassar, which pleases her mother, but decides she wants to major in political science because she wants to help change "the system." This, of course, upsets her mother. Sarah is socially active, and has an affair with a graduate student in political science. Her actions, based on her rebellious nature, become part of her character—she has a unique point of view, a determined attitude. She graduates from college with a degree in political science.

Now what?

She moves to New York to get a job. Her father supports her in this move. Her mother does not; she's upset. She believes Sarah's not doing the things she "should" be doing—finding a stable career, possibly marrying and settling down, as befits an intelligent young woman from Boston.

Remember, I add, drama is conflict. We're searching for ways to generate tension in our material. I explain that the relationship between mother and daughter may be useful during the screenplay, or it may not be. Let's see whether it works or not before we make any decision about it, I advise. The writer always operates from the position of choice and responsibility.

Sarah's move to New York is a major crossroads in our creation of character. So far, we've focused on the *context* of Sarah Townsend. Now we're going to be creating *content*.

Let's define the *exterior* forces working on Sarah. Here's the diagram:

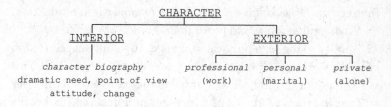

Let's explore the *exterior* forces working on Sarah.

At this point, someone suggests that we create a story using a war as backdrop or as the context of the story. We talk about that for a bit. I ask, *Which* war? The Vietnam War, the Gulf War, the war in Iraq (even the Korean War or World War II)—all of them, no matter in what period of history they occurred, would lend some background tension to our story. We discuss this.

We decide it's a good idea, and I suggest that we could use the Vietnam War as the background of the story. All it means is changing some of the background events and dates working on Sarah. We decide to try it and see what happens. The events we've created are still valid to some degree, and will not have to be changed radically. We change what we need to, get our time lines straight, and decide that Sarah leaves college and moves to New York in the early '70s. So, we research the times.

Slowly, the story begins to take shape. Sarah arrives in New York City in the spring in the early '70s. What does she do? Gets an apartment. Her father sends her some money each month, and does not tell her mother; Sarah prefers it that way. Then what?

She gets a job. What kind of job does she get?

Let's discuss that. We know basically the *kind* of person Sarah is: upper-middle-class, independent, free-spirited, rebellious, on her own for the first time and loving it. Committed to herself and her life. Let's start getting more specific.

New York, 1972. What are the exterior forces working on Sarah? Here's where some research would come in handy.

Nixon is in the White House. The Vietnam War still rages; the country is in a state of nervous exhaustion. Nixon goes to China. McGovern's gaining in the presidential primaries and there's hope "he might be the one." George Wallace is gunned down in a shopping center. *The Godfather* is in release. *Chinatown* is in production.

What kind of job would fit Sarah dramatically?

A job working for a political campaign. Someone suggests Sarah could be working at the McGovern headquarters in New York. This is a point of discussion. (If we wanted to make this a contemporary story, using the war in Iraq as a background force, we could easily have Sarah working for John Kerry's campaign. The context would be the same, only the content would change.) We talk about it. Finally, I explain that for me the job satisfies her rebellious nature; it reflects her first independent step away from home. It satisfies her activist political stance and draws upon her background as a political science major in college, and it gives her parents something to disapprove of—both of them. We're going after conflict, right?

From now on, through a process of trial and error, we're going to be searching for a theme, or dramatic premise: *something* that will move Sarah in a particular direction to generate a dramatic action. The *subject* of a screenplay, remember, is an *action* and a *character*. We've got the character; now we've got to find the action.

This is a hit-and-miss operation. Things are suggested, changed, rearranged; mistakes are made. I'll say one thing, then contradict myself in the next sentence. Don't worry about it. We're after a specific result—a story. We've simply got to let ourselves find it.

New York. 1972. An election year. Nixon versus McGovern. Sarah Townsend is working for the McGovern campaign as a paid staff member. Who are her parents voting for?

What does Sarah discover about politics from her experience in the campaign?

That politics aren't necessarily clean or idealistic. Perhaps she discovers something illegal going on—would she do anything about it?

Maybe something happens, I suggest, that creates a major political issue. Perhaps a friend of hers, someone she sees fairly regularly, resists the draft and flees to Canada. She might become involved in the movement to bring home the draft resisters.

Remember, we're building a character, creating *context* and *content*, searching for a story that will soon appear. Create a character and a story will emerge.

Someone says Sarah's father has a different point of view from hers—he feels draft resisters are traitors to their country and should be shot. Sarah would argue the opposite: that the war is wrong, immoral and illegal, and that the people responsible for it, the politicians, should be the ones taken out and shot.

Suddenly, an amazing thing happens in the room. The air becomes tense, heavy with energy, as the fifty or so people in the class become polarized in their *attitudes* and *points of view* about something that happened several years before they were even born.

Then someone yells out, "Watergate!" Of course! June 1972. Is that a dramatic event that would affect Sarah?

Yes. Sarah would be outraged; it is an event that will generate, or stimulate, a dramatic response in her. It is a potential hook in our as-yet uncreated, untold, and undefined story. This *is* a creative process, remember, and confusion and contradiction are part of it.

Two and a half years later, Nixon is gone, the war is almost over, and the issue of amnesty becomes paramount. Sarah, by virtue of her political involvement, has seen and experienced an event first-hand that will guide her to a form of dramatic resolution, as yet unknown. Sarah, we all realize, is a politically motivated person. Does it work? is my question. Yes.

Would Sarah be motivated enough to enter law school and become an attorney? I ask.

Everybody responds and we have a lot of discussion about this. Several members of the class don't think it works; they can't relate to it. That's okay—we're writing a screenplay. We need a character who is larger than life; I can see several actresses as the lead: Renee Zellweger, Scarlett Johansson, Charlize Theron. As the cliché goes, "It's commercial," whatever that means.

When I was working at Cinemobile back in the '70s, the first question my boss, Fouad Said, asked me about a script was "What's it about?" The second question was "Who's going to star in it?" And at the time I always answered the same thing: Paul Newman, Steve McQueen, Clint Eastwood, Jack Nicholson, Dustin Hoffman, Robert Redford, etc. (Today, it would be Tom Cruise, Tom Hanks, Keanu Reeves, Matt Damon, etc.) That satisfied him. You're not writing a screenplay in order to paper your walls with it. You're writing it, I hope, to sell! And to do that you need a name, a star, especially in today's market.

You may like seeing a woman attorney from Boston as the main character in a movie or you may not. My only comment is that in this exercise, it works!

To me, Sarah goes to law school for a specific reason—to help change the political system! A woman attorney is a good, dramatic choice. Does being a lawyer fit her character? Yes. Let's follow it out, see what happens.

If Sarah is practicing law, something *could* happen, an event or incident that would spark the germ of a story. People start throwing out suggestions. A woman from Boston remarks that Sarah could be involved in the busing issue. It's a very good idea. We're looking for a dramatic premise, remember, something that will trigger a creative response, a hook. Sarah could be working in military law to aid the draft resisters, one person remarks. Another says she might be working in the area of poverty law; or business law, or maritime law, or labor relations. The life of an attorney offers a large range of dramatic possibilities.

That's when it happens—someone mentions he recently heard a news story about a nuclear power plant. That's it! I realize that's what we've been searching for, the hook, the jackpot! Sarah could become involved with the issue of nuclear power plant safety. This *is* what we've been looking for, I say—an exciting, topical story issue; the hook, or gimmick, of our story line. I commit to the choice of Sarah's becoming an attorney.

Everyone now agrees. It's time to expand the exterior forces working on Sarah and fashion our story into a dramatic narrative line.

Suppose we take the premise that Sarah Townsend becomes involved with a movement to redesign safety standards at nuclear power plants. Perhaps she discovers through an investigation that a particular nuclear plant is unsafe. Politics being what they are, maybe a politician supports the plant despite the fact that it is unsafe.

This becomes our story's hook, or dramatic premise. (If you don't agree, find your own hook!) Now we have to create the specifics, the details, the *content,* and we'll have the *subject* for a screenplay—an *action* and a *character.*

The screenplay would focus on the subject of nuclear power plant safety, a major political issue.

What about the story?

Recently, the authorities closed a nuclear power plant in Pleasanton, California, when they discovered it was situated less than two hundred feet from a major fault line, the epicenter of an earthquake. Can you imagine what would happen if an earthquake crumbled a nuclear power plant? Try to put your mind around that!

Let's create an opposite point of view. What would her father say about nuclear power plants? "Nuclear energy must work for us," he might say. "In our energy crisis we have to think ahead, develop an energy source for the future; that future is nuclear energy. We have to insure strict safety standards and create rules and guidelines determined by Congress and the Atomic Energy Commission."

Now, as we all know, these guidelines might be based not on reality, but on political necessity. This might be something Sarah accidentally discovers—possibly a political favor that relates directly to an unsafe condition at a nuclear power plant. But something's got to happen that will trigger the incident that sets the story in motion.

Someone suggests that a person at the nuclear plant is contaminated and the case is brought to Sarah's law firm, and that's how she becomes involved.

It's a very good suggestion! We all agree that this is the dramatic story line we've been looking for: a worker becomes contaminated, the case is brought to Sarah's firm, and she's put on the case. The *Plot Point* at the end of Act I would come when Sarah discovers that the worker's contamination, his fatal illness, is caused by unsafe safety procedures; when, despite threats and obstacles, she decides *to do* something about it.

Act I is the *Set-Up*—we could open with the worker being contaminated. A visually dynamic sequence: The man collapses on the job and is carried out of the plant; an ambulance roars through the streets of the city. Workers gather, protest; union officials meet and decide to file suit for action that will defend the workers from unsafe conditions within the plant.

By circumstances, situation, and design, Sarah is chosen to handle the case. Union officials don't like it—she's inexperienced *and* she's a woman (it's the late '70s, remember), and they don't think she'll be able to handle the pressure. Sarah is determined to make this case her own and prove everybody wrong. The authorities deny her access to the plant, but she manages to explore it anyway and learns firsthand about the unsafe conditions. A brick is thrown through her window. Threats are made. The law firm can't help her. She goes to political representatives, is given the runaround, told it's the worker's fault for getting contaminated.

The media starts sniffing around. She learns there's a political connection between safety standards and plant management. Maybe, someone says, they discover some missing plutonium. It's a good thought, but another story, I reply.

Sarah's uncovering the political connection becomes the *Plot Point* at the end of Act I.

Act II is the *Confrontation*. It's that place in the story line where Sarah confronts obstacle after obstacle in her investigation—so many obstacles, in fact, that she suspects there's some kind of political cover-up. She cannot ignore it any longer. We need to create someone for her to talk to, confide in; maybe a love interest. Perhaps she's involved with a recently separated or divorced attorney with children. Their relationship becomes strained; he thinks she's "crazy," "paranoid," "hallucinating," and they may not be able to keep it together under the pressure of what she's going through. If need be, here's where we can write a two-page essay about Sarah's relationship with men. (How many times has she been in love? What kind of person does she become involved with? And so on.)

She will experience conflict and resistance from members of her law firm; she may be told she's going to be removed from the case if she persists in her investigation. Her parents disagree with her, so she'll have conflict there. The only people who will support and help her are the people who work at the nuclear power plant; they want her to succeed, to expose the unsafe working conditions. We can use the media, and possibly create a reporter who believes she should continue the investigation. He's going to get a story out of it. Possibly there's a romantic link between them.

What about *Plot Point II*? It must be some kind of incident, episode, or event, remember, that hooks into the action and spins it around in another direction.

Perhaps the reporter comes to her with definite proof that there's some kind of political link involving many officials. She has the facts in her hands—what is she going to do about it?

Act III is the *Resolution*. Sarah, with the help of plant workers and the media, exposes political favoritism in the government's regulation of nuclear power safety standards.

The plant is closed until new safety standards are established.

Sarah is congratulated on her persistent, courageous, and victorious stand.

There are different kinds of endings. In "up" endings, things work out. Think of *Erin Brockovich* (Susannah Grant); *Lord of the Rings: The Return of the King; Whale Rider* (Niki Caro); and *The Shawshank Redemption*. In sad or ambiguous endings, it's up to the audience to figure out what happens to the characters. For example, Clarissa (Meryl Streep) in *The Hours;* Bob and Charlotte (Bill Murray and Scarlett Johansson) in *Lost in Translation; Kill Bill II*. In a "down" ending, not everything works out: *American Beauty, The Wild Bunch, Butch Cassidy and the Sundance Kid, Bonnie and Clyde, Thelma & Louise, Cold Mountain, Million Dollar Baby* (Paul Haggis).

If you're ever in doubt about how to end your story, think in terms of a positive ending. We're talking Hollywood here, and I think the purpose of art, or entertainment, is to entertain. That doesn't mean that everybody lives happily ever after, but that people walk away from the theater uplifted, fulfilled, spiritually aligned with their own humanity. As with Jason Bourne searching for the fragments of his life in the *The Bourne Supremacy,* I believe the silver screen is a mirror, reflecting our thoughts, our hopes, our dreams, our successes, our failures.

I once taught a workshop in Germany for some fifty writers, and out of fifty stories, forty-six of them ended in death, suicide, mayhem, and destruction. I told the students that there are better ways to end a screenplay than to have your character caught, shot, captured, die, commit suicide, or be killed. The best ending for your story is an ending that's real, believable, and true, as in *Seabiscuit, Magnolia,* or *Annie Hall. Titanic* had a real, believable ending, in spite of its romanticism. Though money is no criterion of success, it is a criterion of just how many people saw the film and were entertained and uplifted by it. And it's good to remember that the two things that run Hollywood are fear and greed. Everybody wants to be associated with a "winner." That's why weekend grosses are so important in the movie industry.

Resolve your stories any way you want, but be true to your story and characters; if possible, look for the positive, uplifting aspect of the story. A case in point is *Sideways*. In my opinion, it is a beautiful film, well made, well acted, well executed in every aspect, and it leaves us with the hope and possibility that Miles and Maya (Paul Giamatti and Virginia Madsen) may get back together. You might disagree with that and say that life is not like that, but that's only a point of view. We're not talking "life" here; we're talking movies, entertainment.

Which brings us back to our story and Sarah Townsend. And even though the story, at this point, is thin in terms of character and action, we have enough information to start preparing our screenplay.

Here, then, is our story: In the '70s, a young woman attorney discovers unsafe working conditions at a nuclear power plant and, despite political pressure and threats to her life, succeeds in exposing political corruption. The plant is shut down until repairs are made and safe conditions exist to protect the workers and the surrounding community.

Not too bad—considering it took us only a couple of hours to create a character and a story! We even put a working title on it: *Precaution!*

We have an interesting main character: Sarah Townsend; and an action: uncovering a political scandal involving a nuclear power plant. We have the four points needed to anchor our story line; the ending: Sarah exposing the political corruption; and the beginning: a nuclear power plant worker becoming contaminated. *Plot Point I* is when they discover the unsafe conditions, and there's a good source of potential conflict in Act II. The *Plot Point* at the end of Act II comes when Sarah finds the proof that there is a definite political link to the unsafe conditions at the plant.

You may not agree with it or like it—it doesn't matter. The purpose of the exercise is to set into motion a process, to show you how creating a character can generate a dramatic action that leads to a story. Many films, such as *Erin Brockovich*, are structured this way.

As I said at the beginning of this chapter, there are two ways to approach writing your screenplay: One is to create an idea, then create your characters and "pour" your characters into the action. The second way is to create a character and then let the action, the story, emerge out of character. That's what we've just done.

It all came out of "a young woman from Boston."

Try it! See what happens.

6

Endings and Beginnings

> *"Forget it, Jake. . . . It's Chinatown."*
>
> —*Chinatown*
> Robert Towne

Question: What's the best way to open your screenplay?

What scene or sequence would best capture the attention of the reader or audience? Showing your character at work? In a tight or tense dramatic action? A chase scene while delivering pizza? In the heat of passion in a relationship? Arriving at work? Preparing for a day in court? Jogging? In bed, alone, or having passionate sex with someone? Driving down the long, lonely highway as day breaks? Playing golf? Arriving at the airport?

There are, of course, a myriad of different ways to begin your screenplay. Up until now, we've discussed various abstract principles in writing a screenplay in terms of action and character. At this point, we are leaving those general concepts behind and moving into more specific and fundamental parts, or components, of the screenplay.

Let's backtrack a little. All screenplays have a *subject,* and the subject of a screenplay is defined as the *action*—what happens—and the *character*—whom it happens to. There are two kinds of action—*physical* action and *emotional* action; a car chase and a kiss. We discussed character in terms of *dramatic need,* and broke the concept of *character* down into two components—*interior* and *exterior;* your character's life from birth up until the time the movie ends. We talked about *building* character and *creating* characterization and introduced the idea of *context* and *content*.

Now what? Where do we go from here? What happens next? Look at the paradigm:

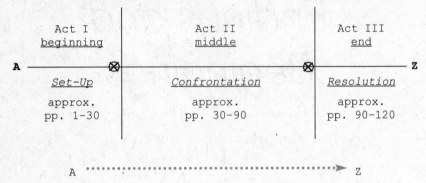

What do you see?

Direction, that's what; your story *moves forward* from point A to point Z, from *set-up* to *resolution*, and it doesn't matter whether it's told in bits and pieces of memory, as in *The Bourne Supremacy*; or in flashbacks, as in *Cold Mountain, Annie Hall,* or *The English Patient*; or in a straight linear story line as in *The Pianist, Chinatown, Spider-Man 2* (Alvin Sargent), or *The Matrix*. Remember that the definition of screenplay structure is "a *linear progression* of *related* incidents, episodes, and events *leading to* a dramatic resolution."

That means your story *moves forward* from beginning to end. You've got approximately ten pages (about ten minutes) to establish three things to your reader or audience: (1) *who* is your main character? (2) *what* is the dramatic premise—that is, what's your story about? and (3) what is the dramatic *situation*—the circumstances surrounding your story?

So—what's the best way to open your screenplay?

KNOW YOUR ENDING!

That's the first thing you have to know: What is the ending of your story? Not the specific shot, scene, or sequence of how the script actually ends, but the resolution. *Resolution means solution;* how is your story resolved? What is the solution? Does your character live or die? Get married or divorced? Win the race or not? Return safely to Cold Mountain or not? Destroy the ring in the fires of Mount Doom or not? Get away with the robbery or not? Go back home or not? Find the criminals and bring them to justice or not?

What is the resolution of your screenplay?

A lot of people don't believe that you need an ending before you start writing. I hear argument after argument, discussion after discussion, debate after debate. "My characters," people say, "will determine the ending." Or, "My ending grows out of my story." Or, "I'll know my ending when I get to it."

Sorry, but it doesn't work that way. At least not in screenwriting. You can do that maybe in a novel, or play, but not in a screenplay. Why? Because you have only about 110 pages or so to tell your story. That's not a lot of pages to be able to tell your story the way you want to tell it.

The ending is the first thing you must know before you begin writing.

Why?

It's obvious, when you think about it. Your story always moves forward—it follows a path, a direction, a line of progression from beginning to end. *Direction* is defined as a *line of development,* the *path along which something lies.*

In the same way, everything is related in the screenplay, as it is in life. You don't have to know the specific details of your ending when you sit down to write your screenplay, but you have to know *what happens* and how it affects the characters.

I use an example out of my own life to illustrate this.

There was a moment in my life when I didn't know what I wanted to do or be. I had graduated from high school, my mother had just died, as my father had some years before, and I didn't want to get stuck in some job or go off to college. I didn't know what I wanted to do with my life, so I decided to travel around the country and see whether I could find a direction. My older brother was in medical school in St. Louis at the time, and I knew I could stay with him or visit friends in Colorado and New York. So, one morning, I packed my bags, got into my car, and headed east on Highway 66.

I never knew where I was going till I got there. I preferred it that way. I had good times and bad times, and loved it; I was like a cloud on the wind, drifting without aim or purpose.

I did that for almost two years.

Then, one day, driving through the Arizona desert, I realized I had traveled that same road before. Everything was the same, but different. It was the same mountain in the same barren desert, but it was two years later. In reality, I saw I was going nowhere. I had spent two years trying to get my head straight, and I still had no purpose, no aim, no goal, no destination, no *direction*. I suddenly saw my future—it was nowhere.

I became aware of time slipping away, almost like an acid trip, and I knew I had to do something. So I stopped wandering and went back to school. At least I'd have a degree after four years, whatever that meant! Of course, it didn't work out the way I expected—it never does. But it was there, at Berkeley, that I met and worked with the man who would change my life forever: my mentor, Jean Renoir. "The future," he told me, "is film."

When you go on a trip, *you are going someplace;* you have a destination. If I'm going to San Francisco, that's my destination. How I get there is a matter of choice. I can fly, drive, take a bus or train, ride a motorcycle or bike, jog, hitchhike, or walk.

I can *choose* how to get there. And life is choice—personal choices, creative choices—and learning how to take responsibility for them.

Understanding the basic dynamics of a story's resolution is essential. By itself, *resolution* means "a solution or explanation." And that process begins at the onset, at the very beginning of the screenwriting process. When you are laying out your story line, building it, putting it together, scene by scene, act by act, you must first determine the resolution. What is the *solution* of your story? At the moment of the initial conception of your screenplay, when you were still working out the idea and shaping it into a dramatic story line, you made a creative choice, a decision, and determined what the resolution was going to be.

Good films are always resolved—one way or another. Think about it.

Do you remember the ending of *Rushmore? Finding Nemo? Spider-Man 2? The Matrix? Bonnie and Clyde? Red River? Butch Cassidy and the Sundance Kid? The Treasure of the Sierra Madre? Casablanca? Annie Hall? Coming Home? Jaws? American Beauty? An Unmarried Woman? The Searchers? Terminator 2: Judgment Day?* These are universally acclaimed films.

A good illustration is Robert Towne's *Chinatown.* One of the true film classics, it incorporates great writing, great filmmaking, and great acting. I've seen *Chinatown* more than thirty times over the years and it still stands up; it's an act of discovery each time I see it. The history of the script is intriguing: There were three drafts of the screenplay, and three different endings.

The first draft of *Chinatown* is much more romantic than the others. In this draft, Robert Towne has Jake Gittes opening and closing the story with a voice-over narration, just the way Raymond Chandler does in most of his stories. When Evelyn Mulwray walks into Jake Gittes's life, he becomes involved with a woman from a different class; she is wealthy, sophisticated, and beautiful, and he falls head over heels in love with her. Near the end of the story, when she learns that her father, Noah Cross (John Huston), has attempted to hire Gittes to find her daughter/sister, she realizes that her father will stop at nothing to get the girl, so she sets out to kill him. She knows it's the only solution. She phones Noah Cross and tells him to meet her along a deserted part of the coast near San Pedro. When Cross arrives, it is raining heavily, and as he walks up the dirt road looking for his daughter, she jams down her car's accelerator and tries to run him over. He narrowly escapes and races to a marshy area nearby. Evelyn leaves the car, pulls a gun, and begins tracking him. Shots are fired. He hides behind a large wooden sign advertising fresh bait. Evelyn sees him and fires again and again into the sign. Blood mingles with the falling rain and Noah Cross falls over backward, dead.

A few moments later, Gittes and Lieutenant Escobar arrive at the scene and we cut to various shots of modern-day Los Angeles and the San Fernando Valley. Gittes, in voice-over narration, tells us that Evelyn Mulwray spent four years in prison for killing her father, that he managed to get her daughter/sister safely back to Mexico, and that the land scheme Noah Cross so brilliantly conceived resulted in a profit of about $300 million. The resolution of this first draft is that justice and order prevail: Noah Cross gets what he deserves, and the graft and corruption of the water scandal leads to Los Angeles becoming what it is today.

That was the first draft.

At that point, Robert Evans, the producer (and the man responsible for *The Godfather* and *Love Story*), brought in Roman Polanski (*The Pianist*) as director. Polanski had his own ideas about *Chinatown*. Changes were discussed, then made, and the relations between Polanski and Towne became tense and strained. They disagreed about many things, mostly about the ending. Polanski wanted an ending in which Noah Cross got away with murder. The second draft is therefore altered considerably. It is less romantic, the action is trimmed and tightened, and the focus of the resolution changed substantially. The second draft is very close to the final one.

In this second draft, Noah Cross gets away with murder, graft, and incest, and Evelyn Mulwray becomes the innocent victim who pays for her father's crime. Towne's point of view when he began writing *Chinatown* is that those who commit certain types of crimes, like murder, robbery, rape, or arson, are punished by being sent to prison, but those who commit crimes against an entire community are often rewarded by having streets named after them or plaques dedicated to them at City Hall. Los Angeles literally owes its survival to the water scandal known as the Rape of the Owens Valley, and it provides the backdrop of the film.

The ending of the second draft now has Gittes planning to meet Evelyn Mulwray in Chinatown; he has arranged for her to be taken to Mexico by Curly (Burt Young), the man in the opening scene, and her daughter/sister is waiting at the boat. Gittes has discovered that Cross is the man behind the murders as well as the water scandal, and when Gittes accuses him, Cross takes him prisoner. They leave for Chinatown, and when they arrive, Cross tries to detain Evelyn, but Gittes manages to subdue the older man. Evelyn races to her car, only to be blocked by Lieutenant Escobar. Gittes makes a drastic move and lunges at the policeman; during the scuffle, Evelyn drives away. Shots are fired and she is killed, shot in the head. This is close to the final draft.

The last scene shows Noah Cross weeping over Evelyn's body while a stunned Gittes tells Escobar that Cross is the man responsible for everything.

In the third, and final, draft, the ending has been modified slightly to accent Towne's point of view, but the resolution is still the same as in the second draft. Gittes is taken to Chinatown, but Lieutenant Escobar is already there, and arrests the private detective for withholding evidence, putting him in handcuffs. When Evelyn arrives with her daughter/sister, Cross approaches the young girl. Evelyn tells him to stay away, and when he doesn't, she pulls a gun and shoots him in the arm. She gets into her car and drives off. There is a shot fired, and Evelyn is killed, shot through the eye. (As a side note, Sophocles has Oedipus tear out his eyes when he realizes he has committed incest with his mother. I find this an intriguing parallel, whether intentional or not.)

Horrified by Evelyn's death, Cross puts his arm protectively around his daughter/granddaughter and forcefully whisks her away into the darkness.

"Forget it, Jake.... It's Chinatown."

Noah Cross, indeed, gets away with it all: murder, the water scandal, the girl. "You gotta be rich to kill somebody, anybody, and get away with it," Gittes tells Curly in the opening scene.

The *resolution* must be clear in your mind before you write one word on paper; it is *context,* it *holds* the ending in place. Billy Wilder once remarked that if you ever have a problem with your ending, the answer always lies in the beginning. To write a strong opening, you must know your ending. This applies to almost everything in life. If you want to cook a meal, or a specific dish, you don't just go into the kitchen, open the refrigerator, and start throwing things together, then see what you've got! You know what you're going to prepare before you go into the kitchen; then all you have to do is cook it.

Your story is really a journey, the end its destination. Take another look at *The Hours,* or at the opening of *American Beauty.* After the short video scene, we see a city and a street, and we hear Lester Burnham's voice-over: "My name is Lester Burnham. I'm forty-two years old. In less than a year I'll be dead.... In a way, I'm dead already." The story then shows us how he comes back to life.

It seems that one of the major difficulties screenwriters deal with is the problem of *endings:* how to end your screenplay so it works effectively, so it's satisfying and fulfilling, so it makes an emotional impact on the reader and audience, so it's not contrived or predictable, so it's real, believable, not forced or fabricated; an ending that resolves all the main story points; an ending, in short, that works.

More easily said than done. What's so interesting about endings is that, in most cases, the ending itself is not really the problem; it's the fact that it *doesn't work effectively.* It's either too soft or too slow, too wordy or too vague, too expensive or not expensive enough, too down, too up, too contrived, too predictable, or too unbelievable. Sometimes it's simply not dramatic enough to resolve the story line, or maybe a surprise twist suddenly comes out of nowhere. Many aspiring screenwriters feel the best way to end their screenplay is by having the main character die, or in some extreme cases, having everybody die. It's tight, complete, easy. But you can do better than that.

Jean Renoir once told me that a good teacher is someone who "shows people the connections between things." I always try to remember that and utilize it in my writings and teachings. In physics, it's a natural law that endings and beginnings are related—cause and effect, like Newton's Third Law of Motion in physics: For every action there's an equal and opposite reaction.

For me, the ending of one thing is always the beginning of something else. Be it a wedding, funeral, or divorce; a career change or the ending of one relationship and the beginning of a new one; a move to a new city or country; or winning or losing your life savings in Las Vegas—it's all the same: The end of one thing is always the beginning of something else. If you overcome a serious medical challenge, like cancer or a heart attack, or go through a near-death experience, it's a brand-new beginning with an awareness that every breath you take is a sacred gift, a blessing of joy and gratitude.

When I was head of the story department at Cinemobile, I was always seventy scripts behind. The pile on my desk rarely got smaller. And if by some miracle I almost caught up, a stack of scripts would suddenly appear from nowhere—from agents, producers, directors, actors, studios. I read so many screenplays that were boring and poorly written that I learned to tell within the first ten pages whether a script was working or not. I gave the writer thirty pages to set up the story, and if it wasn't done by then I reached for the next script on the pile. I had too many scripts to read to waste my time reading material that didn't work. I was reading three scripts a day. I didn't have time to *hope* the writer did his or her job; he either set up his story or he didn't. If he didn't, I threw the script into the large trash bin that served as the "return file."

With that in mind, it's interesting to ask yourself the question: What is the opening of *your* screenplay? How does it begin? What is the opening scene or sequence? What do you write after "fade in"?

You've only got about ten pages to grab the attention of your reader or audience; that's why so many films open with an attention-grabbing sequence like the opening of *Jaws* (Peter Benchley, Carl Gottlieb), *The Shawshank Redemption, The Hours, Raiders of the Lost Ark* (Lawrence Kasdan), the pizza delivery run in *Spider-Man 2,* or the dream sequence that opens *Rushmore.* Once you establish this scene or sequence, usually called the *inciting incident,* you can set up the rest of your story.

Don't worry about where to put the credits. The credits are usually a filmic decision, not a writing one. The placement of credits is the last thing decided on a film, and it's the decision of the film editor and director. Whether it's a dynamic credit montage or simply white cards superimposed on a black background, where to put the credits is not your decision. You can write "credits begin" or "credits end" if you want, but that's it. Write the screenplay; don't worry about the credits.

Nobody sells a script in Hollywood without the help of a reader. I hate to be the one to tell you this, but in Hollywood, "nobody reads"; producers don't read, directors don't read, stars don't read. Readers read. There is an elaborate filtering system regarding screenplays in this town. Everybody says they're going to read your script over the weekend, and that means they're going to give it to somebody to read within the next few weeks: a reader, secretary, receptionist, wife, girlfriend, assistant. If the reader says she likes the screenplay, then she'll pass it on to a creative executive, who'll take the script home over the weekend to read.

The screenwriter's job is to keep the reader turning pages. The first ten pages of your screenplay are absolutely the most crucial. Within the first ten pages, a reader will know whether your story is working or not, whether it's been set up or not. You've got ten pages to grab the attention of your reader. What are you going to do with them? How are you going to hook the reader?

So we go back to the beginning: What's the opening of your screenplay? When you start thinking about how you're going to open your script, the creative choices you make are essential in keeping the reader turning pages. What scene or sequence is on page one, word one? What are you going to show? What image, or action, are you going to visually present that will grab the attention of your reader and audience? Is it going to be a visually exciting action sequence, as in *The Wild Bunch* or *Lord of the Rings* or the battle scene in *Cold Mountain*? Or are you going to create an interesting character introduction, as Robert Towne does in *Shampoo:* a darkened bedroom, moans and squeals of pleasurable delight—the phone rings, loud, insistent, shattering the mood. It's another woman—for Warren Beatty, who's in bed with Lee Grant. It shows us everything we need to know about his character. In *The Royal Tenenbaums,* Wes Anderson and Owen Wilson use a voice-over narration to introduce the family background while showing us the four main characters growing up. It sets up the entire film and establishes the theme of family, failure, and forgiveness.

Shakespeare is a master of openings. Either he opens with an *action* sequence, like the ghost walking the parapet in *Hamlet,* or the witches foretelling the future in *Macbeth,* or he uses a scene revealing something about the character: Richard III is hunchbacked and laments about the "winter of our discontent"; King

Lear demands to know how much his daughters love him, in terms of material goods, in dollars and cents. Before *Romeo and Juliet* begins, the chorus appears, bangs for silence, and synopsizes the story of the "star-crossed lovers."

Shakespeare knew his audience: the groundlings standing in the pit, the poor and oppressed, drinking freely, talking boisterously to the performers if they didn't like the action onstage. He had to grab their attention and focus it on the action.

An opening can be visually active and exciting, grabbing the audience immediately. Another kind of opening is expository, slower-paced in establishing character and situation: *Thelma & Louise, Y Tu Mamá También, American Beauty, Sideways,* or *Mean Girls.*

Your story determines the type of opening you choose.

The Watergate break-in opens *All the President's Men* (William Goldman) with a tense and dramatic sequence. *Lord of the Rings: The Fellowship of the Ring* sets up the history of the ring and the situation in Middle Earth; *Close Encounters of the Third Kind* opens with a dynamic, mysterious sequence where we don't know what's going on. *Rushmore* is a story about a dreamer, so it opens with the main character in a dream sequence that illuminates the character's affinity for living in fantasy. The opening of *Julia* (Alvin Sargent) is moody, reflective, establishing a character enmeshed in the strands of memory. *An Unmarried Woman* (Paul Mazursky) opens with an argument, then reveals the life of the married woman.

The opening of your screenplay has to be well thought out and visually designed to illustrate what your story is about. Many times I read screenplays and the writer has not really thought out his/her opening; there are scenes and sequences that don't have anything to do with the story. It's like the writer is searching, through dialogue and explanation, for his/her story. Before you write one shot, one word of dialogue on paper, you must know four things: your ending, your beginning, Plot Point I, and Plot Point II. In that order. These four elements, these four incidents, episodes, or events, are the cornerstones, the foundation, of your screenplay.

Endings and beginnings are related in the same way that an ice cube and water are related: Water is composed of a definite molecular structure, and an ice cube has a definite crystalline structure. But

when an ice cube melts in water, you can't tell the difference between the elements that were water and those that were the ice cube.
They are part and parcel of the same thing; they exist in the relationship between the parts and the whole. The opening of your
script will determine whether the reader continues reading your
screenplay or not. He or she must know three things within these
first few pages of the script: the character—*who* the story is about;
the dramatic (or comedic) premise—*what* the story is about; and the
situation—*the circumstances* surrounding the action. Within those
first ten pages, the reader is going to make a decision about whether
he/she likes or dislikes the material. If you don't believe me, check it
out at the next movie you see. More about this in a later chapter.

Robert Rossen's *The Hustler,* one of the great classics of the '60s,
opens with Eddie (Paul Newman) arriving to play pool at a pool
hall with Minnesota Fats (Jackie Gleason); it ends with Eddie leaving the pool hall after winning the game, in a self-imposed exile
from the world of pool. The film opens with a pool game and closes
with a pool game.

In Sydney Pollack's excellent *Three Days of the Condor,* one of the
unheralded great films of the '70s, Joseph Turner (played by Robert
Redford) raises the dramatic premise of the entire film in his first
line: "Anything in the pouch for me, Dr. Lapp?" The answer to that
question results in several people being brutally murdered and in
Turner almost losing his life. He has uncovered a "CIA" within the
CIA—and he doesn't know it until the end of the movie. His discovery is the final key that resolves the movie.

The ending of *Condor* (Lorenzo Semple Jr. and David Rayfiel,
from the novel *Six Days of the Condor* by James Grady) is an excellent example of story resolution. Ably directed by Sydney Pollack, it
is a fast-moving, well-constructed thriller that works on all levels—
the acting is excellent, the cinematography effective, the ending
tight and lean; there is no "fat" in this film.

By the end of the movie, Turner has tracked down the mysterious Lionel Atwood—a high-level executive in the CIA—but he
doesn't know *who* Atwood is or *what* his connection is, if any, to
the murders. In the resolution scene, Turner establishes Atwood as

the man who ordered the murders, determining that he is responsible for establishing a secret cell of the CIA within the CIA because of the world's oil fields. This now established, Joubert (Max von Sydow) appears, the hired assassin of the intelligence underworld, and abruptly kills Atwood. Turner is now back in the employ of the "company," the CIA. He breathes easier; he's alive—"at least for now," as Joubert reminds him.

No loose ends. Everything is resolved dramatically, in terms of action and character; all questions raised are answered. The story is complete.

The filmmakers added a "tag" scene at the end. Joe Turner and Higgins are standing in front of the New York Times Building, and Turner states that if anything happens to him, the *Times* has the story. But "will they print it?" Higgins asks.

It's a good question.

If we think about the relationship between the ending and beginning, the parts and the whole, we can look at the story's resolution as a whole made up of the ending, the parts. The resolution is the seed of the ending, and if planted and nurtured correctly, it can sprout into a full-fledged dramatic experience. That's what we all strive for. Endings are manifested in the resolution and the resolution is conceived in the beginning.

If you don't know your ending, then ask yourself *what you would like the ending to be,* regardless of whether it's too simple, too trite, too happy, or too sad. And please, please, don't get caught up in the game of "What kind of an ending would *they* like?"—whoever *they* are. What ending do *you* want? It doesn't matter whether it's "commercial" or not, because nobody knows what's commercial or not anyway.

You might find it necessary to write an essay about what happens in Act III so that the story line is clear and defined. Then go through the action and in free association, in a one- or two-page essay, begin to list the ways this film can end. Don't be attached to any single shot, scene, or sequence. Just list the various ways the endings can be achieved. If that doesn't clarify the action, and you're still unclear about how the material should end, simply write down how you would like it to end, regardless of budget, believability, or anything else that gets in the way. Just throw down any thoughts, words, or ideas, without any regard as to how to do it. That's really the first step in the completion process. It's important to tie together all the loose ends of the narrative line so the screenplay becomes a complete reading and visual experience (in the mind's eye) that rings true and is integral to the action and the characters.

There are other ways to end your screenplay as well. There may be an instance where Act III becomes an entire sequence, a full and complete unit of action. The ending of *Apollo 13* is such a case; as are the endings of *Witness* and *Crimson Tide*. And if you look at *Pulp Fiction*, the ending is really a "bookend": the Pumpkin and Honey Bunny (Tim Roth and Amanda Plummer) robbery attempt in the restaurant—which, coincidentally, opens the movie. Endings and beginnings are connected, right? In each of these scripts the ending completes the action of Act III.

In *Apollo 13*, the entire third act focuses on the astronauts' return to Earth, as we follow the action from the moment the LEM separates from the spacecraft, cutting back and forth to the command center, to the anxious three minutes that turns out to be four, waiting for them to plunge through the atmosphere, not knowing whether the heat shield will protect them or not. When they finally do break through the cloud cover and land safely in the ocean and are rescued, that is the resolution; the ending is simply the voice-over of Jim Lovell telling us what happened to the three astronauts after their ordeal in space. It's played over shots of them on the aircraft carrier.

The Plot Point at the end of Act II in *Witness* has John Book (Harrison Ford) and Rachel completing their relationship as they embrace underneath the birdhouse that Book had broken when he first arrived, and that has now been restored. Act III opens when the three crooked cops pull over the ridge, park their car, pull out their weapons, and make their way down to the farmhouse. Once there, they break into the farmhouse and hold Rachel and the grandfather hostage while they hunt for Book and young Samuel, trying to kill them. So the entire third act is really a shoot-out, and the end emerges from that action; John Book says good-bye to Rachel and young Samuel, and over the end credits, as he drives the car up the long dirt road leading back to Philadelphia, Daniel, Rachel's suitor (Alexander Godunov), walks toward the farmhouse. *Witness* is a great little film that works on all levels. The ending of one thing is always the beginning of something else.

It's a little different with *Crimson Tide* (Michael Schiffer). At Plot Point II, the emergency action message has been partially received, and while it is being deciphered, the Denzel Washington and Gene Hackman characters are at an uneasy standoff as the countdown to launch the nuclear missiles continues. Act III is an entire sequence, and ends when they finally receive the complete message telling them to cancel the nuclear strike. That's the resolution.

The ending is something else. There is a little tag added on after the action is complete: A naval inquiry is held, and it is decided that both men were right in their actions, because the naval regulations were unclear on this situation. The Gene Hackman character retires from active duty, and the Denzel Washington character will be promoted to captain and receive command of his own ship.

Two different points of view, resolved, effective, complete. It's what a good ending is meant to provide.

So what makes a good ending? It has to work, first of all, by satisfying the story; when we reach the final fade-out and walk away from the movie experience, we want to feel full and satisfied, much as if we were leaving the table after a good meal. It's this feeling of satisfaction that must be fulfilled in order for an ending to work effectively. And, of course, it's got to be believable.

What you want in your screenplay is the best possible ending that works. You want to be true to your story line and not have to resort to any tricks, gimmicks, or contrived elements in order to make it work. Sometimes you start out writing with a specific ending in mind and you base the structure and story line around it, but as you're writing the story, you suddenly get a better idea about how to end the script. Go with it. Let it change. It probably *is* a better ending. That's where you have to trust your creative self, your intuition. But, though it's good to accept that your ending may change as you're writing, that doesn't mean you should begin writing without knowing your ending.

If I could sum up the concept of endings and state the one most important thing to remember, I would say: *The ending comes out of the beginning.* Someone, or something, initiates an action, and how that action is resolved becomes the story line of the film.

The Chinese say that "the longest journey begins with the first step," and in many philosophical systems "endings and beginnings" are connected; as in the concept of yin and yang, two concentric circles joined together, forever united, forever opposed.

If you can find a way to illustrate this in your screenplay, it is to your advantage.

This is something you can study. Read as many scripts as you can. There are several Web sites that offer downloadable screenplays. Just Google "screenplays" and check out the sites. And you should be seeing and analyzing as many films as you can, at least two movies a week, either in movie theaters or on DVD or video. Movies are available to everyone now. You should see all kinds of movies: good films, bad films, foreign films, old films, new films. Every film you see becomes a learning experience; if you examine it, it will generate a process, giving you an expanded awareness of the screenplay. A movie should be viewed as a working session: Talk about it, discuss it with friends or loved ones; see whether you can isolate its structure; see whether it fits the paradigm or not.

So, what's the best way to open your screenplay?

KNOW YOUR ENDING!

Cat Stevens sums it up in his song "Sitting":

Life is like a maze of doors,
and they open from the side you're on.
Just keep on pushin' hard, boy, try as you may,
you might wind up where you started from.

Endings and beginnings: two sides of the same coin.

———————

Determine the ending of your screenplay, then design your opening. The primary rule for the opening is: Does it set your story in motion? Does it establish your main character? Does it state the dramatic premise? Does it set up the situation? Does it establish or set up a problem that your character must confront and overcome? Does it state your character's need?

Setting Up
the Story

There's a law in physics called Newton's Third Law of Motion, which states that "for every action, there is an equal and opposite re-action." Which means, basically, that everything is related. We exist in relationship to each other, we exist in relationship to the Earth, we exist in relationship to all living things, and we exist in relation-ship to the universe. "There's a special providence in the fall of a sparrow..." is the way Shakespeare puts it.

In a screenplay the same principle holds true: Everything is re-lated. If we go back to the second definition of structure, it states that there is a causal "relationship between the parts and the whole." If you change a scene or a line of dialogue on page 10, it impacts and influences a scene or a line of dialogue on page 80. Change a few elements in the ending, and you have to add or delete a few ele-ments in the beginning. A screenplay is a whole, and exists in direct relationship to its parts. Therefore, it becomes essential to introduce your story from the very beginning, from page one, word one. As mentioned, you've got about ten pages or less to grab your reader, so you've got to set up your story right away.

The reader must know what's going on immediately, from the very first words on the page. Setting up your story by explaining things through dialogue slows down the action and impedes the story progression. A screenplay is a story told with pictures, remember, so it's important to set up your story visually. The reader must know *who* the main character is, *what* the dramatic premise is, what the story is about, and the dramatic *situation*—the circumstances surrounding the action.

These elements must be introduced within the first ten pages, whether you open your screenplay with an action sequence, as in *Raiders of the Lost Ark, The Matrix,* or *Lord of the Rings: The Fellowship of the Ring,* or with a dramatic sequence, as in *The Shawshank Redemption, The Pianist,* or *Mystic River* (Brian Helgeland). The reader has to know *what* the story is about and *who* it's about. I tell my students you have to approach the first ten pages of your screenplay as a *unit,* or *block,* of dramatic action. It must be designed and executed with efficiency and dramatic value because it sets up everything that follows.

I thought about this as I was preparing this chapter. When I first wrote *Screenplay,* I used *Chinatown* as an illustration of the best way to set up your screenplay, interrelating story with character and situation. I examined other films as well, but I kept coming back to *Chinatown.* The first ten pages of this film still work perfectly as an example of setting up your story.

Chinatown is now considered one of the classic American screenplays; conceived in the 1970s, it was written and produced during a virtual renaissance of American screenwriting. Not that it's any "better" set up than *The Godfather,* or *Apocalypse Now,* or *All the President's Men,* or *Close Encounters of the Third Kind,* or *Five Easy Pieces* (Carol Eastman, aka Adrien Joyce), or *Annie Hall,* or *Julia,* or *Coming Home,* or later films such as *Raging Bull* (Paul Schrader and Mardik Martin), or *An Officer and a Gentleman* (Douglas Day Stewart), or *Dances With Wolves,* or *Thelma & Louise,* or *Forrest Gump* (Eric Roth), or *Pulp Fiction* (Quentin Tarantino), or *The Usual Suspects* (Chris McQuarrie), and so many others. All of these films are outstanding examples of how screenplays are set up. But after looking at them all, as well as many others, I decided *Chinatown* was still the most effective.

Why? Because *Chinatown* is a film that works on all levels: story, characters, historical perspective, visual dynamics, and above all, the basic essentials that illustrate screenwriting as a craft. The film is a mystery-thriller in the style and tradition of Raymond Chandler; Robert Towne used the Owens Valley Scandal of the early 1900s as the dramatic backdrop to the story, but updated the action from the turn of the century to Los Angeles in 1937. In this way, Towne achieved the same revolutionary shift in filmmaking as did the Flemish painters of the fifteenth and sixteenth centuries, who placed the portraits of their Belgium patrons against the backdrop of Italian landscapes, a move that changed the course of art history.

I've written a lot about my experience of *Chinatown,* and I still vividly recall the first time I saw it, at an industry screening at Paramount. I was working at Cinemobile at the time, and there was a light rain falling as I pulled into the Paramount lot. As I walked through the dampness of early evening, I did not want to be there. It had been an extremely full and stressful day. I had read my usual quota of scripts, attended my usual quota of meetings, and had a large and late lunch with a writer during which I drank a little too much wine. My throat was raw, and I felt I was coming down with a cold. Nothing would be better, I thought, than soaking in a long hot bath, having a nice cup of tea, and crawling into bed.

The film began, and as the story unfolded, my critical mind kicked in and I started a little dialogue in which I was complaining about the movie. I thought it was flat, the characters dull and one-dimensional. Before I knew it, I had nodded off. I don't know how much of the film I missed, I just knew it was one of those evenings where my body was in the screening room, but I certainly was not.

When I heard the last lines of the film, "Forget it, Jake.... It's Chinatown," that's exactly what I wanted to do. By the time I got home, I had already forgotten about it.

So much for my introduction to *Chinatown.*

A short time later, I had the opportunity to interview Robert Towne, and during the course of our conversation I asked how he went about creating his characters, especially how he conceived Jake

Gittes, the Jack Nicholson character. He replied that the first question he often asks himself when approaching his character is "What is this character afraid of?" In other words, what is his/her deepest fear? Gittes, a private detective who specializes in "discreet investigation," has a certain reputation to uphold, so he always wants to "look good." He does everything to make a good impression. He dresses immaculately, has his shoes shined every day, and has his own code of ethics. Gittes's unspoken, deep-seated fear is not being taken seriously, looking foolish.

I was very impressed with Bob Towne, both by what he said and how he said it. He was open, insightful, articulate, engaging, and extremely literate, qualities I genuinely admire. I was so impressed that I wanted to see *Chinatown* again; I wanted to see if I'd be able to catch those little nuances of character and story that Towne had spoken about that I had missed during my first viewing of the film.

So, one night after work, I went to see it again. And this time, by the end of the film, when Evelyn Mulwray, the innocent victim, is killed in Chinatown, I felt I had really seen the movie. When I heard that familiar last line, "Forget it, Jake.... It's Chinatown," I was touched, moved, and inspired. The film lingered with me over the next few days, and various scenes kept coming back to mind.

My experience of *Chinatown* was literally a voyage of discovery. Against the backdrop of water runoff and several murders, we follow Jake Gittes as he uncovers the puzzle, one piece at a time. We learn what's going on at the same time that Gittes does; audience and character are linked together as they connect the bits and pieces of seemingly unrelated information, as they assemble this giant jigsaw puzzle.

From the very first images on screen—a series of photographs showing a man and woman having sex in the park—we know this is a story told in pictures. Over these pictures, we hear the moans and groans of Curly, the husband of the woman, played by Burt Young. What does this show? What Jake Gittes, the main character, does for a living. He's a private detective specializing in divorces, unfaithful spouses, and "going through other people's dirty linen," as one of the characters remarks. It's his métier.

Jake's character is defined by what he does, his actions. Towne sets up the story in the very first scene. When the phony Mrs. Mulwray (Diane Ladd) hires Jake to find out who her husband is having an affair with, he begins his surveillance of Hollis Mulwray. As he does, the audience learns what Gittes learns.

After Gittes follows Mulwray to the dried-out Los Angeles River bed, then to the ocean, his long surveillance is rewarded when he witnesses water being dumped into the ocean. Several hours later, when Gittes returns to his car, he picks a leaflet off the windshield declaring, "Our city is dying of thirst!" and "Save our city."

This theme of water is an organic, thematic thread, woven through the story. As I began tracing the connection of water to the story, I felt like Gittes when Noah Cross (John Huston) tells him, "You may think you know what's going on, but believe me, you don't."

When Gittes finds "the girl" at the end of Act I and closes the case, he sees the pictures he had taken on the front page of the newspaper. (And if you look closely in the background of this scene, you'll see a car overheating from lack of water.) The headlines scream "scandal," and when Jake returns to his office, he finds a woman waiting for him: Faye Dunaway. She confirms they've never met, then declares she could never have hired him to find out who her husband is having an affair with. "You see, my name is Mrs. Evelyn Mulwray": the real Mrs. Mulwray.

This is the key incident in the movie. It is the "key" that unlocks the story. If Faye Dunaway is the real Mrs. Mulwray, who is the Diane Ladd character who hired Gittes, claiming to be Mrs. Mulwray? And who hired the phony Mrs. Mulwray? And why? That's the question that shocks Gittes into action. It is the *true* beginning of the story.

The relationship between these scenes of seemingly unrelated information sets up the entire story. Every scene, every piece of information, no matter how seemingly small, reveals something about the story and leads to that moment when the real Evelyn Mulwray shows up. This entire unit of dramatic action serves to establish three things: *who* the main character is, *what* the story is about, and *what* the dramatic situation is, the circumstances surrounding the action; i.e., "L.A. is dying of thirst."

The first ten pages set up the entire screenplay. What follows are these first ten pages of *Chinatown* as they appear in the screenplay. Read them carefully. Notice how Towne sets up his *main character*, how he introduces the *dramatic premise* and reveals the *dramatic situation*.

(NOTE: All questions about screenplay form will be discussed in Chapter 10.)

(page 1 of screenplay)

CHINATOWN

by Robert Towne

FADE IN

FULL SCREEN PHOTOGRAPH

grainy but unmistakably a man and woman making love. Photograph shakes. SOUND of a man MOANING in anguish. The photograph is dropped, REVEALING another, more compromising one. Then another, and another. More moans.

                    CURLY'S VOICE
                      (crying out)
          Oh, no.

INT. GITTES' OFFICE

CURLY drops the photos on Gittes' desk. Curly towers over GITTES and sweats heavily through his workman's clothes, his breathing progressively more labored. A drop plunks on Gittes' shiny desktop.

Gittes notes it. A fan whirrs overhead. Gittes glances up at it. He looks cool and brisk in a white linen suit despite the heat. Never taking his eyes off Curly, he lights a cigarette using a lighter with a "nail" on his desk.

Curly, with another anguished sob, turns and rams his fist into the wall, kicking the wastebasket as he does. He starts to sob again, slides along the wall where his fist has left a noticeable dent and its impact has sent the signed photos of several movie stars askew.

Curly slides on into the blinds and sinks to his
knees. He is weeping heavily now, and is in such
pain that he actually bites into the blinds.

Gittes doesn't move from his chair.

>   GITTES
>   All right, enough is enough—you can't
>   eat the Venetian blinds, Curly. I just
>   had 'em installed on Wednesday.

Curly responds slowly, rising to his feet, crying. Gittes reaches into his desk and pulls out a
shot glass, quickly selects a cheaper bottle of
bourbon from several fifths of more expensive
whiskeys.

Gittes pours a large shot. He shoves the glass
across his desk toward Curly.

                                              (2)

>   GITTES
>   Down the hatch.

Curly stares dumbly at it. Then picks it up, and
drains it. He sinks back into the chair opposite
Gittes, begins to cry quietly.

>   CURLY
>   (drinking, relaxing a little)
>   She's just no good.

>   GITTES
>   What can I tell you, kid? You're
>   right. When you're right, you're
>   right, and you're right.

>   CURLY
>   Ain't worth thinking about.

Gittes leaves the bottle with Curly.

>   GITTES
>   You're absolutely right, I wouldn't
>   give her another thought.

> CURLY
> *(pouring himself)*
> You know, you're *okay*, Mr. Gittes. I
> know it's your job, but you're okay.

> GITTES
> *(settling back, breathing a little easier)*
> Thanks, Curly. Call me Jake.

> CURLY
> Thanks. You know something, Jake?

> GITTES
> What's that, Curly?

> CURLY
> I think I'll kill her.

(3)

INT. DUFFY & WALSH'S OFFICE

noticeably less plush than Gittes'. A well-
groomed, dark-haired WOMAN sits nervously between
their two desks, fiddling with the veil on her
pillbox hat.

> WOMAN
> I was hoping Mr. Gittes could see to
> this personally—

> WALSH
> *(almost the manner of someone comforting the
> bereaved)*
> If you'll allow us to complete our
> preliminary questioning, by then
> he'll be free.

There is the SOUND of ANOTHER MOAN coming from
Gittes' office—something made of glass shatters.
The Woman grows more edgy.

INT. GITTES' OFFICE—GITTES & CURLY

Gittes and Curly stand in front of the desk,
Gittes staring contemptuously at the heavy
breathing hulk towering over him. Gittes takes a
handkerchief and wipes away the plunk of perspiration on his desk.

CURLY
(crying)
They don't kill a guy for that.

GITTES
Oh they don't?

CURLY
Not for your wife. That's the
unwritten law.

Gittes pounds the photos on the desk, shouting:

GITTES (Con't)
I'll tell you the unwritten law, you
dumb son of a bitch, you gotta be rich
to kill somebody, anybody, and get
away with it. You think you got that
kind of dough, you think you got that
kind of class?

(4)

Curly shrinks back a little.

CURLY
... No ...

GITTES
You bet your ass you don't. You can't
even pay me off.

This seems to upset Curly even more.

CURLY
I'll pay the rest next trip—we only
caught sixty ton of skipjack around
San Benedict. We hit a chubasco, they
don't pay you for skipjack the way
they do tuna or albacore-

GITTES
(easing him out of his office)
Forget it. I only mention it to
illustrate a point ...

INT. OFFICE RECEPTION

He's now walking him past SOPHIE, who pointedly
averts her gaze. He opens the door where on

the pebbled glass can be read: J.J. GITTES and
Associates—DISCREET INVESTIGATION.

> GITTES
> I don't want your last dime.

He throws an arm around Curly and flashes a dazzling smile.

> GITTES
> *(continuing)*
> What kind of a guy do you think I am?

> CURLY
> Thanks, Mr. Gittes.

> GITTES
> Call me Jake. Careful driving home,
> Curly.

He shuts the door on him and the smile disappears.

                                                    (5)

He shakes his head, starting to swear under his
breath.

> SOPHIE
> A Mrs. Mulwray is waiting for you,
> with Mr. Walsh and Mr. Duffy.

Gittes nods, walks on in.

INT. DUFFY & WALSH'S OFFICE

Walsh rises when Gittes enters.

> WALSH
> Mrs. Mulwray, may I present Mr.
> Gittes?

Gittes walks over to her and again flashes a warm,
sympathetic smile.

> GITTES
> How do you do, Mrs. Mulwray?

                         MRS. MULWRAY
          Mr. Gittes ...

                         GITTES
          Now, Mrs. Mulwray, what seems to be
          the problem?

She holds her breath. The revelation isn't easy
for her.

                         MRS. MULWRAY
          My husband, I believe, is seeing
          another woman.

Gittes looks mildly shocked. He turns for confir-
mation to his two partners.

                         GITTES
                        (gravely)
          No, really?

                         MRS. MULWRAY
          I'm afraid so.

                         GITTES
          I am sorry.

Gittes pulls up a chair, sitting next to Mrs.
Mulway—between Duffy and Walsh. Duffy cracks his
gum.

                                              (6)

Gittes gives him an irritated glance. Duffy stops
chewing.

                         MRS. MULWRAY
          Can't we talk about this alone, Mr.
          Gittes?

                         GITTES
          I'm afraid not, Mrs. Mulwray. These
          men are my operatives and at some
          point they're going to assist me. I
          can't do everything myself.

                         MRS. MULWRAY
          Of course not.

> GITTES
> Now—what makes you certain he is
> involved with someone?

Mrs. Mulwray hesitates. She seems uncommonly nervous at the question.

> MRS. MULWRAY
> A wife can tell.

Gittes sighs.

> GITTES
> Mrs. Mulwray, do you love your
> husband?

> MRS. MULWRAY
> *(shocked)*
> . . . Yes, of course.

> GITTES
> *(deliberately)*
> Then go home and forget about it.

> MRS. MULWRAY
> But . . .

> GITTES
> *(staring intently at her)*
> I am sure he loves you, too. You know
> the expression, "let sleeping dogs
> lie"? You're better off not knowing.

(7)

> MRS. MULWRAY
> *(with some real anxiety)*
> But I have to know!

Her intensity is genuine. Gittes looks to his two partners.

> GITTES
> All right, what's your husband's first
> name?

> MRS. MULWRAY
> Hollis. Hollis Mulwray.

> GITTES
> *(visibly surprised)*
> Water and Power?

Mrs. Mulwray nods, almost shyly. Gittes is now casually but carefully checking out the detailing of Mrs. Mulwray's dress—her handbag, shoes, etc.

> MRS. MULWRAY
> He's the Chief Engineer.

> DUFFY
> *(a little eagerly)*
> *Chief* Engineer?

Gittes' glance tells Duffy Gittes wants to do the questioning. Mrs. Mulwray nods.

> GITTES
> *(confidentially)*
> This type of investigation can be hard on your pocketbook, Mrs. Mulwray. It takes time.

> MRS. MULWRAY
> Money doesn't matter to me, Mr. Gittes.

Gittes sighs.

> GITTES
> Very well. We'll see what we can do.

EXT. CITY HALL—MORNING

already shimmering with heat.

(8)

A drunk blows his nose with his fingers into the fountain at the foot of the steps.

Gittes, impeccably dressed, passes the drunk on the way up the stairs.

INT. COUNCIL CHAMBERS

Former Mayor SAM BAGBY is speaking. Behind him is a huge map, with overleafs and bold lettering:

"PROPOSED ALTO VALLEJO DAM AND RESERVOIR"
Some of the councilmen are reading funny papers
and gossip columns while Bagby is speaking.

                    BAGBY
        Gentlemen, today you can walk out that
        door, turn right, hop on a streetcar
        and in twenty-five minutes end up smack
        in the Pacific Ocean. Now you can
        swim in it, you can fish in it, you can
        sail in it—but you can't drink it, you
        can't water your lawns with it, you
        can't irrigate an orange grove with
        it. Remember—we live next door to the
        ocean but we also live on the edge of
        the desert. Los Angeles is a desert
        community. Beneath this building,
        beneath every street, there's a
        desert. Without water the dust will
        rise up and cover us as though we'd
        never existed!
        (pausing, letting the implication sink in)

CLOSE—GITTES

sitting next to some grubby farmers, bored. He
yawns—edges away from one of the dirtier farmers.

                    BAGBY (O.S.)
                    (continuing)
        The Alto Vallejo can save us from
        that, and I respectfully suggest that
        eight and a half million dollars is a
        fair price to pay to keep the desert
        from our streets—and not on top of
        them.

                                            (9)

AUDIENCE—COUNCIL CHAMBERS

An amalgam of farmers, businessmen, and city employees have been listening with keen interest. A
couple of the farmers applaud. Somebody shooshes
them.

COUNCIL COMMITTEE

in a whispered conference.

                        COUNCILMAN
                    (acknowledging Bagby)
            Mayor Bagby . . . let's hear from the
            departments again—I suppose we better
            take Water and Power first. Mr.
            Mulwray.

REACTION—GITTES

looking up with interest from his racing form.

MULWRAY
walks to the huge map with overleafs. He is a
slender man in his sixties who wears glasses and
moves with surprising fluidity. He turns to a
smaller, younger man, and nods. The man turns the
overleaf on the map.

                        MULWRAY
            In case you've forgotten, gentlemen,
            over five hundred lives were lost when
            the Van der Lip Dam gave way—core
            samples have shown that beneath this
            bedrock is shale similar to the
            permeable shale in the Van der Lip
            disaster. It couldn't withstand that
            kind of pressure there.
                    (referring to a new overleaf)
            Now you propose yet another dirt-
            banked terminus dam with slopes of two
            and one half to one, one hundred
            twelve feet high and a twelve-
            thousand-acre water surface. Well, it
            won't hold. I won't build it. It's
            that simple—I am not making that kind
            of mistake twice. Thank you,
            gentlemen.

                                                    (10)

Mulwray leaves the overleaf board and sits
down. Suddenly there are some whoops and hollers
from the rear of the chambers and a red-faced
FARMER drives in several scrawny, bleating sheep.
Naturally, they cause a commotion.

                    COUNCIL PRESIDENT
                  (shouting to farmer)
What in the hell do you think you're
doing?
                  *(as the sheep bleat down the aisle
                     toward the Council)*
Get those goddam things out of here!

                      FARMER
                   (right back)
Tell me where to take them! You don't
have an answer for that so quick, do
you?

Bailiffs and sergeants-at-arms respond to the im-
precations of the COUNCIL and attempt to capture
the sheep and the farmers, having to restrain one
who looks like he's going to bodily attack
Mulwray.

                      FARMER
            (through above, to Mulwray)
You steal the water from the Valley,
ruin the grazing, starve my livestock—
who's paying you to do that, Mr.
Mulwray, that's what I want to know!

OMITTED

The scene ends and we cut to Los Angeles River bed
where Gittes watches Mulwray through binoculars.

Let's take a look at these first ten pages, which set up the story.

The main character, Jake Gittes, is introduced in his office, show-ing photographs of Curly's wife being unfaithful.

We learn things about Gittes. On page 1, for example, we find that he "looks cool and brisk in a white linen suit despite the heat." He is shown to be a meticulous man who uses his "handkerchief to wipe away the plunk of perspiration on his desk." When he walks up the steps of City Hall a few pages later, he is "impeccably dressed." These *visual* descriptions convey character traits that reflect his per-sonality. Notice how Gittes is *not physically described* at all; he's not tall, thin, fat, short, or anything else. He seems like a nice guy. "I wouldn't take your last dime," he says. "What kind of a guy do you think I am?" Yet he offers Curly a drink from a "cheaper bottle of bourbon from the several fifths of more expensive whiskeys." He's vulgar, yet exudes a certain amount of charm and sophistication. He's the kind of man who wears monogrammed shirts and carries silk handkerchiefs, who has his shoes shined and hair cut at least once a week.

On page 4, Towne reveals the dramatic situation *visually* in the stage directions: "on the pebbled glass can be read J.J. GITTES and Associates—DISCREET INVESTIGATION." Gittes is a private detective who specializes in divorce work, or "other people's dirty linen," as the cop Loach says about him. Later, we'll learn he's an ex-cop who left the force; when Escobar tells him he made lieutenant, Gittes suffers a twinge of envy.

The dramatic premise is established on page 5 when the phony Mrs. Mulwray informs Jake Gittes, "My husband, I believe, is seeing another woman." That statement sets up everything that follows: Gittes, the ex-cop, "checks out the detailing of Mrs. Mulwray's dress—her handbag, shoes, etc." That's his job, and he's very good at what he does.

When Gittes tracks down and takes pictures of "the little twist" Mulwray is supposedly having an affair with, as far as he is concerned, the case is closed. The next day he's surprised to find the pictures he took on the front page of the newspaper, with headlines declaring that the head of the Department of Water and Power has been "caught" in a love nest. He doesn't know how his pictures got into the paper. When he returns to his office he is further surprised to find the real Mrs. Mulwray there to greet him—the key incident and the Plot Point at the end of Act I.

"Do you know me?" she asks.

"No," Gittes replies. "I would have remembered."

"Since you agree we've never met, you must also agree that I haven't hired you to do anything—certainly not spy on my husband," she says. As she leaves, her attorney hands Gittes a complaint that could take his license away and smear his name and reputation.

Gittes doesn't know what's going on. If this woman is the *real*

Mrs. Mulwray, *who* was the woman who hired him, and *why*? More important, *who* hired the woman to hire him? Someone has gone to a lot of trouble to set him up. "I'm not the one who's supposed to be caught with my pants down," he says. He's going to find out who's responsible, and why. That is Jake Gittes's dramatic need, and it drives him through the story until he solves the mystery.

The dramatic premise—"My husband, I believe, is seeing another woman"—sets up the *direction* of the screenplay. And direction, remember, is "a line of development."

In the interview I did with Robert Towne, he said he approached *Chinatown* from the point of view that "some crimes are punished because they can be punished. If you kill somebody, rob or rape somebody, you'll be caught and thrown into jail. But crimes against an entire community you really can't punish, so you end up rewarding them. You know, those people who get their names on streets and plaques at City Hall. And that's the basic point of view of the story."

"You know something, Jake?" Curly tells Gittes on page 2. "I think I'll kill her," meaning his wife.

Gittes responds with the prophetic lines that illustrate the script's point of view. "You gotta be rich to kill somebody, anybody, and get away with it. You think you got that kind of dough, you think you got that kind of class?"

Curly certainly can't get away with murder, but Noah Cross, Evelyn Mulwray's father and former head of the Department of Water and Power along with Hollis Mulwray, can and does get away with it. The ending of the film shows Noah Cross whisking his daughter/granddaughter into the night after Evelyn Mulwray is killed trying to escape. That is Towne's point of view: "You gotta be rich to kill somebody, anybody, and get away with it."

That brings us to the "crime" of *Chinatown,* a scheme based on the water scandal known as the Rape of the Owens Valley. It is the backdrop of *Chinatown.*

In 1900, the city of Los Angeles, "a desert community," as former mayor Bagby reminds us, was growing and expanding so fast it was literally running out of water. If the city was to survive, it had to find another source of water. L.A. is right next door to the Pacific Ocean. "You can swim in it, you can fish in it, you can sail on it, but you can't drink it, you can't water your lawns with it, and you can't irrigate an orange grove with it," Bagby argues.

The closest water to L.A. is the Owens River, located in the Owens Valley, a green and fertile area about 250 miles northeast of Los Angeles. A group of businessmen, community leaders, and politicians—some would call them "men of vision"—saw the need for water and conceived a marvelous scheme. They would buy up the river rights to the Owens River, by force if necessary, then buy up all that worthless land in the San Fernando Valley, about 20 miles outside L.A. Then they would place a bond issue on the ballot that would fund building an aqueduct from the Owens Valley across 250 miles of blazing desert and jagged foothills to the San Fernando Valley. Then they would turn around and sell the now "fertile" land of the San Fernando Valley to the city of Los Angeles for an enormous sum of money, about $300 million.

That was the plan. The government knew about it, the newspapers knew about it, the local politicians knew about it. When the time was right, the authorities would "influence" the people of Los Angeles to pass the proposed bond issue.

In 1906, Los Angeles was in the middle of a drought. Things got bad, then worse. People were forbidden to wash their cars or water their lawns; they couldn't flush their toilets more than a few times a day. The city dried up; flowers died, lawns turned brown, and scare headlines declared, "Los Angeles is dying of thirst!" and "Save our city!"

To underscore the drastic need for water during the drought and to make certain the citizens passed the bond issue, the Department of Water and Power dumped thousands of gallons of water into the ocean.

When it came time to vote, the bond issue passed easily. The Owens Valley aqueduct took several years to complete. When it was finished, William Mulholland, then head of the Department of Water and Power, turned the water over to the city: "There it is," he said. "Take it."

Los Angeles flourished and grew like wildfire; the Owens Valley withered and died. No wonder it was called the Rape of the Owens Valley.

Robert Towne took this scandal from 1906 and used it as the backdrop in *Chinatown*. He changed the time period from the turn of the century to 1937, when the visual elements of Los Angeles had the classic and distinctive look of Southern California.

The water scandal that Noah Cross (how appropriate his name) conceives and executes, the crime that causes the deaths of Hollis Mulwray, Leroy the drunk, Ida Sessions, and finally Evelyn Mulwray, the scandal that Jake Gittes uncovers, is woven with great subtlety and skill through the entire screenplay.

And Noah Cross gets away with murder.

All this is established and set up on page 8, when Gittes is in the council chambers and we hear Bagby arguing that "eight and a half million dollars is a fair price to pay to keep the deserts from our streets—and not on top of them."

Hollis Mulwray, the character modeled on William Mulholland, replies that the dam site is unsafe, as proven by the previous Van der Lip Dam disaster, and says, "I won't build it. It's that simple—I am not making that kind of mistake twice." By refusing to build the dam, Hollis Mulwray becomes a target for murder; he is an obstacle that must be eliminated.

Again, on page 10, the dramatic question of the screenplay is raised: "You steal the water from the Valley, ruin the grazing, starve my livestock," yells the farmer who invades the chambers. "Who's paying you to do that, Mr. Mulwray, that's what I want to know!"

So does Gittes.

It is *the* question that propels the story to its final resolution, and it is all *set up* from the very beginning, in the first ten pages, and moves forward in a *linear* direction to the end.

"Either you bring the water to L.A., or you bring L.A. to the water," Noah Cross tells Gittes.

That is the foundation of the entire story. That's what makes it so great.

It's that simple.

Watch *Chinatown*. See how the backdrop of the action, the scandal, is introduced. See if you can design your opening ten pages in such a way that you introduce the main character, state the dramatic premise, and sketch the dramatic situation in the most cinematic way.

8

Two Incidents

"Incident: A specific occurrence or event
that occurs in connection to something
else."

—*The New World Dictionary*

A few years ago I was given the opportunity of working with the writer Joe Eszterhas in a complicated legal case. Called as an expert witness, I was engaged to go through the entire work of this noted screenwriter, analyze the material, and then, in outline form, lay out "the structural essence" of his screenplays. In other words, what was it that made Joe Eszterhas's material so singular and unique; what made Joe Eszterhas "Joe Eszterhas"?

It was a daunting and intriguing assignment. I didn't know what to do or how to begin, except to begin at the beginning, by reading his screenplays and noting the similarities and distinctions in the creation of Eszterhas's style.

As I began reading and analyzing his work, I became aware of several factors that seemed to make his scripts so powerful, whether they were action-thrillers like *Basic Instinct, Jagged Edge, Jade,* and *Sliver,* or dramatic and contemporary pieces like *Music Box, Flashdance,* and even the ill-wrought *Showgirls.*

In all his work I saw he was dealing with real people in real situations, and his characters were interesting, tough, with a sense of bravado that covered a deep well of insecurity and sometimes a lack of self-respect. For instance, the Jennifer Beals character in *Flashdance* had a sense of creative and defiant confidence within her that engaged reader and audience. And there was the music, of course, woven into the story of the girl who overcame all odds—physical, mental, and emotional—to achieve her dream. A steelworker by day and a pole dancer by night, she had a visual appeal to a vast moviegoing audience. The film was an enormous hit.

As I began to get more familiar with Joe Eszterhas's scripts, I noticed that he thrust the reader and audience into the story line immediately. In most cases, he began his stories with an action sequence that plunged the main character directly into the story line.

In *Basic Instinct,* the first words of the script—"It is dark; we don't see clearly"—set the tone. The visual directions continue. "A man and woman make love on a brass bed. There are mirrors on the walls and ceiling. On a side table, atop a small mirror, lines of cocaine. A tape deck PLAYS the Stones: 'Sympathy for the Devil.' "

It is a graphic, wild, and erotic sex scene, the tempo tight and passion high; as it builds in rhythm, the words get shorter and shorter. "He is inside her...arms tied above him...on his back... eyes closed...she moves...grinding...he strains for her...his head arches back...his throat white...she arches her back...her hips grind...her breasts are high..." and then, at the height of the sexual frenzy, "Her back arches back...back...her head tilts back...she extends her arms...her right arm comes down suddenly...the steel flashes...his throat is white...he bucks, writhes, bucks, convulses..." and the ice pick flashes up and down, "and up...and down...and up...and...."

When I first read this opening scene I was totally riveted, focused, eager to continue reading and see what happened. The more I read, the more I was hooked. I had been attracted, engaged, and totally captured by the visual action of the first page.

It's a perfect example of what I call a visual "grabber," an opening that grabs you by the throat and seizes your attention. What better elements can you open a screenplay with than intense passion, wild sex, horrific murder, and visual mayhem, set to the music of The Stones, to boldly establish the style and tone of an entire screenplay? It's just a great opening.

The next morning, the main character, Nick Curran (Michael Douglas), a tough, hard-nosed, cynical cop with too many years on the force for his relatively youthful age, investigates the crime scene along with his partner and learns that the likely suspect, Catherine (Sharon Stone), is a smart, beautiful, and accomplished novelist. And while he questions her, Nick is immediately attracted as she daringly flaunts her sexuality at him. It's easy to see why he's smitten and intrigued by her, and we know the temptation she offers is going to hook him. It doesn't take too long before he becomes so infatuated with her that he can't listen to his voice of reason, or his associates' warnings, as he plunges headlong into a tumultuous affair that costs him his job and may wind up costing him his life.

I began to understand that this opening sex/murder scene is the incident that sets the story in motion and directly draws the main character into the story line. The murder is committed to grab our attention and show us the reason Nick is called upon to investigate the crime. When he leaves the scene of the crime, we follow him and his partner and begin to learn more about this man and the choices he makes. The opening scene and the story that's going to unfold are directly linked.

This incident—the murder—and the story of a cop giving in to his temptations epitomize the illumination of character and incident. Remember Henry James: "What is character but the determination of incident? And what is incident but the illumination of character?" You can't reveal a character dramatically (or comedically) unless you have him/her react to a particular incident; the nature of drama, after all, is to show the universal connection between all humans, regardless of race, color, gender, or cultural differences.

The incident of the murder leads directly to the infatuation Nick feels for Catherine. And that attraction is reinforced when the police question Catherine as the prime suspect. There is a relationship between these two incidents. One incident, the opening sex/murder, is called the *inciting incident,* because it *sets the story in motion;* it is the first visual representation of the *key incident, what the story is about,* and draws the main character into the story line. Remember the definition of incident: "a specific event or occurrence that occurs in relation to something else."

When I understood this connection, it was almost a revelation. Using an opening sequence to draw the main character into the story line is pure cinema. From here on through the rest of the screenplay, the story is set up, the characters and premise are established, and there is a story line, a direction to follow—and all because of the connection between these two incidents. This new understanding gave me another tool to use in the craft of screenwriting.

I went back through all of Eszterhas's scripts and began to examine his screenplays, focusing on how he wrote and structured opening scenes or sequences. And I saw, in most cases, that the opening scene, the *inciting incident,* was a cinematic tool he used to set up the story from page one, word one.

I began to see that in certain kinds of movies—action films, action-thrillers, mysteries, action-adventures, sci-fis, even dramas—writers structure their stories so that this opening, the inciting incident, serves two distinct functions. First, it grabs or hooks the audience immediately—just look at the opening scenes or sequences of *The Matrix, Jaws, Cold Mountain, The Bridges of Madison County, American Beauty, Pulp Fiction, Lord of the Rings: The Fellowship of the Ring, Rushmore, The Royal Tenenbaums,* and other films, and you'll see that this opening scene or sequence is what sets the entire story in motion.

For example, in *The Matrix,* a squad of policemen confronts Trinity, and as we watch her defy all known laws of physics and gravity, leaping over buildings to escape, we are drawn into a world of cyberspace that grabs our attention immediately. The inciting incident anchors us to the edge of our seats, and lets us know that we're in for an incredible adventure. In *Jaws,* the late-night beach party and a nude swimming lark turn into a horrifying experience as the great white attacks.

In *Cold Mountain,* Union troops burrow underground and plant explosives beneath the Confederate camp; when the charge is detonated the result illustrates the total madness of war, just as in the classic *The Bridge on the River Kwai* (Michael Wilson and Carl Foreman). In *The Bridges of Madison County* (Richard LaGravenese), after the death of Francesca (Meryl Streep), her two grown children are going through her things and uncover a hidden diary. As they read, they discover that their mother had a love affair with a man named

Robert (Clint Eastwood) many years earlier. The story of that affair becomes the entire movie. Discovering the diary, which sets the story in motion, is the inciting incident. In *American Beauty*, we see the "dead" life of Lester Burnham as he begins another day of remorse, regret, and failed dreams. In *Pulp Fiction*, we see Honey Bunny and Pumpkin discuss holding up the restaurant; when they pull out their guns we freeze the action and cut away to Jules and Vincent, driving to their assignment, recovering a briefcase for Marcellus Wallace. In *Lord of the Rings*, we open with the history of the ring, then watch as Bilbo Baggins finds it at the bottom of the river. This is the inciting incident that sets the entire trilogy in motion.

I could cite example after example of the inciting incident, but what I feel is most important is the understanding that this incident serves two important and necessary functions in the craft of storytelling: (1), it sets the story in motion; and (2), it grabs the attention of the reader and audience. Seeing the relationship between this first incident and the story line is essential to an understanding of good screenwriting.

The next time you go to a movie, or watch one on DVD or on television, see if you can identify the inciting incident and notice how it sets things in motion. *Crimson Tide* is one of my favorite examples. In the opening sequence, a CNN news reporter is stationed on the deck of a French aircraft carrier and shows us actual newsreel footage of Russian rebels forcefully occupying the Kremlin in an attempt to take over the government. We then cut to a shot of the rebel leader stating emphatically that the rebel forces will not tolerate any U.S. intervention and, having occupied a Russian nuclear base, feel no hesitation in launching a nuclear missile attack against the United States. Then we cut to a TV screen, with Ron Hunter (Denzel Washington) and Weps (Viggo Mortensen) watching the news story during a birthday party for Ron's three-year-old daughter.

Why is this the inciting incident? Because it sets the story in motion. (It's also a good illustration of the Henry James quote.) *Crimson Tide* is constructed around the way two people see the world. In response to the Russian rebel threat, a U.S. submarine, the

Alabama, carrying live nuclear warheads, is sent out as a precautionary measure—either launch a "first-strike" missile or retaliate against Russian missiles. The Captain (Gene Hackman) believes that "war is an extension of politics," and it is his duty to carry out his orders even if it means a nuclear holocaust. Ron, the executive officer, on the other hand, believes that because of nuclear weapons, war is an outmoded concept. The purpose of war, he says, is to win, and if both sides launch nuclear weapons, there will be no winner, only losers. War, he believes, is no longer a viable option.

That's when the *Alabama* receives orders to launch a first-strike nuclear attack against the Russians rebels. As they are preparing to launch the weapons, the men on the submarine receive another emergency message that is cut off before the entire text can be transmitted. What do these second orders say? Should they continue to follow the first orders and launch a first strike? Or will they delay the launch to confirm or deny the first order?

These two differing points of view, these two belief systems, generate the conflict that drives the script forward. Both points of view are right within the framework of character. There is no right and wrong here, no good or bad. Hegel, the great eighteenth-century German philosopher, maintained that the essence of tragedy derives not from one character being right and the other being wrong, or from the conflict of good versus evil, but from a conflict in which *both characters are right,* and thus the tragedy is one of "right against right," being carried to its logical conclusion.

Both characters in *Crimson Tide* operate from that sense of truth within themselves. The Captain maintains that the situation demands that he follow the first orders received. The executive officer does not agree, and claims that the second order, even though not completely received, overrides the first and must be confirmed before they launch their first-strike missiles. Nobody is right or wrong in this conflict, because both men's actions are determined by their point of view, the way they see the world.

As I repeat often, *all drama is conflict:* Without conflict you have no action; without action you have no character; without character you have no story; and without story you have no screenplay.

The Russian rebels have threatened to launch a nuclear missile attack on the U.S., and this conflict becomes the foundation of the entire film. And it's all set up in the inciting incident that opens the film. *It sets the story in motion.* That is its function.

Depending on the kind of story you're writing, the inciting incident will either be action-driven or character-driven. It does not have to be a tense action or dramatic sequence—it can be a scene involving a situation. In *Chinatown,* the inciting incident is Gittes's being hired by the phony Mrs. Mulwray, and the key incident comes when the real Mrs. Mulwray confronts Gittes. The inciting incident always leads us to the *key incident,* which is the hub of the story line, the engine that powers the story forward. The *key incident* reveals to us what the story is about.

In *Lord of the Rings: The Fellowship of the Ring,* the history of the ring is revealed in the first few pages as it is being forged in the fires of Mount Doom: There were "20 rings made, three were given to the Elves...seven to the Dwarf-Lords,...and nine rings were gifted to the race of Men...but they were all of them deceived..." Another ring was made: "One Ring to rule them all..." Then, in a series of cinematic vignettes, we trace its path of power and evil: "And some things that should not have been forgotten...were lost." We see Gollum worship the ring, then lose it, and it lies there, forgotten, until Bilbo Baggins finds it at the bottom of a murky pool and takes it home to the Shire.

So it begins. This prologue, this inciting incident, is what grabs our attention, and through the voice-over narration and various images it gives us the information we need to know, thus setting up the entire story of the three episodes of *Lord of the Rings.*

Once we've established the inciting incident, the story begins. The Wizard Gandalf arrives in the Shire and we're introduced to him as well as to Frodo, Sam, and the others as Bilbo throws his birthday celebration. Time for him to move on, Bilbo tells Gandalf. When the Wizard hears Bilbo's farewell and watches him disappear at his birthday celebration, he demands to see the ring. Immediately, we see the effect the ring has on Bilbo; he's rude, mean, and turns nasty until Gandalf confronts him. And then, when Bilbo leaves on his journey, his nephew Frodo inherits the ring. It is the *key incident* in the story line; Frodo's inheritance, his dramatic need, is to return the ring to the fires of Mount Doom and destroy it. That is what the story is all about. And when Gandalf learns the origins, history, and mystery of the ring, when he learns of its power, only then does he realize that Sauron's riders, the dark forces of evil, are at this very moment searching for the ring. It is too dangerous for it to remain in the Shire. Frodo, by fate, destiny, or karma, becomes the ring bearer; the ring now becomes his physical, emotional, and mental burden to bear.

This is the *key incident* of the screenplay. It begins Frodo's journey to Mount Doom. The journey begins and the Fellowship of the Ring is formed.

The inciting incident and the key incident—Bilbo's finding the ring and Frodo's, by necessity and design, inheriting it and taking responsibility for it—are related. These two incidents are essential parts of the whole that must be established when you are setting up the screenplay.

Many times the key incident and Plot Point I are the same. *American Beauty* represents this very well. When we first meet Lester Burnham, he tells us in voice-over narration, "I'm forty-two years old. In less than a year, I'll be dead....In a way, I'm dead already." We're introduced to his family, watch as they prepare for the day. As they drive to work and school, Lester says in a voice-over: "My wife and daughter think I'm this gigantic loser, and they're right....I have lost something. I'm not sure what it was, but...I feel sedated....But you know, it's never too late to get it back."

American Beauty is a story of resurrection and rebirth, of finding a reason, or purpose, for living. Lester's loaded little statement is what sets the story in motion; it is the inciting incident. In voice-over narration, it tells us that Lester Burnham is a man who wants to regain his sense of aliveness, his sense of well-being, his sense of contentment. That's his dramatic need. Once this is established in the opening scenes, we follow Lester, wife Carolyn, and daughter Jane as they go through their "day in the life." Lester goes to his job, which he hates; real estate agent Carolyn is determined to sell a house; and Jane goes off to school. Then, in one of my favorite scenes, they come home and we see them at dinner. From the outside it looks warm and inviting, like a Norman Rockwell picture of the ideal American family. But that's only on the outside; on the inside, they're totally dysfunctional.

Later, Jane and her friend Angela are preparing to perform their cheerleader routine at the basketball half-time festivities. Carolyn insists on coming to watch because she wants to "support" their daughter. Lester doesn't want to be there: "I'm missing the James Bond marathon on TNT." They arrive, get settled, then watch the group perform their routine. Lester's attention is drawn to Angela, and as he focuses on her, we get closer and closer to her and enter the subjective realm of Lester's head. In a dazzling cinematic display, we see his vision of Angela. The external sound stops, the music gets wacky, and we zoom in close on Angela. Now her routine turns into an erotic, hypnotic display of fantasy and suggestion.

This is a marvelous filmic presentation of the *key incident* of the movie, because it is this incident that totally turns Lester's life around. Not only is it the key incident of the film, it's also Plot Point I. Seeing Lester's fantasy is the incident, episode, or event that hooks into the action and spins it around in another direction, in this case Act II. Lester is suddenly brought back to life. It is a sequence that visually illustrates what the story is all about: Angela becomes the focus of Lester's fantasy, his infatuation, the very reason and purpose of his being alive, something to live for. This is shown after the half-time festivities, when Lester makes a fool of himself fawning over Angela. "Could he be any more pathetic?" Jane asks her friend after her parents leave.

Of course, he is pathetic, but Lester's reawakening is the key incident in the screenplay. To show this we cut to Lester lying awake in the glow of his fantasy, watching, in his mind's eye, Angela beckoning to him on a carpet of rose petals. He says, "I feel like I've been in a coma for about twenty years and I'm just now waking up." His journey into "life" is about to begin. How he does this and the changes and obstacles he confronts are what this story is all about.

At the end, he is happy and content as he sits in the kitchen looking at pictures of his family taken many years before, when they were "startlingly happy." He stares at these photographs, and a smile appears on his face, a "deep satisfied smile" of peace and contentment. And then the gun enters the frame and the trigger is pulled.

The key incident is what literally spins Lester's life around in an-other direction and initiates his emotional journey, his transformation from despair to happiness. In this case, the key incident and Plot Point I happen to be the same thing. There are times when this happens, and other times when it doesn't. The inciting incident and the key incident are related, but not always in the same way. It all depends on the story you're telling. There are no magic formulas in screenwriting.

In *Mystic River,* the inciting incident is in the past, when Dave (Tim Robbins) was abducted by the two perverts; it sets the story in motion and leads to the key incident: the discovery of Jimmy's (Sean Penn's) murdered daughter. It connects the story line in terms of "Who committed the murder?" to the inciting incident with Dave that opened the movie. In *The Shawshank Redemption,* we see the inciting incident wrapped in three different events: Andy on trial, Andy drunk in his car loading his gun, and Andy watching his wife and her boyfriend in a sexual embrace.

Many people wonder about the distinctions between the dramatic premise—what the story is about (as mentioned in Chapter 2)—and the key incident we're talking about. Are they the same? Both deal with the foundation of the story line, but the dramatic premise could be said to be a *conceptual description* of what the story is about, while the key incident would be that *specific scene or sequence* that is the dramatic visualization of what the story is about.

Sometimes the key incident will be something that has affected your character's life at an earlier time, as in *Mystic River.* Sometimes the story is about the person trying to piece together the fragments of his or her life. In *The Bourne Supremacy,* for example, the key incident is the murders Jason Bourne committed as a member of the Treadstone mission years earlier. He's on a quest to rediscover his past. Everything bounces off and revolves around this key incident; the whole story leads up to it.

The Manchurian Candidate (Daniel Pyne and Dean Georgaris; original screenplay by George Axelrod, based on the novel by Richard Condon) is very much the same; a key incident is "buried" within Ben Marco's (Denzel Washington's) mind and he has to unlock its mysteries before he can achieve his dramatic need. The same with *Ordinary People;* the entire screenplay revolves around the key incident of the drowning, which occurs before the story begins but is emotionally pieced together like a jigsaw puzzle and finally seen in its totality at Plot Point II.

When you begin writing your screenplay, it's essential that you know the distinctions between the inciting incident and the key incident. Why are they so important in setting up and establishing your story line? If we go back to Henry James's statement—"What is character but the determination of incident? And what is incident but the illumination of character?"—we see that the force of the key incident affects both the internal and external aspects of your character and story, as in *Mystic River* and *Finding Neverland* (David Magee).

Act I is a unit of dramatic action that is approximately twenty or thirty pages long; it begins at the beginning of the screenplay and goes to the Plot Point at the end of Act I. It is held together with the dramatic context known as the *setup.* If you recall, context is the empty space that holds the content in place. This unit of dramatic action sets up your story; it sets up the situation and the relationships between the characters, and establishes the necessary information so the reader knows what's happening and the story can unfold clearly.

The first ten pages of your screenplay, as mentioned, establish three specific things. The main character is introduced so we know *who* the story is about. In *Basic Instinct,* after the murder, Michael Douglas is brought into the story when he investigates the crime scene. Who committed the murder and why? In *American Beauty* we know immediately that the story is about Lester Burnham; he is the main character. In *Lord of the Rings: The Fellowship of the Ring,* we immediately meet Frodo as Gandalf rides into the Shire.

The second thing we create within this first ten-page unit of action is the dramatic premise. What is this story about? We can state it through dialogue, as in *Chinatown,* or show it visually, through the inciting incident, as in *Crimson Tide.* The third thing we need to establish is the situation, the circumstances surrounding the action, as in *Mystic River,* or *Finding Neverland,* or *Sideways.*

The two incidents provide the foundation of the story line. The inciting incident sets the story in motion and the key incident establishes the story; it is the dramatic premise executed. If the key incident is the hub of the story, then all things—the actions, reactions, thoughts, memories, or flashbacks—are tethered to this one incident. So, you can tell your story in a linear fashion, as in *Basic Instinct;* or in flashback, as in *American Beauty, The Bourne Supremacy,* or *The Manchurian Candidate;* or even in a nonlinear way, as in *Pulp Fiction.*

Pulp Fiction is an interesting film to examine within the context of these two incidents. When I first considered trying to identify and define them in Tarantino's movie, I thought I was trying to put a round peg into a square hole. Was I trying to force the issue? Or was it something that I could now see differently as a result of my new awareness? I didn't really have an answer, so I decided to just take a look and see what I came up with.

So I traced my history with *Pulp Fiction.* To begin with, everybody knows *Pulp Fiction* has had a tremendous impact on world cinema. When it first came out, you either loved it or hated it. When I first saw it I hated it. But everyone kept telling me how wonderful it was, how different and intriguing, definitely a landmark film. Though I didn't agree with that, I had to acknowledge that *Pulp Fiction* sparked a new awareness in the filmgoer's consciousness. In my workshops and seminars around the world, everyone was talking about its impact.

Even though we were riding the wave of a technology revolution in the mid-'90s, as far as I was concerned the real revolution was going to manifest itself more in terms of technology than in form and content—that is, *what* you showed and *how* you showed it. *Pulp Fiction* was definitely a part of that.

When I began to reexamine it, I asked myself what made *Pulp Fiction* so influential. The answer, I knew, was in the screenplay. Was it the structure? Was it one of the characters getting killed in the middle of the movie and then the film's coming back to the events that led up to his death? Was it the three stories? The bookend opening and closing?

When you read the screenplay of *Pulp Fiction,* the first thing you see is the title page; it states that *Pulp Fiction* is really "three stories ... about one story." When you turn the page, there are two dictionary definitions of *Pulp:* "a soft, moist, shapeless mass of matter," and "a magazine or book containing lurid subject matter and being characteristically printed on rough, unfinished paper." That's certainly an accurate description of the film. But on the third page, you might be surprised to find a Table of Contents. *Kill Bill I* and *II* is that way too; in fact, it has not only a Table of Contents, but chapter headings as well.

I thought that was odd; who puts a Table of Contents in a screenplay? It states very clearly that the film is broken down into five individual parts: Part I, the Prologue; Part II, Vincent Vega and Marcellus Wallace's Wife; Part III, The Gold Watch; Part IV, The Bonnie Situation; and Part V, the Epilogue.

As I studied the script, I saw that all three stories really bounce off the key incident: Jules and Vincent retrieving Marcellus Wallace's briefcase from the four kids. I saw that this one incident was really the hub of all three stories, and noticed that each story is structured as a whole, in linear fashion; it starts at the beginning of the action, goes into the middle, then proceeds to the end. Each section is like a short story, presented from a different character's point of view.

Thinking in terms of "three stories about one story" allowed me to see the film as one unified whole. *Pulp Fiction* is three stories surrounded by a prologue and an epilogue, what screenwriters call a bookend technique. *The Bridges of Madison County, Sunset Boulevard* (Billy Wilder and Charles Brackett), *Saving Private Ryan,* and *American Beauty* use this technique as well.

The Prologue sets up Pumpkin and Honey Bunny in a coffee shop discussing various types of small-time robbery. It sets the first and last stories in motion. When the two finish their meal, they pull out their guns and announce the robbery. The film freezes and we cut to the main titles. Then we cut into the middle of a dialogue between Jules (Samuel L. Jackson) and Vincent (John Travolta) as they are driving, having an enlightening discussion about the relative merits of a Big Mac here and abroad.

This little exchange sets up their characters, and when they stop and pull out their weapons we see the contradiction between their words and their actions. It literally sets up the film and tells us everything we need to know: The two men are killers working for Marcellus Wallace; their job, their dramatic need, is to retrieve the briefcase. That's the true beginning of the story. In Part I, Jules and Vincent arrive, state their position, reclaim the briefcase, then kill three of the four guys they encounter. It's only by the grace of God they're not killed themselves. Only one other person, Marvin, survives, at least for the moment.

Vincent takes Mia Wallace (Uma Thurmond) out to dinner, and after she accidentally overdoses, they say good night. Part III is about Butch and his gold watch and what happens when he wins the fight instead of losing it as he had agreed to do. In the middle of this section Butch (Bruce Willis) kills Vincent, who is at his apartment looking for him. Part IV deals with cleaning up Marvin's remains, which are splattered all over the car, a continuation of Part I. That's followed by the Epilogue, where Jules talks about his transformation and the significance of Divine Intervention and then Pumpkin and Honey Bunny resume the holdup that began in the Prologue. *Pulp Fiction* is a very novelistic presentation, as are *Kill Bill I* and *II*.

It became very clear that no matter what form a film takes, whether linear or nonlinear, there is always going to be an inciting incident and a key incident. *Kill Bill I* and *II* is based entirely on the key incident of the story—the killing of The Bride's (Uma Thurman's) wedding party—and like *Pulp Fiction* is driven by the theme of revenge and unfolds in a novelistic way, complete with a Table of Contents and individual chapters, one of the interesting changes happening in the form right now.

Structuring a nonlinear movie means defining each part, then structuring each section, whether in present time or past time, from beginning to end, at which point the screenwriter can build and arrange the parts in any order he or she desires. *Courage Under Fire* (Patrick Sheane Duncan) is a good example of this, as is *Groundhog Day* (Danny Rubin, Harold Ramis), *The Usual Suspects, The English Patient,* and *Sliding Doors* (Peter Howitt). These screenplays are introduced with the inciting incident, then structured around the key incident. Take a look at any of these films and see if you can identify and make the distinction between the inciting incident and the key incident.

In my screenwriting workshops, I have my students focus on and define these two incidents before they write one word of screenplay. Once they know what the incidents are, they can fuse the action, characters, and events into a structured line of dramatic action, whether using a linear or nonlinear story line. It's important to remember that structure is not something embedded in concrete, or something that is unbending, or unyielding; rather, it is flexible, like a tree that bends in the wind but doesn't break. Understanding this concept allows you to play with the plotline so you can tell your stories visually, with narrative action rather than explanation.

This is a relatively new shift in the craft of screenwriting. It wasn't too long ago that characters had to explain who they were, what their background was, and what their motivation or purpose was. Things were explained through the character's dialogue. As a matter of fact, explaining their story line through dialogue was one of the chief problems that aspiring screenwriters had when writing their screenplays. But there is a new generation of young people growing up with television, wireless technology, and PlayStation, and it's pretty obvious their visual sense is heightened; as a result, we're expanding the craft with stories that are more visual, while unfolding with clarity and simplicity. It is a clear sign of evolution at work.

But though the form may be evolving, the simple tools of story-telling remain the same. What you write is just as important as how you write it.

And that's what it's all about.

9

Plot Points

> "Writing a screenplay is in many ways simi-
> lar to executing a piece of carpentry. If
> you take some wood and nails and glue and
> make a bookcase, only to find when you're
> done that it topples over when you try to
> stand it upright, you may have created some-
> thing really very beautiful, but it won't
> work as a bookcase."
>
> —*Adventures in the Screen Trade*
> William Goldman

The hardest thing about writing is knowing what to write. When you sit down in front of 120 blank sheets of paper, the only way you can get through that intricate tangle of seemingly endless creative decisions, solutions, and choices is by knowing what you're doing and where you're going. You need a road map, a guide, a *direction*— a line of development leading from beginning to end.

You need a story line.

If you don't have one, you're in trouble. That's why it's so easy to get lost in the maze of your own creation. James Joyce, the great Irish novelist, once remarked that the experience of writing is like climbing a mountain: When you're in the middle of your climb, you can only see what's directly in front of you and what's directly above you. You can plan only one move at a time. You can't see two or three moves above you or how you're going to get there. Only when you reach the top of the mountain can you look down and gain some kind of an overview of the landscape you've negotiated.

It's a good analogy. When you're writing a screenplay, you can see only the page you're writing and the pages you've written. Most of the time you can't see where you're going or how you're going to get there. Sometimes you can't even see that. The scene you're going to write next is only some kind of vague notion, and you don't know whether it will work or not. You literally have no objectivity at all—no overview.

That's why the *paradigm* is so important—it gives you a direction, a line of development. It's like a road map. On the road, driving through Arizona, New Mexico, on through the vast reaches of Texas, and across the high plains of Oklahoma, you don't know where you are, much less where you've been. All you can see is a flat, barren landscape, broken only by silver flashes of the sun bouncing off the windshields of passing cars.

When you're *in* the paradigm, you can't *see* the paradigm. That's why Plot Points are so important. As defined, the Plot Point is "any incident, episode, or event that hooks into the action and spins it around in another direction." There are many Plot Points scattered throughout the screenplay, but when you're confronting 120 blank sheets of paper, you need to know only four things to structure your story line: the ending, the beginning, and Plot Points I and II.

The function of the Plot Point is simple: *It moves the story forward.* Plot Point I and Plot Point II are the story points that *hold the paradigm* in place. They are the anchors of your story line.

Take another look at the *paradigm:*

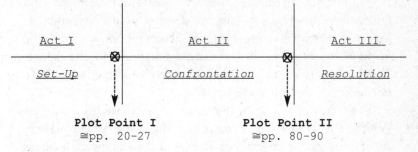

If you look at the screenplay as a series of story points, or story progressions, your story line begins at the beginning and ends at the end, whether in linear form as in *Collateral, Thelma & Louise,* or *Million Dollar Baby,* or in nonlinear form as in *Cold Mountain, Pulp Fiction,* or *The Hours.* No matter what form your story line is in, linear or nonlinear, it is anchored in place by Plot Points I and II.

Structure is the foundation, the base, the blueprint of the screenplay; as William Goldman says, "Screenplay is structure." If you don't know the basic structure of your story line, you're not really ready to start writing. That's why I stress the importance of the four things you need to know before you put one word down on paper: the ending, beginning, and Plot Points I and II. If you don't know those four points, you're in trouble. This does not mean that there are only two Plot Points in your screenplay. That's not the case at all. We're dealing with the preparation you need to make before you begin writing. Once you know what these two Plot Points are, they will anchor your story line, hold it in place so you can begin the writing process with freedom and creativity. When the screenplay is completed, it may contain as many as ten to fifteen Plot Points, most of which will be in Act II. How many you have, again, depends upon your story. The purpose of the Plot Point is to *move* the story *forward,* toward the resolution. That is its purpose.

In Michael Mann's high-powered thriller *Collateral* (tautly written by Stuart Beattie), the action moves forward on both a physical and emotional level. The Tom Cruise character, Vincent, has a job to do—five contracted murders in one night. He forces Max (Jamie Foxx) to be his driver, makes physical threats on his life, but pays him well to drive him around. We discover what's happening as Max discovers what's happening. The action moves forward to the final shoot-out with clarity, ingenuity, character insight, and change. The film itself is "clean, lean and tight"; there's not an ounce of "fat," or padding, in the entire screenplay.

The thrust of the script moves relentlessly forward from Plot Point to Plot Point. As a matter of fact, the characters' arc and the arc of the story line impact each other, so that each physical incident reveals a different aspect of the characters. Foxx's cabbie goes through a strong dramatic arc: from passive wimp to man of action; from dreamer to achiever. And the irony, of course, is that Max is forced into these changes by the villain of the piece; when Cruise destroys his old life, Foxx is forced to grab the new.

The script opens with Vincent arriving at LAX and exchanging a black bag with an unknown accomplice; then we cut to and set up Max cleaning his taxi as he readies himself for the night shift. He picks up a fare, Annie (Jada Pinkett Smith)—the inciting incident—and during the ride downtown they develop an easy-going familiarity, an attraction, for each other. He delivers Annie to the Federal Building, and as she gets out she tells him she's a prose-cutor working an "all-nighter" on a big case and gives Max her card. He picks up another fare, Vincent, who hires him for the night to make the five stops to get "signatures" on a real estate deal he's clos-ing. So far, it's just another night in L.A.

As Vincent and Max banter about the state of L.A., they get to know each other a little more. They make stop number one, and Max is waiting in the alley behind the building when suddenly there's a loud crash and a dead body plunges onto the front wind-shield. Shocked, stunned, disbelieving, Max is astonished to learn that Vincent killed the man, though the hit man claims "it was the bullet and the fall that killed him."

That's Plot Point I, the key incident of the script. This is the inci-dent that sets in motion the entire screenplay, because Max is now forced against his will to drive Vincent to his other "appointments." He's virtually a prisoner. Now, the true story begins.

Two physical actions are going on in this story: (1), Max trying to escape from Vincent as they roam through the city; and (2), Vincent doing his job and honoring his contracts. As they make their appointed rounds, we watch Max reacting to the physical ac-tion by going through an emotional change that, step by step, leads to his transformation. In the beginning, he's passive and weak, a wimp, afraid to stand up to his boss at the cab company. Then he begins to gain a little courage and tries to escape, but winds up watching helplessly as Vincent kills two guys trying to rip off his briefcase. They make a "random" visit to a nightclub, ostensibly to listen to some good jazz, but in fact it's a cover for Vincent to score his next hit. This is a nice touch, setting us up to expect one thing, then turning it around. Then Max is made to visit his mother at the hospital, and once again tries to escape by running away with

Vincent's briefcase and, in defiance, tossing it onto the freeway. His attitude, his strength, is beginning to emerge; he's starting to stand up for himself.

After the briefcase episode Vincent forces Max, as a sort of punishment or test, to pose as him and meet Felix, the crime boss, to get the new information about the last two hits of the night. Max, in a tense and dramatic moment, rustles up his strength, threatens Felix, and manages to walk out of the meeting alive. This is another incident where the physical action triggers an emotional response.

The cops, who think Max is the hit man responsible for all these murders, follow him to a nightclub, and there, on a crowded dance floor, there is a violent shoot-out. Max tries to get away, and when he is spotted by a cop who believes in his innocence, he's hustled off to safety. When Vincent sees him with the cop, however, the hit man kills the cop and "rescues" Max.

There's one more hit for Vincent to fulfill. At this point, two things are left unresolved. One, how is Max going to get away from Vincent alive? And two, how is he going to prevent Vincent's last hit? Racing away from the big shoot-out at the nightclub, Vincent says that Max's dream of starting a limo company is only a dream, a "someday" excursion into a fantasy that will never happen. Max, for the first time, realizes that he has been living a dream for twelve years. Now his dream shattered, and knowing he'll probably be killed by Vincent when this ordeal is over, he decides to give it all up and live for the moment. Otherwise, "What's the point?" It is this insight that gives him the strength to put his foot on the gas for a wild speed run through the streets of L.A. He loses control of the wheel and crashes the car, hitting a divider. The car leaps into the air, hits the ground with a tremendous crash, and rolls. Plot Point II.

Vincent crawls out of the torn and twisted wreckage, and runs. Max manages to crawl out of the overturned taxi, sees a picture of Annie, the woman he met earlier that evening, and realizes that she is the last victim on Vincent's list. Which happens to be the reason why Vincent was at the Federal Building in the first place: She was supposed to be his first hit of the night. Max races on foot to warn Annie, and then we go into a chase sequence that ends the film.

These two Plot Points anchor the story in place. Plot Point I is the true beginning of the story: the first murder and Max's realization that Vincent is responsible for it. At Plot Point II, he crashes the car and stands up to Vincent, ready to kill him if need be, in order to save Annie. Each Plot Point is geared by both the emotional and physical forces working on the character; the outside events affect the interior, emotional life of the character and move the script to its next level of action.

Once again, a Plot Point is a function of the main character and moves the story forward. It amps up the action and underscores the arc of the character: Vincent is a cynical, amoral person with no values of right and wrong; he's merely doing a job, and he's very good at it. He views the world and everyone in it as "a cosmic accident," the product of random chance. There's no meaning or significance to our lives because we're nothing more than an infinitesimal speck of dust in the vast universe. If there's no meaning to our existence, then our lives mean nothing, so taking a human life has little consequence. As Tolstoy said, without God, without a moral system of right and wrong, "anything is permissible."

Collateral is a very good example of how Plot Points hook into the story line and move it forward, influencing both the emotional and physical arc of the characters. The choices your characters make may very well determine the course and outcome of the story. The interplay between Max and Vincent and the choices they make bind them together in a unique and unusual situation that expresses the story's dynamic in a visual, suspenseful way.

The connections and interplay between the characters, of course, are essential to the movement and plotline of the story. Let's take another look at *Chinatown*. As a mystery-detective story, *Chinatown* is structured from Plot Point to Plot Point, each Plot Point carefully moving the action forward from the beginning, when Gittes is hired by the phony Mrs. Mulwray, to the end, when Evelyn Mulwray is killed.

The script opens with the question: Who is Mrs. Mulwray's husband having an affair with? Gittes follows Mulwray to a number of the city's reservoirs, then discovers him in the company of a young woman. He takes pictures and returns to the office, and as far as he's concerned, the case is closed. But the next day, he learns someone has released the story, along with his pictures, to the newspaper.

Who did it? And why?

When Gittes returns to his office he finds a woman waiting to see him. "Have you ever seen me before?" she asks. She then tells him she is the *real* Mrs. Mulwray; since she did not hire him, she's going to sue him and take away his detective license. But if she's the *real* Mrs. Mulwray, who hired him to find out who Mulwray was having an affair with? And why? With the "love scandal" front-page news, he knows he's been set up—framed. Someone wants him to take the fall. He's going to find out who set him up. And why.

End of Act I.

What moment in this block of dramatic action hooks into the action and spins it around in another direction? When the real Mrs. Mulwray shows up. That's the key incident in the story line.

When the real Mrs. Mulwray enters the picture, the action shifts from a job completed to possible legal action and the loss of Jake's license. He'd better find out who set him up—then he'll find out *why*.

Act II opens with Gittes driving up to the Mulwray house. Mrs. Mulwray tells him her husband might be at the Oak Pass Reservoir. Gittes goes to the reservoir, and there meets Lieutenant Escobar, a former colleague, who tells him that Mulwray is dead—drowned, apparently in an accident.

Mulwray's death presents another problem, or obstacle, for Gittes. Remember, the dramatic *context* for Act II is *Confrontation*.

Gittes's dramatic need is to find out *who* set him up, and *why*. So screenwriter Robert Towne creates obstacle after obstacle to keep the action going. Remember, if you know your character's dramatic need you can create obstacles to it, and the story becomes your character's overcoming these obstacles to achieve his/her dramatic need. Mulwray is dead. Murdered, Gittes finds out later. Who did it? And why? This is a Plot Point within the structure of Act II to keep the story moving forward. There are ten such Plot Points in the second act of *Chinatown*.

Mulwray's death is an incident that *moves the story forward*. Gittes is totally involved now, whether he likes it or not. Later, he receives a phone call from a mysterious "Ida Sessions": the phony Mrs. Mulwray. She tells him to look in the obituary column of the paper for "one of those people," whatever that means. Then she hangs up. Soon after, Ida Sessions is found murdered, and Escobar is certain Gittes is involved.

The theme of water has been introduced several times before, and Gittes follows it. He checks out the owners of the land in the Valley and discovers that most of the acreage has been sold within the last few months.

Gittes investigates, but is attacked by farmers who think he's the man who's been poisoning their water. When he regains consciousness, Evelyn Mulwray is there—called by the farmers. As they drive back to L.A., Gittes discovers that one of the names in the obituary column mentioned by Ida Sessions is cited as being the owner of a large parcel of land in the Valley. Strange. He died at a place called the Mar Vista Home for the Aged. Together, Gittes and Evelyn Mulwray drive to the retirement home. Gittes learns that most of the new owners of the land parcels in the Valley are living at the home, unaware of their purchases. It's phony—the whole thing's a giant scam. As they're leaving, his suspicions confirmed, thugs attack him, but Evelyn drives up, steps on the gas, Gittes jumps on the running board, and they manage to get away.

These incidents, episodes, and events are all Plot Points, all story progressions that move the story forward.

Back at her house, Evelyn cleans Gittes's nose wound (for being "too nosy"); he notices something in her eye, a slight color defect. He leans over and kisses her. They have sex.

Afterward, they lie in bed making small talk.

The phone rings. She answers it, suddenly becomes agitated, hangs up. She tells Gittes he must leave. Immediately. "Something important" has come up.

At this point in the story, we still don't know two things: (1) who the girl was who was with Mulwray in the beginning before he was murdered; and (2) who set up Gittes, and why. Gittes knows that the answers to the two questions are related. There's a good chance that whoever killed Mulwray set him up. Why, we don't know yet.

Something has come up. What? Gittes wants to find out, so he tails Evelyn to a house in the Echo Park section of Los Angeles. When he returns to Evelyn's house, he discovers a pair of bifocals in the bottom of the fish pond. He returns to the Echo Park house and confronts Evelyn. She tells him the girl is her sister, then says she's her daughter. Gittes slaps her. "I want the truth," he says. He slaps her again, and she finally confesses that the girl is "my daughter *and* my sister." At fifteen, she was the victim of incest, and now cares for her daughter and refuses to speak to her father, Noah Cross. So, now we know who the girl is. The second point: Who wore the bifocals, victim or killer? Once Gittes learns the truth, he wants to help Evelyn get away. But before he leaves, at the end of the scene, in what seems to be a throwaway line, she tells Gittes that her husband did not wear bifocals. There is only one conclusion: The glasses were worn by the killer. Now Gittes knows the truth: Noah Cross had a motive for murder. It is the final answer he's seeking and the *Resolution,* the solution of the story.

Gittes calls Noah Cross and tells him he has "the girl," and to meet him at Evelyn's house. And here Gittes learns that the man responsible for the death of Mulwray and the others, the man responsible for the entire water scandal, is Noah Cross. Why? "Because it's the future, Mr. Gittes. The future." The way to create it, Cross says, is simple: "Either you bring the water to L.A., or you bring L.A. to the water."

That's the dramatic hook of the movie. And it works, beautifully. The premise that money, power, and influence are corruptive forces is established; as Gittes says: "You gotta be rich to kill somebody, anybody, and get away with it." If you've got enough money and power, you can get away with anything—even murder.

Gittes, now a prisoner, is taken to Chinatown so that Cross can claim his daughter/granddaughter. When Evelyn dies at the end of the film, Cross spirits his daughter/granddaughter away, and does indeed get away with murder. Ironically, the incident that drove Gittes off the police force in Chinatown has repeated itself: "I tried to help someone and all I ended up doing was hurting them," he had said earlier.

Full circle, turn. Gittes can't deal with it. He has to be restrained; the last words of the script are forged in filmic consciousness: "Forget it, Jake.... It's Chinatown."

The Plot Points at the end of Acts I and II are there to hook in the action and spin it around in another direction. They are the hub of the story progression, amp the story up to the next level, and move it forward to its dramatic resolution.

As a simple exercise, the next time you go to the movies or watch a film on DVD or cable (without commercial breaks), see if you can locate the Plot Points at the end of Act I and Act II. Every film you see will have definite Plot Points; all you have to do is find them. If you want, take a look at your watch anywhere from twenty to thirty minutes into the film (depending on its length, of course) and see if you can determine what the action point is; ask yourself what's happening, or what's going on in the story around this point in the action. There will be some kind of incident, episode, or event that will occur. Discover *what* it is, and *when* it occurs.

Do the same for Act II. Around eighty or ninety minutes into the feature, check out what's happening in the story line. What incident, episode, or event occurs that will lead us into Act III, the *Resolution*? What happens around this time in the movie? It's an excellent exercise. The more you do it, the easier it gets. Pretty soon it will be ingrained in your consciousness; you'll grasp the essential nature of the relationship between structure and story. Then you'll see how the definition of dramatic structure—"a series of related incidents, episodes, and events leading to a dramatic resolution"— guides you through the story line. Plot Points are those incidents, episodes, and events that anchor your story line; they provide the foundation of the narrative line of action.

Let's take a look at the Plot Points in a couple of other films: *The Matrix* and *Thelma & Louise.*

Here's the *paradigm:*

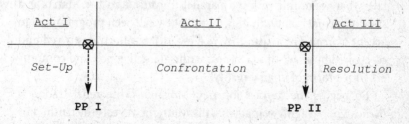

We're looking for the Plot Points at the end of Acts I and II.

In *The Matrix,* the opening scene shows us that this is no ordinary action sequence of flying fists, fired shots, and a few explosions. This is a totally unique sequence; it pits Trinity, a lone woman, against several armed policeman, all wearing bulletproof vests. Right before our eyes, in the most amazing physical feats, Trinity leaps up, is suspended in midair, then runs up walls and across ceilings in order to escape. She leaps from rooftop to rooftop, building to building, totally disregarding gravity as she flies through the air to reach the other side. From there, it's a race against a huge garbage truck to reach the ringing telephone. She makes it in the nick of time and answers the phone just as the truck slams into the telephone booth.

Whoa . . . if that's not a grabber, I don't know what is. In terms of information, we don't know who Trinity is, whether she's a "good guy" or a "bad guy," nor do we know what the story's about, or how she managed to escape the way she did. But as an opening this inciting incident certainly grabs our attention.

At this point, we don't know *what* the story is about or *who* it's about. We need some exposition here, defined as *the information needed to move the story forward,* and that's exactly what we get next. Neo, the main character, wakes up to the words "Follow the white rabbit" on his computer screen. There's a knock on the door; it's a girl with a white rabbit tattooed on her shoulder. He follows her to a club. There he meets Trinity and asks her about the Matrix. But she doesn't explain anything; she only warns him that he's in danger: "They're watching you." And, she stresses, "The truth is out there, Neo, and it's looking for you and will find you, if you want it to." Then she's gone.

What is the Matrix? Morpheus (Laurence Fishburne) explains later that we're inhabiting a parallel universe and the Matrix is a state of virtual reality, an illusion that we've all been programmed to accept as *real.* The truth, the "real" world, has been destroyed and re-created by a race of machines, artificial intelligence, and computers into a form of virtual reality.

So begins the heroes' journey. Morpheus, the rebel leader, is dedicated to waging war against the Matrix to reveal "the truth," liberating humanity from the bondage of the machines. Morpheus believes in the prophecy that their only hope of winning is by finding "The One," a human being endowed with godlike powers who will lead them in their war of liberation. And he believes Neo is "The One." As Morpheus tells Neo, the mind and body are intertwined, and even though they are separate entities, if you can control your mind you can control reality, and thus control your destiny.

That's an ancient teaching from Eastern philosophy, brought into a contemporary situation, futuristic in thought and execution. Neo, like Hamlet or the warrior Arjuna in the classic Indian tale the Bhagavad Gita, must choose his own destiny. This theme of choice, of choosing the reality you wish to inhabit, is a recurring motif throughout the film. When Neo goes to work the next day, he is told he has to make a choice: to either be Thomas Anderson by day, or Neo, the self-styled rebel, his true self, by night. When he gets to his office, Neo receives a package and a cell phone pops out, ringing. Morpheus is on the line. He tells Neo, "They're after you. There are only two ways for you to leave the building—either you choose to leave by the scaffolding hanging outside the window, or you choose to leave as a prisoner." Like Hamlet and Arjuna, Neo embodies the stance of the reluctant hero: Before he can rise to another, higher level of consciousness, he must first accept himself and his destiny.

He leaves as a prisoner, and is later wired, a bug planted deep within him. Trinity and the others pick Neo up under the bridge, but only after he is "debugged" will he be taken to meet Morpheus. This fusion of the ancient and the futuristic is embodied in the various names used in *The Matrix*. The rebel ship, the *Nebuchadnezzar*, for example, is named after the famed Babylonian king of the fifth century B.C. who is credited with tearing down and rebuilding the ancient temples; so he's both a destroyer and builder. The name fits the ship's destiny, for it houses the small rebel band determined to destroy the Matrix. In Greek mythology *Morpheus* is the god of Sleep, responsible for weaving the fabric of our dreams in the deep sleep state. *Neo*, of course, means "new," and *Trinity* has several religious implications. These mythological echoes are simply a way of adding more insight and dimension to the story line.

At this point, the story progresses by action and explanation. Only when Neo can accept being "The One" can he really *be* "The

One." In other words, what we believe to be true, is true. And this sets up Plot Point I.

He has his first face-to-face meeting with Morpheus at Plot Point I. During the meeting, the key incident, Morpheus offers Neo a choice: Either take the Blue Pill and get ordinary reality or take the Red Pill and get the truth. Neo doesn't hesitate—he takes the red one. Reality distorts as he falls between the corridors of virtual reality and the netherworld. In a sequence as bizarre and evocative as an H. R. Giger painting, Neo is reborn as a man freed from the restraints of his limited mind. As the embryo of himself, Neo must retrain both his body and his mind until he is capable of exploring the untapped resources of his unlimited self as seen in martial arts contests with Morpheus.

Plot Point I is the true beginning of the story; it is the incident that hooks into the action and spins it around into Act II. The context of Act II is *Confrontation,* so Neo encounters obstacle after obstacle to achieve his dramatic need: to know the Matrix and to be self-realized. Plot Point I fulfills this function.

Neo's encounter with the Oracle is the Mid-Point of the story. She's a great character. When I first saw the film I expected an old, old man, extremely wise, with white hair and possibly a long straggly beard. Instead, I was delightfully surprised to discover a middle-aged woman baking cookies. When she casually asks if he believes he's "The One," Neo shakes his head and says, "I'm just an ordinary guy." Once again, his belief systems, the limitations of his mind, imprison him. Too bad, she says. Why? Neo asks. "Because Morpheus believes in you, Neo, and no one, not even you or me, can convince him otherwise," she says. "He believes it so blindly that he's going to sacrifice his life for you. You're going to have to make a choice. On one hand, you'll have Morpheus's life...and on the other hand, you'll have your own....One of you is going to die....Which one, will be up to you."

She is his "mirror," reflecting what he believes, telling him what she sees within him. His struggle guides him to the understanding that he can wear the mantle of "The One" only if he chooses to. Only when we can give up the concepts of our limited self can we attain enlightenment and liberation. The reluctant hero must accept the challenge of being who he or she really is, in much the same way that Hamlet and Arjuna must choose to honor themselves and accept their destiny. Whether he likes it or not, Neo is "The One" who has been chosen to "set the times right."

When Agent Smith takes Morpheus prisoner, Neo makes his decision to rescue him. "The Oracle told me this would happen," Neo says. "She told me I would have to make a choice...." He pauses, and in an early draft of the script says, "I may not be what Morpheus thinks I am, but if I don't try to help him, then I'm not even what I think I am.... I'm going in after him." When he declares himself in this fashion, it is the first step of accepting himself as "The One." This, then, is Plot Point II. It leads to the *Resolution* of the story.

At Plot Point I, Morpheus had asked Neo if he believed in fate. No, Neo had replied—"Because I don't like the idea that I'm not in control of my life." Whether he believes it or not, whether he knows it or not, he's now in the hands of his fate, his destiny.

After rescuing Morpheus, Neo doesn't make it out of the Matrix in time and, in a tremendous fight scene, dies at the hands of Agent Smith. As Trinity stands over Neo's inert body, she tells him what the Oracle has told her: that she would fall in love with the man who was "The One." Even though Neo's dead, she believes with all her heart that love is stronger than the physical body. She kisses him, then demands that he "get up." Neo's eyes flip open, and he's resurrected. A miracle? Of course. But as Joseph Campbell states in *The Power of Myth,* the true hero has to die in order to be reborn. Once again, Neo has died so he can be reborn. How? It doesn't matter. Either we believe it or we don't; it is the willing suspension of disbelief. He has overcome the limitations of his mind; he has chosen to wear the mantle of "The One."

The Matrix was one of the first blockbuster films influenced by Asian filmmaking, and it portends a future direction in movies: technology integrated into a classical, mythical story line that is larger than life. It's too bad that *The Matrix: Reloaded* and *The Matrix: Revolutions* don't live up to the quality or creativity of the original.

Thelma & Louise, like *Collateral,* is a story that deals with character change and transformation. When the film begins, Louise is finishing up her night shift at the restaurant where she works. It is early morning, and she calls Thelma, who is in the kitchen preparing breakfast. We immediately *see* who Thelma is. Her breakfast is a bite out of a frozen candy bar. From our very first glimpse, Thelma appears to be a little bit ditzy. Louise asks if she's ready to go for their weekend trip to the mountains. Thelma replies she hasn't asked her husband Darryl yet, but when he appears, she hangs up hastily. Our impression of her husband is that he's a pompous, self-centered ass. Thelma hesitates to ask him, finally decides not to, and makes up her mind on the spot to go away with Louise for the weekend anyway.

After her husband leaves for work, Thelma starts packing, and, in a beautiful display of film as behavior, we see two people doing the same thing in totally different ways; we *see* who they are by what they *do*. Here's the way Thelma packs: She stands in front of her closet, and though she's going away for only a couple of days, she doesn't know what to take. So, she takes everything: bathing suits, wool socks, flannel pajamas, jeans, sweater, T-shirts, a couple of dresses; she grabs most of her closet and dumps it in her suitcases. Then she takes a lantern and several pairs of shoes, and, as an afterthought, grabs a gun by the handle, holding it like a rat by the tail, and drops it in her purse. What do we know about her from the way she packs?

Here's the way Louise packs: She puts the suitcase on the bed; everything is perfectly ordered. She neatly folds, as the script puts it: "three pairs of underwear, one pair of long underwear, two pairs of pants, two sweaters, one furry robe, one nightgown. She could be packing for camp. Her room is as orderly as the suitcase. As an afterthought, she throws in an extra pair of socks and closes the suitcase." On the way out, she calls her boyfriend Jimmy, and when his answering machine picks up, she angrily turns his picture facedown. She goes to the sink, rinses the only glass that's on the counter, wipes it, puts it back in the cupboard, and leaves in her beautiful T-Bird. Spotless. What do we know about her character from the way she packs? Film is behavior.

She picks up Thelma and they drive toward their weekend retreat. But along the way Thelma begs her to stop so they can get something to eat. They pull into a bar called, appropriately enough, the Silver Bullet. That occurs on about page 10 of the screenplay. We already know who the story is about, as well as their relationships with the men in their life. We learn they are on this weekend holiday because Louise wants to prove a point to her boyfriend Jimmy. A musician, he's been on the road for three weeks, and has not called her once. She's so pissed that she's not going to be home when he returns. Let's see how he likes that!

In an interview I had with writer Callie Khouri for my book *Four Screenplays,* she told me, "Jimmy is a guy who's afraid to make a commitment. She wants to get married, wants all the conventional things, yet she's being denied them because of the choice she's made in this man. Basically, his shortcoming is holding her back from what she really wants.

"I wanted to show her feelings because she feels responsible for everything that happens. She plays a game with him; when he comes back from his trip, she's not going to be in town, and this is what happens when she's not being honest."

Not being honest in her relationship leads to what eventually happens. It's not dharmic, meaning it's not the "right action" based on the moral and ethical principles of the universe. In other words, it's uncool. Thelma and Louise go into the bar, order drinks, talk about their relationships. Then a stranger named Harlan approaches, makes himself comfortable at their table, and starts hustling Thelma. Louise shoos him away, but later he comes back and he and Thelma step onto the dance floor. He plies her with drinks, gets her so dizzy she thinks she's going to be sick, then takes her outside to the parking lot.

And there, what starts as a "friendly" little kiss turns into a pretty ugly scene. He attempts to rape Thelma, and almost gets away with it. After slapping her around, he flips up her dress, knocks her legs apart, unzips his pants. We hear the crunch of gravel, and then a gun enters the frame at his head. Louise. She tells him to stop, adding, "You've got a pretty fucked-up idea of fun." He mouths off to her and says one thing too much, and Louise "raises the gun, and fires a bullet into his face." He's killed instantly.

Plot Point I—the true beginning of the story; the "incident, episode, or event that hooks into the action and spins it around in another direction." What began as a nice weekend trip to the mountains ends up in an attempted rape and murder. From here on out, Thelma and Louise are on the run, and as they race down the highway, like so many other characters in so many other movies, they come to grips with themselves, find out who they really are, and ultimately end up taking responsibility for their lives and actions. *Thelma & Louise* is a road movie, yes, but it's really a journey of enlightenment and self-discovery.

Their dramatic need has changed now and there is no turning back as they race toward Mexico a step ahead of the law. As they drive through Monument Valley in Utah, Louise stops the car. In the vast and towering silence, she steps out of the car and drinks in this most memorable sight. She now knows that this might be her last night on Earth, at least in this lifetime. That realization, experienced in total silence, is Plot Point II. In the next scene, she shares this insight with Thelma. Thelma thanks her for what she did, because Harlan was hurting her. The two women are bonded together in friendship and forgiveness.

It's a beautiful moment. In silence, underneath a blanket of stars, in a place that exists beyond time, they accept themselves and their destiny. For the first time, they understand there may be no way back. The stillness of the scene is the pause before the storm, and the silence works better and more effectively than words ever could.

This little scene is the Plot Point at the end of Act II. It spins the story line into Act III, the *Resolution,* because at this point in the story, we don't know what's going to happen. Will they get caught or escape safely to Mexico? More important, will they live or die? From now on, through the rest of the story line, they resolve their feelings for each other and take full responsibility for their actions. From here on, there's no turning back for Thelma and Louise. There are no options left: It's death or it's death.

It should be noted that a Plot Point does not have to be a dramatic moment, or a major scene or sequence. A Plot Point can be a quiet moment, as in Plot Point II in *Thelma & Louise,* or an exciting action sequence, as in Plot Point I in *Collateral,* or a line of dialogue, as in *The Matrix,* or a decision that affects the story line, as in

Chinatown. A Plot Point is whatever you choose it to be—it could be a long scene or a short one, a moment of silence or of action; it simply depends on the script you're writing. It's the choice of the screenwriter, but it is always an incident, episode, or event that is dictated by the needs of the story.

Knowledge and mastery of the Plot Point is an essential require-ment of writing a screenplay. As you approach the 120 blank sheets of paper, the Plot Points at the end of each act are the anchoring pins of dramatic action; they hold everything together. They are the signposts, the goals, the objectives, the destination points of each act—forged links in the chain of dramatic action.

10

The Scene

RICK:
"Inside both of us, we both know you belong
with Victor. . . . If that plane leaves the
ground and you're not with him, you'll regret
it—oh, maybe not today, maybe not tomorrow,
but soon, and for the rest of your life."

ILSA:
"What about us?"

RICK:
"We'll always have Paris. We didn't have it;
we'd lost it before you came to Casablanca.
We got it back last night. . . . Ilsa, I'm no
good at being noble, but it doesn't take
much to see that the problems of three little people don't amount to a hill of beans
in this crazy world. . . . Someday you'll understand that. Here's looking at you, kid."

—*Casablanca*
Julius and Philip Epstein,
Howard Koch

Casablanca is an extraordinary film experience, one of those rare and magical moments that reside deep within our collective film consciousness. What makes it such a great film? What makes it stand out so vividly in the fabric of our film experience? Many things, of course, but in own my personal opinion, Rick is a charac-ter who, through his words and actions, sacrifices his life for the higher good. In *The Hero with a Thousand Faces,* Joseph Campbell says the hero has "to die in order to be reborn." When *Casablanca* begins, Rick has been living in the past, harboring the emotional pain of his lost love affair with Ilsa. When she reenters his life, Rick laments, "Of all the lousy gin joints, in all the towns in all the world, she walks into mine," and we know it's time for him to deal with, confront, and embrace the past.

What makes Bogart so memorable in this film? I think it's a combination of two things: his screen persona and the part itself, which morphs into Bogart's mythological stature. In their screenplay, Julius and Philip Epstein and Howard Koch have fashioned a character who is tough and fearless and possessed of a strong moral center and the proverbial heart of gold. He's one of the "good guys," and his action at the end of the film, letting Victor Laszlo (Paul Henreid) and Ilsa (Ingrid Bergman) escape to Lisbon to continue their fight against the Germans, serves a much higher purpose than would his and Ilsa's personal love affair. "I'm no good at being noble," he tells Ilsa, "but it doesn't take much to see that the problems of three little people don't amount to a hill of beans in this crazy world."

By his actions, Rick is transformed; he has sacrificed his own personal love for Ilsa to aid and benefit the Allies in defeating the Nazis.

"A hero is someone who has given his or her life to something bigger than oneself," Joseph Campbell says. If you look at the template of the classical "hero" throughout myth and literature, Rick's action elevates him to the stature of a contemporary hero. "Life consists in action," Aristotle said, "and its end is a mode of action, not a quality." The same with Hamlet, or Arjuna in the Bhagavad Gita, or Neo in *The Matrix:* characters who have overcome their doubts and fears, then pushed them aside and acted. It is this action that elevates them into the realm of "heroic figures."

No matter what's in Rick's heart, it's his quality of character, his action, that drives the story line forward. The ancient Indian scriptures call it dharma, or righteous action, and it thrusts Bogart, in this case, to the level of a heroic figure. His stature, his personification of the nobility of the human spirit, stands as a beacon of humanity that crosses all barriers of time, culture, and language.

Good scenes make good movies. When you think of a good movie, you remember *scenes,* not the entire film. Think of *Psycho.* What scene do you recall? The shower scene, of course. It's a classic.

The scene is the single most important element in your screenplay. It is where something happens—where something *specific* happens. It is a particular unit, or cell, of dramatic (or comedic) action—the place in which you tell your story.

The way you present your scene on the page ultimately affects the entire screenplay. A screenplay is a reading experience before it becomes a movie experience.

The purpose of the scene is twofold: Either it *moves the story forward* or it *reveals information about the character*. If the scene does not satisfy one, or both, of these two elements, then it doesn't belong in the screenplay.

A scene can be as long or as short as you want it to be. It can be an essential story beat (progression), or it can be a transition, a way to bridge the elements of place and time. It can be a complicated three-page dialogue scene or as simple as a single shot, like a car streaking down the highway. It can be a complicated flashback scene (or as I like to call it, a *flashpresent* scene) like the jailbreak scene in *The Shawshank Redemption* where Andy Dufrense escapes. The scene can be anything you want it to be. That's the beauty of it.

It is the story that determines how long or how short your scene is. There is only one rule to follow: Tell your story. The scenes will be as long or as short as they need to be; just trust the story and it will tell you everything you need to know.

Throughout my many years of teaching, I've noticed that some people have a tendency to want to make a rule for everything. If there happens to be eighteen scenes in the first act of a screenplay or movie, they feel *their* first act must have eighteen scenes. I can't tell you how many times I've been awakened in the middle of the night by a hysterical writer on the phone saying, "My pages are too long," or "Act I is thirty-five pages long," or "My Plot Point I happens on page nineteen"; then I hear labored breathing in my ear, followed by a plaintive cry: "What do I do?"

I listen and always give them the same answer: "So what!" So what if your first act is too long; so what if Plot Point I occurs on page 19. So what! You can't write a screenplay following numbers as you would a drugstore painting. It is the form of the screenplay that's important—beginning, middle, and end—not the numbers on the page. The *paradigm* is only a guide, not an absolute! Writing a screenplay that way doesn't work—trust your story to tell you what you need to know, what scenes you need to write, or what scenes not to write.

We're going to approach our analysis of the scene from two different perspectives. First, we're going to explore the *generalities* of the scene—that is, the *form;* then we'll examine the *specifics,* how you create a scene from the elements, or components, you have within that scene.

First, the form. Two things are necessary in every scene—*place* and *time.* They are the two components that hold things in context. Every scene occurs at a specific *place* and at a specific *time.*

Where does your scene take *place*? In an office? A car? At the beach? In the mountains? On a crowded city street? What is the *location* of the scene? Does the scene take place inside or outside, *interior* or *exterior*? Designate *interior* by INT. and *exterior* by EXT.

The other element is *time.* What time of the day or night does your scene take place? In the morning? Afternoon? Late at night? All you have to do is specify either day or night. But sometimes you may want to be more specific: sunrise, early morning, late morning, midafternoon, sunset, or dusk. These distinctions are necessary, because the light is different at each time of the day. The delineations allow the director of photography to set up his or her lights for the scene properly. And that can be a big job. All you need to indicate is DAY or NIGHT.

So the heading of the scene (the slug line) becomes, for example, INT. LIVING ROOM—NIGHT or EXT. STREET—DAY.

That's the context: *place* and *time.* These two ingredients are what you must know before you start writing and constructing your scene. If you change either *place* or *time,* it becomes a new scene. Why? Because each time you change one of these elements, you have to change the lighting of the scene and, almost always, the camera placement, which means the lights, dolly tracks, electrical equipment, and many other things.

For example, we saw in the first ten pages of *Chinatown* that Curly, in Jake's office, is upset because Gittes showed him that his wife was having sex with a stranger. Gittes gives him a drink of cheap whiskey, then escorts him out of his office into the reception area.

When they move from Gittes's office into the reception area, it is a new scene. Why? Because they have changed *place*, gone from one place, the office, to another place, the reception area. New scene. That requires a new setup of lights and camera.

Gittes is then called into his associates' office, where we meet the phony Mrs. Mulwray. The scene in the associates' office is also a new scene, even though it's the same action. Once again, they have changed the *place* of the scene; one scene takes place inside Gittes's office, another in the reception area, and another in his associates' office. There's one line of action—Gittes's being hired by the phony Mrs. Mulwray—but there are three different scenes that make up this *office sequence*.

If your scene takes place in a house, and you move from the bedroom to the kitchen to the living room, you have three individual scenes. Your scene might take place in the bedroom between a man and a woman. They kiss passionately, then move to the bed. At the window we see the light change from night to day, then when we cut back to our couple waking up, it is another, new scene. Why? You have changed the *time* of your scene. That means lights have to be changed and repositioned. It becomes a new location.

If your character is driving a car up a mountain road at night and you want to show him at different locations, you must change your scenes accordingly: EXT. MOUNTAIN ROAD—NIGHT to EXT. MOUNTAIN ROAD, FARTHER—NIGHT.

The physical necessity of changing the position of the CAMERA (the word CAMERA is always capitalized in the screenplay) or the physical *location* requires striking one set and building another. Each scene requires a change in CAMERA position and therefore requires a change in the physical components of the scene. That's why movie crews are so large and the cost of filming a movie has become so expensive. As the price of labor escalates, the cost per minute increases and we end up paying more at the box office. At this writing, it costs $10,000 or more per minute to film a major movie production. (Independent film is different, of course.)

Scene changes are essential to your screenplay. The scene is the cell, or kernel, of the action, where it all happens—where you tell your story in *moving pictures.*

A scene can be constructed in several different ways, depending on the type of story you're telling. For many types of scenes you can build the action in terms of beginning, middle, and end; a character enters the place—restaurant, school, home—and the scene unfolds in linear time, much the way a screenplay unfolds. The opening scene in *Chinatown* between Gittes and the phony Mrs. Mulwray starts at the beginning and ends at the end. Many times one might show a snippet of an action at the beginning, a major portion of it in the middle, and another part of it at the end. Or you can begin a scene, cut away to a flashback, as in *The Bourne Supremacy* or *Ordinary People,* then bring it back to the present and end it in real time. The scene in *Thelma & Louise* where Thelma robs a convenience store is a good example of this. The scene starts with Thelma racing out of the convenience store yelling to Louise to "go ... go." Louise asks what's happening and we cut to a video scene of Thelma robbing the store; then we pull back and we're in police headquarters, with the police watching the video; then we cut back to Louise and Thelma and they're again in present time, still on the run.

Again, there's no rule—it is your story, so you make the rules. Sometimes, in certain situations, it's good to lay out the action line of the scene in terms of beginning, middle, and end, and then use only portions, or bits and pieces, of the action line to present the scene.

Every scene must reveal one element of necessary story information to the reader or audience; remember, the purpose of the scene is to either move the story forward or to reveal information about the character. Rarely does a scene provide more than one piece of information. Many times I'll read scenes where the writer includes two, sometimes three pieces of information, and it's way too much. It bogs down the narrative line and can be confusing.

Generally, there are two kinds of scenes. One is where something happens *visually,* like an action scene—the opening of *The Matrix,* for example, or the battle scenes in *Cold Mountain.* The other is a *dialogue* scene between two or more characters, as in *Casablanca,* or the famous "slapping" scene in *Chinatown,* or the various wonderfully inventive scenes in *The Royal Tenenbaums* and *Magnolia.* Most scenes are a combination. In a dialogue scene, there's usually some action going on, and in an action scene, there's usually some dialogue.

Since one page of screenplay equals approximately one minute of screen time, most dialogue scenes need be no longer than two or three pages. That's two or three minutes of screen time, and believe it or not, that's an enormous amount of screen time. I had a student once who wrote a seventeen-page dialogue scene in a romantic comedy. Needless to say, it was way, way too long. I made cuts to the scene and it ended up a little over three and a half pages. This is a general rule, of course, and there are always exceptions. There are times when a dialogue scene is highlighted by strong background action, like the scene in *Collateral* where Max drives faster and faster until he crashes the cab into the street barrier.

Within the body of the scene, something specific happens— your *characters* move from point A to point B in terms of emotional growth or reaching a decision; or your *story* links point A to point B in terms of the narrative line of action, the plot. Your story always moves forward, even if parts of it are told in flashback, as in *The English Patient, The Bourne Supremacy, Casablanca, Memento, The Hours,* and many other films.

In *The Hours,* the three stories are interrelated with flashbacks that move the story forward. All three stories begin with the main characters waking up in the morning and end during the evening hours. Basically, it's one day in the life of three characters. The entire piece is structured to include flashbacks as an integral part of the story. The flashback is a technique used to expand the audience's comprehension of story, characters, and situation. The purpose of the flashback is the same as the scene—either it moves the story forward or it reveals information about the characters.

How do you go about creating a scene?

First create the *context* of the scene, then determine the *content,* what happens. What is the *purpose* of the scene? Why is it there? How does it move the story forward? What happens within the body of the scene? Where has the character just been before he or she enters the scene? What are the emotional forces working on the character during the scene? Do they impact the purpose of the scene?

Sometimes an actor approaches a scene by finding out what he's doing there—his purpose—then where he's coming from, and then where he's going after the scene concludes. What is his/her purpose in the scene? Why is he/she there? To move the story forward or to reveal information about the character?

As writer, it's your responsibility to know why your characters are in a scene, what the purpose of the scene is, and how the characters' actions, or dialogue, are relevant to the story. You've got to know what happens to your characters *in* the scenes, as well as what happens to them *in between* the scenes: What happened during the time between the office Monday afternoon and the next scene, Thursday night at dinner? If you don't know, who does?

By creating *context,* you determine dramatic purpose and can build your scene line by line, action by action. By creating *context,* you establish *content.*

How do you do this?

By finding the *components* or *elements* within the scene. What aspect of your character's *professional* life, *personal* life, or *private* life is going to be revealed?

Let's go back to the story of three people stealing moon rocks from NASA's Houston complex. We need to write a scene showing our characters committing to the caper. Up to this point, they've only talked about it. Now they decide to do it. That's the *context.* Next, *content.*

Where does the scene take place?

At home? In a bar? Inside a car? Walking in the park? Maybe a quiet location, like a rented van on the highway? That might work, but maybe there's a more visual approach we can take—this is, after all, a movie.

Actors often play "against the grain" of a scene; that is, they approach the scene not from the obvious approach but from the unobvious approach. For example, they'll play an "angry" scene smiling softly, hiding their rage or anger beneath a façade of niceness. Brando was a master at this.

When you're approaching a scene, look for a way that dramatizes the scene "against the grain" or a location that could make it visually interesting. In *Silver Streak,* Colin Higgins wrote a love scene between Jill Clayburgh and Gene Wilder in which they talk about flowers! It's beautiful. Orson Welles, in *The Lady from Shanghai,* plays a love scene with Rita Hayworth in an aquarium, in front of sharks and barracudas.

In our moon rock story, instead of setting the "decision" scene in a quiet location like the van, suppose we wrote it in a crowded pool hall, at night. We could introduce an element of suspense into the scene as well; as our characters shoot pool and discuss the decision of pulling the job, suppose an off-duty security cop enters and starts wandering around, adding a touch of dramatic tension. (Hitchcock did this kind of thing all the time.) We might open with a shot of the eight ball, then pull back to reveal our characters leaning over the table, talking about the job.

Suppose we wanted to write a scene establishing the disintegrating emotional connections in a family. How could we do it?

First, establish the purpose of the scene. In this case we want to show the relationship of the family, how its members relate to themselves and each other. Second, *where* does the scene takes place, and *when,* either day or night. It could take place anywhere: in a car, on a walk, in a movie theater, in the family dining room.

In *American Beauty* there's a great scene illuminating the dysfunctional aspects of Lester and his family. Lester, his wife, Carolyn, and their daughter, Jane, are having dinner together after a day we've observed. Screenwriter Alan Ball sets the scene in the dining room, a place that *looks* beautiful: low lighting, a marvelously set table, candles burning, a romantic version of "You Are Too Beautiful" playing in the background, vibrant roses on the table. In short, everything "looks" great; at least, on the outside. It could be a scene from a Norman Rockwell painting. That's the *context.*

What's the purpose of the scene? To show the family dynamic. So while everything looks great on the outside, what's going on inside? First, Jane complains about the music: "Mom, do we have to listen to this elevator music?" To which Carolyn replies, "No. As soon as you've prepared a nutritious yet flavorful meal that I'm about to eat, you can listen to whatever you like." Lester inquires about Jane's day at school, to which she replies: "It was okay." "Just okay?" Lester asks. She looks at her parents, then sarcastically says: "It was spec-tac-ular." Lester complains about his job, then whines that Jane doesn't even listen to him anymore. She replies, "You've barely even spoken to me for months." And she gets up and leaves the table. Carolyn looks at Lester critically, and he mumbles: "What, you're Mother of the Year? You treat her like an employee.... You treat us both like employees." And he abruptly leaves the table and tries to mend things with Jane in the kitchen, leaving Carolyn sitting alone in this beautiful space, listening to the haunting musical refrains of John Coltrane and Johnny Hartman: "You are too beautiful..."

It's an extraordinary scene! It shows us the outside as well as the inside. Inside, we see a totally dysfunctional family. The characters are illuminated by their contained dissatisfaction, with themselves as well as each other. It says so much with so little. It is a perfect illustration of setting up the context and revealing the dysfunctional aspects of the family through the content.

When you're preparing to write a scene, first establish the purpose, then find the components, the elements contained within the scene. Then determine the content. Suppose you wanted to set a scene in a restaurant. What components could you effectively use? Possibly the waiter has a cold, or is starting to come down with one; or maybe he or she is overworked, has too many stations to cover; maybe he had a disagreement with his significant other just before he came to work; or maybe a couple at a nearby table is having an argument that begins in a subdued fashion, but soon escalates and intrudes on the characters in your scene. Let something happen that could possibly impact the characters. Look for any ingredients you might use that could generate some form of conflict, either inside the characters or within the restaurant itself.

The *content* of the scene now becomes part of the *context*.

This allows you to stay on top of your story, and not let the story be on top of you. As a writer, you must exercise *choice* and *responsibility* in the creative decisions you make and in the construction and presentation of your scene. After all, it's the character's choice within the narrative that determines the flow of the story line.

Within the context of the scene you can influence tone, feeling, and mood by the descriptions you write. In *Collateral*, screenwriter Stuart Beattie sets up Los Angeles in short, choppy strokes: "Shades of yellow. Ribbons of silver. Shimmers of chrome. Headlights sweeping past, flaring to white. Brake lights flashing, halating red. Reflections of overhead fluorescence flowing like liquid along the windshields of glass ..." The style, the descriptions of the city portray a heightened sense of filmic reality, something we can see, a feeling experienced, the pounding pulsations of the city at night. And Michael Mann, the director, brilliantly brings it to life.

In *Collateral*, the Plot Point at the end of Act II is an action-charged scene where Vincent shatters Max's dream during a wild taxi ride after the chaotic shoot-out at the Korean nightclub. It's a great example of how dialogue can reveal character as well as amp up the tension within a scene. The scene begins after Vincent "rescues" Max from the LAPD detective, Fanning (Mark Ruffalo). Vincent yanks Max back into the cab and they take off, heading downtown.

```
EXT. AERIAL SHOT: LOS ANGELES CITYSCAPE—NIGHT

STRAIGHT DOWN from above. Acid-mint streetlight
in pools on Olympic Blvd. The yellow cab is the
only vehicle heading east. Everything else
streams west. Emergency vehicles. Flashers.

INT. MAX'S CAB—MAX

In shock. Back in purgatory . . . eternally in his
cab's front seat. As the lone yellow cab drives
east . . .

                     VINCENT
          What a clusterfuck. Only thing didn't
          show was the Polish cavalry.

Max's life, controlled by Vincent, is a night-
mare, perpetual and eternal. Now Vincent realizes
he's getting the silent treatment.
```

(Continued)

                    VINCENT
You're alive. I saved you. We're
BREATHING. Do I get any thanks? No.
All you can do is clam up. You don't
wanna talk, tell me to fuck off ...

                    MAX
                 (inaudible)
... fuck off.

Vincent's attention goes to the window, out which
are streams of emergency vehicles ... looks to the
airspace, filled with LAPD and news helicopters.

EXT. STREET—THE ANONYMOUS YELLOW CAB

heads east. All other traffic races to the debacle
left behind ...

                VINCENT (O.S.)
Okay.
                 (beat)
... blood, bodily fluid and death get
to you?
Try deep breathing. Or remember, we
all die anyway ...

                MAX (O.S.)
You had to kill Fanning?

                VINCENT (O.S.)
Who the fuck is Fanning?

INT. CAB

                    MAX
That cop!
                 (beat)
Why'd you have to do that? You coulda
wounded him. Maybe he had a family,
parents, kids who gotta grow up without
a dad, he believed me, he was a good
guy ...

                    VINCENT
I shoulda saved him 'cause he believed
you ...?

                    MAX
No, not just that.

                  VINCENT
Yeah, that . . .

                    MAX
Yeah, so, what's wrong with that?

                  VINCENT
It's what I do for a living . . .

                    MAX

Some living.

                  VINCENT
Head downtown.

                    MAX
What's downtown?

                  VINCENT
How are you at math? I was hired for
five hits. I did four.

                    MAX
                  (grim)
One more.

                  VINCENT
There you go . . . !

                    MAX
Whyn't you kill me and find another
cab?

                  VINCENT
'Cause you're good. And we're in this
together. You know . . .
                  (beat)
. . . fates intertwined. Cosmic
coincidence. All that crap . . .

                    MAX
You're full of shit.

                  VINCENT
I'm full of shit?

(beat)
                    VINCENT (CONT'D)
You're a monument of it. You even
bullshitted yourself, all I am is
taking out the garbage. Killing bad
people . . .

                                        (Continued)

                    MAX
'Cause that's what you said . . .

                    VINCENT
And you believed me . . . ?

                    MAX
What'd they do?

                    VINCENT
How do I know?
                    (beat)
But, they all got that "witness
for the prosecution" look to me.
It's probably some major federal
indictment against somebody who
majorly does not want to get in-
dicted . . . I dunno.

                    MAX
That's the reason?

                    VINCENT
That's the "why." There is no reason.
                    (beat)
No good reason; no bad reason. To live
or to die.

                    MAX
Then what are you?

                    VINCENT
                    (looks up)
. . . indifferent.

Vincent looks out the window.

                         VINCENT (CONT'D)

C'mon, man. Get with it. Millions of
galaxies of hundreds of millions of
stars and a speck on one. In a
blink...that's us. Lost in space.
The universe don't care about you. The
cop, you, me?
                    (beat)
Who notices?

                         MAX
How much they pay you? They pay you a
lot?

                         VINCENT
Yeah.

                         MAX
What do you do afterwards?

                         VINCENT
After what?

                         MAX
When enough's enough. When you got
enough money. What do you do then?

                         VINCENT
Make that light.

                         MAX
You got a plan? You got like an
exit strategy, don't you?

Vincent has no game plan. There is no objective
towards which his life is moving. He is a subject
in meaningless motion.

                         MAX (CONT'D)
Or you doin' the same thing again and
again, pointlessly. 'Cause you're
damaged goods? When you wake up in the
morning? Open your eyes in the a.m.,
is there anybody there? Anybody home?

                    VINCENT
No, I just put on a happy face and go
on with my day.

                    MAX
'Cause I think you are low. I think
you are really low, my brother, and
some standard parts that are supposed
to be there in people . . . with you,
aren't. So what happened to you, man?
And why haven't you killed me?

                    VINCENT
Of all the cabbies in LA, I pull Max.
Sigmund Freud meets Dr. Ruth . . .

                    MAX
Answer the question.

                    VINCENT
Look in the mirror
              (on the attack)
. . . with your paper towels . . . a clean
cab . . . your own limo company someday.
How much you got saved?

                    MAX
None of your business.

                    VINCENT
Someday? "Someday my dream will
come . . . ?"
              (beat)
But one night you will wake up and
discover it all turned around on
you. Suddenly you are old. And it
didn't happen. It never will. 'Cause
you were never going to do it, anyway.
The dream became yesterday and got
lost. Then you'll bullshit yourself,
it could never have been. And you'll
push it into memory . . . and zone out
in a Barcalounger with daytime TV on
for the rest of your life . . .
              (beat)

                  VINCENT (CONT'D)
    Don't talk to me about murder. You're
    killing yourself in this cab. Bit by
    bit. Every day.

Max is soaking up every word.

                  VINCENT (CONT'D)
    All it ever took was a down payment.
    On a Lincoln Town Car. What the hell
    are you still doing in a cab? Or that
    girl. You can't even call that girl
    [referring to Annie—Jada Pinkett
    Smith—whom Max met in the beginning of
    the story].

The needle on the speedometer is creeping past
forty...

                  MAX
    'Cause I never straightened up and
    looked at it, you know...?

                  VINCENT
    Slow down.

                  MAX
            (ignoring him)
    ...myself, I should have. My
    brothers did...
                (beat)
    Tried to gamble my way out from under.
    Another born-to-lose deal! Then,
    "It's gotta be perfect to go!" You
    know? Risk all torqued-down. I coulda
    done it anytime...

Needle pushing sixty...

                  VINCENT
    Red light.

                    MAX
    But you know what? It doesn't matter.
    What's it matter, anyway? 'Cause we
    are...insignificant out here in this
    big-ass nowhere. *Twilight Zone* shit.
    Says the badass sociopath in my
    backseat. So that's one thing I got to
    thank you for, bro...Until now, I
    never saw it that way...

The cab goes blasting through an intersection on
a red light. A *LOS ANGELES TIMES* DELIVERY TRUCK
SLAMS ON ITS BRAKES as Max swerves, barely avoiding a collision.

                    VINCENT
    That was a red light!

Max glances in the rearview.

                    MAX
    ...not until now. So what's it all
    matter? It don't. So, fuck it. Fix it.
    Nothing to lose. Right?

Vincent's H+K's aimed at Max's head. Max almost
laughs.

                    VINCENT
    Slow the hell down!

                    MAX
    Why? What are you gonna do? Pull
    the trigger? Kill us? Go ahead, man!
    Shoot...my ass.

                    VINCENT
    Slow down!

                    MAX
    Vincent?

Their eyes meet in the rearview mirror. Vincent
is arrested by a look in Max that he's not seen
before. It's the even, confrontational look of a
man with nothing to lose.

```
                    MAX (CONT'D)
         Go fuck yourself.

     Max slams on the brakes and cranks the steering
     wheel hard right...

     EXT. STREET—RIGHT WHEEL

     hits a low divider...rear end comes unstuck,
     rotating over the front right and flipping the cab
     into a violent roll onto its roof, spinning down
     the street, SMASHING off other cars, pieces
     falling off, spewing glass...and then settling
     upside down, revolving slowly to a creaking stop,
     anti-freeze spilling across the pavement.

     And then everything goes silent, motionless,
     still.
```

And then we're into the aftermath. Wow! A virtual assault of words—explosive, fast, visually dynamic, and emotionally insightful; the dialogue is crisp, sharp, and carries us like lightning across the page. More than anything, it's an epiphany for Max. It's a grabber, in more ways than one.

The scene starts in the aftermath of the shoot-out at the Korean nightclub. It begins surrounded in tension, like an echo of the chaotic shoot-out that preceded it. The strain inside the cab gradually picks up as the car increases speed and Max and Vincent go after each other. Max's choices are few if he hopes to walk away from this nightmare alive.

First, not only is it exciting, filled with friction and suspense, but it illustrates the true purpose of a scene: It *moves the story forward* as well as *revealing information about the main character*. It does this both physically and emotionally. During the scene, as Max and Vincent race toward downtown, layer after layer of character is stripped away to reveal their personal histories and divergent points of view. According to Vincent, we are insignificant here, a tiny speck in the galactic expanse of space. Basically, life is meaningless, with no design, no purpose. The scene is the Plot Point at the end of

Act II and leads us into Act III, the *Resolution*. After the car crashes, the only question that remains is simple: Can Max walk away alive, and can he stop Vincent from fulfilling his fifth hit, who, he now learns, is Annie?

The scene *reveals character*, as Vincent probes and bursts Max's dream balloon. Up until now, as Vincent says, Max has lived in a dream, in a "someday" state; someday he's going to fulfill his dream of starting Island Limousine; someday he's going to meet the woman of his dreams; someday he'll have it all and be fulfilled as a person. It's a pretty big Someday. Vincent shows him that there is only now, today, this present moment, this point in time. Waiting for "someday" is, like striving for perfection, really just an excuse. "Someday" is a concept that, to quote my mentor, Jean Renoir, "exists only in the mind, not in reality."

What forces are working on these two characters as they engage in their personal duel? In the nightclub, the hit man, against all odds, has completed his fourth hit, and now Max is driving him toward number five. Once again, Max is virtually a prisoner, his choices few; either he finds some way to escape safely, Vincent kills him after the final hit is completed, or he manages to kill Vincent.

You'll notice that this scene is not a simply just another dialogue scene; Max and Vincent are in a speeding taxi, escaping from the frenetic shoot-out at the Korean nightclub. So there is an outside, external tension—the police, other cars, helicopters, traffic lights—that impedes their action and becomes a source of conflict, adding tension to the harsh verbal exchange between Max and Vincent.

There's another thing that's revealed in this scene. In the beginning, Max was portrayed as something of a wimp, a man afraid to stand up to his boss, the cab dispatcher, a man who lives a "someday" dream pictured in a postcard. But he has been transformed, and finally stands up to and confronts his nemesis.

This does not happen spontaneously but has been gradually built up to, step by step, from the beginning of the screenplay. It is Vincent who stands up to the dispatcher when he gives Max a bad time, and shows Max how to defend himself against his superior. Max gathers enough strength to throw Vincent's briefcase onto the freeway, ruining it. Then he's forced to confront the drug warlord, Felix, and walks out alive. Though some might say that these elements are too unbelievable to be taken seriously, to my mind, they work effectively. Now, prompted by Vincent's prodding, Max has found enough courage to flip the cab, possibly killing himself and Vincent but at least stopping Vincent from completing his last hit of the evening.

In short, this scene, set amid the fury and confusion of the speeding cab, allows us to watch Max's transformation and ultimately leads to the conclusion of the film. Max has completed his character arc.

It's a marvelous scene.

Do these same principles work with comedy? Comedy creates a situation, then lets people act and react to the situation and each other. In comedy, you can't have your characters playing for laughs; they have to believe what they're doing, otherwise it becomes forced and contrived, and therefore unfunny.

Remember the scene at the outdoor restaurant in *Annie Hall*? Annie (Diane Keaton) tells Alvy (Woody Allen) that she just wants to be his "friend" and not continue their romantic relationship. Both are uncomfortable, and this adds tension to the scene by heightening the comedic overtones; when he leaves the restaurant he collides with several cars, then tears up his driver's license in front of a policeman. Woody Allen utilizes the situation for maximum dramatic effectiveness.

In the Italian film *Divorce—Italian Style*, a classic comedy with Marcello Mastroianni, only a thin line separates comedy from tragedy. But, after all, comedy and tragedy are two sides of the same coin. Mastroianni is married to a woman who makes enormous sexual demands on him, and he can't cope with it—especially when he meets a voluptuous young cousin who's crazy about him. He wants a divorce but, alas, the Church won't recognize it. What's an Italian man to do? The only way the Church will recognize the end of his marriage is for his wife to die. But she's as healthy as a horse.

So he decides to kill her. But under Italian law, the only way he can kill her with honor and get away with it is if she's unfaithful; he has to be cuckolded. So he sets out to find a lover for his wife.

That's the situation!

After many, many funny moments, she *is* unfaithful to him, and his Italian honor demands he take action. He tracks her and her lover to an island in the Aegean Sea and searches for them, gun in hand.

The characters are caught within the web of circumstances and play their roles with exaggerated seriousness, and the result is film comedy at its best. For in comedy, Woody Allen says, "Acting funny is the worst thing you can do."

Comedy, like drama, depends on "real people in real situations."

When you set out to write a scene, find the purpose of the scene and root it in place and time. Then establish the context and determine the content, and find the elements or components within the scene to build it and make it work.

Every scene, like a sequence, or an act, or an entire screenplay, has a definite beginning, middle, and end. If you break the components of the scene down into beginning, middle, and end, you can establish the bits and pieces of action that are visually effective. In *Collateral,* we saw the entire scene: the beginning, when Max and Vincent head downtown; the middle, when they exchange conversation; and the end, when Max steps on the gas and flips the car.

You don't always need to show the entire scene. You can choose to show a few parts from the beginning, or just the middle, or maybe only the end. Only rarely is a scene depicted in its entirety. William Goldman, who wrote *Butch Cassidy and the Sundance Kid* and *All the President's Men,* among other films, once remarked that he doesn't enter the action until the last possible moment—that is, just before the purpose of the scene is revealed.

You, as writer, are completely in control of how you create your scenes to move your story forward. You *choose* what part of the scene you are going to show.

Create a scene by creating a *context,* then establish the *content.* Find the purpose of the scene, then choose the *place* and *time* for the scene. Find the *components* or *elements* within the scene to create inner or outer conflict to generate drama. Drama, remember, is conflict; seek it out.

Your story always moves forward, step by step, scene by scene, toward the resolution. Once you know what you're doing, you're ready for the next step—writing the sequence.

11

The Sequence

"Form follows structure; structure doesn't
follow form."

—I. M. Pei
Architect

"Synergy" is the study of systems, the behavior of systems as a whole, independent of their working parts. R. Buckminster Fuller, the noted scientist and humanitarian, creator of the geodesic dome, stresses the concept of synergy as the *relationship* between the whole and its parts; that is, a system.

The screenplay is comprised of a series of elements that can be compared to a system, a number of individually related parts arranged to form a unity, or whole: The *solar system* is composed of planets orbiting the sun; the *circulatory system* works in conjunction with all the organs of the body; a *stereo system,* either analog or digital, is made up of amplifier, preamp, tuner, CD/DVD player, cassette player, speakers, turntable, cartridge, needle, and/or other technology. Put together, arranged in a particular way, the system works as a whole; we don't measure the individual components of the stereo system, we measure the system in terms of "sound," "quality," and "performance."

A screenplay is really a system of sorts, comprised of specific parts that are related and unified by action, character, and dramatic premise. We measure it, or evaluate it, in terms of how well it works or doesn't work.

The screenplay, as a system, is made up of specific elements: endings, beginnings, scenes, Plot Points, shots, special effects, locations, music, and sequences. Together, unified by the dramatic thrust of action and character, the story elements are arranged in a particular way and then revealed visually to create the totality known as the screenplay.

As far as I'm concerned, the *sequence* is perhaps the most important element of the screenplay. A *sequence* is *a series of scenes connected by one single idea with a definite beginning, middle, and end.* It is a unit, or block, of dramatic action unified by *one single idea.* It is the skeleton, or backbone, of your script and, like the nature of structure itself, holds everything together.

Remember the War Admiral race sequence in *Seabiscuit*? It's a lengthy sequence, leading up to the match race between War Admiral and Seabiscuit. It's really a sequence within a sequence. It begins with the agreement by the owner of War Admiral, Samuel Riddle, to race his champion Thoroughbred against Seabiscuit. The Seabiscuit team journeys across the country, then arrives at Pimlico and watches War Admiral work out. The group is so impressed with his size and speed that they know Seabiscuit needs "an edge." That's the beginning of the sequence.

The middle—the team members train Seabiscuit at night, away from the frenzy of media attention; they "borrow" a fire bell and familiarize the horse with breaking from the start at the sound of the bell. Shortly before the race is set to begin, Red (Tobey Maguire), the jockey, breaks his leg while doing a favor for an old friend, and another rider has to be found. Seabiscuit trains some more and Red, in the hospital, coaches George Woolf, the new rider, on Seabiscuit's racing quirks.

The end of this section is really a sequence within the sequence. It is the race itself, which is broken down into beginning, middle, and end.

We could call it "The Race." The beginning of the race sequence is the day of the race; the fans arrive, and excitement runs high as the infield fills up. We cut to the locker room as the team, Tom Smith (Chris Cooper), jockey George Woolf (real-life jockey Gary Stevens), and Charles Howard (Jeff Bridges) prepare for this incredible race and discuss their last-minute preparations.

The middle is the actual race itself: The horses are led to the starting line, settle down, and the bell sounds. The race begins and we see how focused the national attention has become on these two horses running around the track: "The race was broadcast on NBC and businesses around America scheduled a half day of work so their employees could hear the call...," the narrator tells us in voice-over. Writer-director Gary Ross even cuts away to stills of the people of Depression America huddled together, listening to their radios. That's how important this race was to the people of the Depression. It's even said that President Franklin D. Roosevelt stopped doing the business of the country to tune in to the race.

The race itself is a dazzling display of cinematic style and suspense. Back and forth we go, the two horses head-to-head. Then Seabiscuit kicks into another gear and leaves the larger horse behind, and wins by more than five lengths. Joy abounds as people embrace, yelling and screaming. Red listens from his hospital bed as the sequence ends with Seabiscuit in the Winner's Circle, surrounded by the owners and media.

It's an incredible sequence, and you can see that it has a definite beginning, middle, and end. The race sequence itself also has a beginning, middle, and end. That's the value of a well-constructed sequence. It moves the story forward while revealing information about the characters.

A sequence is a *series* of scenes connected by one single idea, usually expressed in a word or two: a wedding, a funeral; a chase; a race; an election; a reunion; an arrival or departure; a coronation; a bank holdup. The context of the sequence is the specific idea that can be expressed in a few words or less. The race between Seabiscuit and War Admiral, for example, is a *unit,* or *block,* of *dramatic action;* it is the *context,* the idea that holds the *content* in place, like an empty coffee cup holds coffee, tea, water, milk, juice, or whatever. Once we establish the *context* of the sequence, we build it with *content,* the specific details, or ingredients, needed to create the sequence.

The sequence is a key part of the screenplay because it *holds* essential parts of the narrative action in place, much like a strand holds a diamond necklace in place. You can literally string or hang a series of scenes together to create chunks of dramatic action.

Remember the wedding sequence that opened *The Godfather*?

The final action sequence in *Collateral* as Vincent hunts Annie and Max tries to save her? The opening battle sequence in *Cold Mountain,* integrating two distinct time periods, time present and time past? The real estate sequence in *American Beauty* where Carolyn is determined that "I will sell this house today"? The opening sequence of *The Royal Tenenbaums* where we are introduced to the family? Or the final battle sequence from *Lord of the Rings: The Return of the King*?

Remember *The Matrix* when Neo and Trinity rescue Morpheus? They arrive in the lobby of the building where he's being held, blast their way inside, and run up to the floor where Agent Smith is holding Morpheus. They fight their way in, rescue Morpheus, then fight their way out and make their escape. Beginning, middle, and end, all designated and held in place by one word—"rescue."

It's an important concept to understand in the writing of a screenplay. It is the organizational framework, the *form,* the *foundation,* one of the major building blocks of the screenplay.

The contemporary screenplay, as practiced by such modern screenwriters as Alan Ball, Richard LaGravenese, Wes Anderson, Robert Towne, Steven Kloves, Frank Darabont, Ron Bass, James Cameron, Gary Ross, Stuart Beattie, to name just a few, might be defined as *a series of sequences tied together, or connected, by the dramatic story line.* Stanley Kubrick's epic *Barry Lyndon* is a series of sequences; so is James Cameron's *Terminator 2: Judgment Day* and Steven Spielberg's *Close Encounters of the Third Kind.*

Why is the sequence so important?

Look at the *paradigm:*

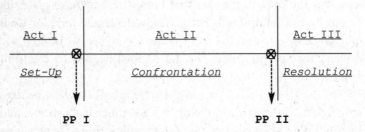

As already discussed, when you begin writing your screenplay, you need to know four things: the *opening,* the *Plot Point* at the end

of Act I, the *Plot Point* at the end of Act II, and the *ending*. When you know what those four elements are, and have done the necessary preparation on action and character, *then* you're ready to start writing.

Sometimes, but not always, these four story points are sequences. You might open your film with a wedding sequence, as in *The Godfather*. You might use a sequence like Neo meeting Morpheus and choosing the Red Pill in *The Matrix* as the Plot Point at the end of Act I. You might want to write a sequence like Paul Thomas Anderson does in *Magnolia*, when nine characters, all in states of deep emotional stress, sing the lyrics of Aimee Mann's song "Wise Up." It's a wonderful illustration of how inventive a sequence can be. You might use a dramatic sequence to end the film, like Gary Ross does in *Seabiscuit*, or resolve your script with the performance of a play, like Wes Anderson and Owen Wilson do in *Rushmore*.

Sequences can be written any way you want; they are a creative, limitless context within which to paint your picture against the canvas of action. It should be noted that there are no specific number of sequences in a screenplay; you don't need exactly twelve, eighteen, or twenty sequences to make up your script. Your story will tell you how many sequences you need. Frank Pierson conceived and wrote *Dog Day Afternoon* with just twelve sequences. He started off with four: the opening, the two Plot Points at the end of Acts I and II, and the ending. He added eight sequences throughout the narrative line and built that into a complete screenplay.

Think about it!

You can have as many or as few sequences as you want. There's no rule about the number you need. All you need to know is the idea behind the sequence, the *context;* and then you can create a series of scenes, the *content*.

Most action films are held together by a series of sequences that keep the story moving forward. The action genre is a significant staple of our film fare, and if you look at any film company's production schedules for the upcoming year, you'll see at least half of its production slate is devoted to the action film.

Writing the action film, and the action sequence, is really an art unto itself. So many times I read screenplays whose pages are filled with nonstop action—in fact, there is so much action, with little or no characterization, that it becomes dull and repetitive. The reader and viewer become overwhelmed and numb from the onslaught of words and pictures. Sometimes you can have a good action script with strong individual action sequences, but the premise is weak and derivative of earlier films. It needs a "new look," or a more interesting concept.

Why? Because there are problems: with the plot, or the characters, or the action itself. Some writers have a natural ability to write action, and others are more comfortable writing character. It's important to note that before you can write any kind of action film, or action sequence, you must understand what the action film is, what its essential nature is. Once I had a student who wrote a screenplay about a navy pilot sent on a mission to a foreign country to rescue a kidnapped scientist being held hostage. It's a good premise, and there are several opportunities to create notable action sequences that keep the story moving forward at a fast pace. That's what he did, and his entire screenplay was one action sequence after another; the story moved like lightning, but it didn't work at all. Why? Because he didn't create an interesting main character. And because he didn't know his main character, most of the dialogue consisted of expository elements designed to keep the story moving forward. It didn't work. We didn't know anything about this person sent to rescue the scientist, who he was or where he came from; we had no idea about his thoughts or feelings, or the forces working on his life.

This is not all that uncommon. When you're writing an action screenplay, like *The Bourne Supremacy* or *Collateral*, the focus must be on action *and* character; the two must reside in and interact with each other. Otherwise there are going to be problems. What usually happens is that the action overpowers the story and diminishes the characters, resulting in a screenplay that, no matter how well written, is flat and uninteresting. There has to be an appropriate balance of peaks and valleys, places in the material where the reader and audience can pause and catch their collective breath.

Writing an action sequence is a definite skill, and good action scripts are written with color, pacing, suspense, tension, and, in most cases, humor. The interchanges between Max and Vincent in *Collateral* were often humorous as well as insightful. Remember Bruce Willis's character mumbling to himself in *Die Hard* (Jeb Stuart and Steven de Souza) or the bus making that leap across the enormous freeway chasm in *Speed* (Graham Yost)? We remember good action films like *Jurassic Park* (David Koepp) or *The Fugitive* (David Twohy and Jeb Stuart) or *The Hunt for Red October* (Larry Ferguson and Donald Stewart) by the uniqueness of their action and the characters who take part in that action. But we usually forget all the cool car chases and explosions that occupy the majority of action films that fill our theaters. They all look alike.

The key to writing any action film lies in writing the action sequence. In an action film like *Terminator 2: Judgment Day* (James Cameron and William Wisher), one of the most influential films of the '90s, everything is structured and anchored around six major action sequences. After the introduction of the Terminator, the T-1000, and John and Sarah, the *first* major sequence is where young John Connor is rescued by the Terminator; the *second* is when the Terminator and John break his mother out of prison; the *third,* the "rest period" at Enrique's gas station where they load up with weapons; the *fourth,* Sarah's attempt to kill Miles Dyson, creator of the microchip that makes the future Age of Machines possible; the *fifth,* the siege at Cyberdyne Systems; and the *sixth* sequence is their breakout and chase, winding up in the steel factory. The entire third act is literally one long nonstop action sequence.

These six key sequences *hold* (the function of the structure) the entire story together, but within this structural framework James Cameron and William Wisher have created a dynamic and intriguing premise, as well as some interesting characters. That, along with the special effects, makes this a truly memorable action film. And let's not forget the "rest period" at the abandoned gas station so we can "breathe" and learn more about the characters. Then we're off and running again.

What makes a good action film great? The electricity of the action sequences. Remember the chase scenes from *Bullitt* and *The*

French Connection? Or the start of the cattle drive in Howard Hawks's *Red River*? Or "the walk" at the end of *The Wild Bunch*? Or the last sequence of *The Matrix*? Or Butch and Sundance jumping into the river gorge after being relentlessly chased by the Super Posse in *Butch Cassidy and the Sundance Kid*? The list goes on and on.

The key to writing a great action sequence is the way it's *designed*. A sequence, remember, is *a series of scenes connected by one single idea, with a definite beginning, middle, and end.* As mentioned, a sequence is a complete entity, held together by one *single idea:* a chase sequence, wedding sequence, party sequence, fight sequence, love sequence, storm sequence.

What's nice about designing a sequence is that you can play with many different elements to make it catchy, exciting, dynamic. One of the things I like the most about Sam Peckinpah as a filmmaker is the way he designs his sequences in what I call "the contradiction of image." Things we don't expect begin to play upon and affect the central core of action. One of my favorite examples is the opening sequence of *The Wild Bunch*. It can be described simply: a holdup, or bank robbery. That's the context.

The script opens with the outlaws, led by Pike Bishop (William Holden), wearing soldier uniforms and riding into a small town. They pass a group of kids setting fire to a scorpion, a little visual aside about what's to come.

When the Wild Bunch rides into town, they pass a preacher standing underneath a tent, denouncing the evils of alcohol in an abbreviated Leviticus 10:9: "Do not drink wine or strong drink … least ye die…it biteth itself like a serpent and stingeth like an adder." In almost every Peckinpah film, there is some kind of reference to the evils of alcohol. But of course, he never just throws in a scene like this; he includes it as an integral part of the action that erupts once the Temperance Parade begins.

The stage description sets up Pike's character immediately.

Pike is a *thoughtful, self-educated top gun with a penchant for violence who is afraid of nothing—except the changes in himself and those around him. Make no mistake, Pike Bishop is not a hero—his*

values are not ours—he is a gunfighter, a criminal, a bank robber, a
killer of men. His sympathies are not for fences, for trolleys and
telegraphs or better schools. He lives outside and against society be-
cause he believes in that way of life....

Pike's character reveals his sympathetic side immediately; as the
group prepares to enter the bank, he inadvertently bumps into a little old lady and knocks her parcels to the ground. Everybody
freezes, but with the decorum of a gentleman, Pike picks up the
packages, extends his arm, and helps the lady across the street.

The bank robbery does more than just set us up for an action sequence. Peckinpah sets up his characters and situations in order to
illustrate his theme, which is "unchanged men in a changing land."
The relationship between the two main characters, Pike and Dutch
(Ernest Borgnine), is established immediately. In the first scene we
see they've ridden together, stood by each other, and fought each
other; they have a history between them. They know that the days of
robbing banks and railroads are "closing fast," and they're locked
into a dead-end future where the only alternatives are death, prison,
or living out a meager kind of existence in a small Mexican village.

There are three separate elements in the opening sequence: the
holdup, the Temperance Parade, and the scavenger bounty hunters
waiting to ambush the Wild Bunch. On a roof across from the bank,
the bounty hunters, led by Deke Thornton (Robert Ryan), have
been waiting hours for the Wild Bunch to arrive. The sun is boiling
and they're hot and tired and ornery, but there are large rewards for
the capture or killing of the Wild Bunch.

All these elements are set up and established as the holdup begins to unfold. It's only a matter of time before it all explodes into
one kaleidoscopic action sequence.

Integrating these different elements into an action sequence is
what places Peckinpah head and shoulders above most other action directors. Inside the bank, Angel, one of the Bunch, notices
sunlight on the roof reflecting off rifle barrels across the street.
Pike and Dutch immediately know it's an ambush, and using the
Temperance Parade as a cover they make their break, joining the elderly marchers and children and band members. That's when all

hell breaks loose. The street becomes a confused melee as bandits run for their horses, bounty hunters open fire, and men, women, and children collide with each other, caught in the crossfire.

It's an extraordinary sequence that utilizes all the visual components to capture our attention and keep us glued to the edge of our seats. Sometimes, if a script does not seem to be working as well as it should, or you feel there's a problem in terms of pacing, or things seem dull and boring, you might think about adding some kind of action sequence to keep the story moving and the tension taut. Sometimes you have to make some drastic creative choices to pump up the story line. If you do, you need to examine the material and see whether the proposed action will blend in with your original concept. The material has to be designed for and incorporated into your story line, then executed to the best of your ability. Often the easy way out—a car chase, or a kiss, or a shoot-out, or a murder attempt—draws attention to itself and therefore doesn't work.

David Koepp, who wrote *Spider-Man, Mission: Impossible, Jurassic Park,* and *The Lost World,* to name just a few of his credits, says the key to writing a good action sequence is finding more ways to say that someone "runs." "Action sequences use a lot of verbs," he says. "Look at the possibilities: He runs to hide behind the rock. He races over to the rock. He scrambles over to the rock. He crawls frantically on his belly over to the rock . . . Things like that can drive me crazy. Hurries, trots, sprints, dives, leaps, jumps, barrels, slams. The word *slams,* that'll appear a lot in an action script."

In an action scene, Koepp says, "The reader is sometimes forcing their eyes along because what's tremendously entertaining to watch on film is not necessarily so thrilling to read. I think the challenge is to make that stuff fly by at the pace you would like it to fly by in the movie. So you've constantly got to find ways to make the action sequences readable and easy for the reader to picture in his mind."

So what's the best way to write an action sequence?

Design it; choreograph the action from the beginning, through the middle, and on to the end. Choose your words carefully when you're writing. Action is not written with a lot of long and beautifully styled sentences. Writing an action sequence has got to be intense, visual. The reader must see the action as if he or she were seeing it on the screen. But if you write too little, and don't flesh out the action as much as you should, the action line becomes thin and doesn't carry the gripping intensity that you must have in a good action sequence. We're dealing with moving images that you hope will keep people glued to the edge of their seats, filled with excitement, or fear, or great expectation, locked in that great "community of emotion" that unites everybody in a darkened movie theater. Just look at some of the great action sequences: the opening of *Cold Mountain,* the shoot-out in Act III in *Witness,* the action sequences in *Terminator 2: Judgment Day,* the ending of *Lord of the Rings: The Two Towers,* the final battle sequence in *Lord of the Rings: The Return of the King,* the last act of *Collateral,* the train robbery and final shoot-out in *The Wild Bunch.* These are all action sequences that have been designed and choreographed with immense care and strict attention to detail.

Here's an example of an excellent action sequence; it's lean, clean, and tight, totally effective, extremely visual, and not bogged down with details. This is a little piece out of *Jurassic Park.* The scene takes place on the island off Costa Rica just as it has been hit by a violent tropical storm, and an employee trying to smuggle out dinosaur embryos has shut down the security systems. The two remote-controlled electric cars, one carrying two children and the attorney Gennaro, the other the Sam Neill and Jeff Goldblum characters, are stalled next to the massive electric fence that keeps the dinosaurs enclosed in their restricted area. The power is out all over the island, and the kids are scared. They wait nervously.

```
Tim pulls off the goggles and looks at two clear
plastic cups of water that sit in recessed holes
on the dashboard. As he watches, the water in the
glasses vibrates, making concentric circles—

—then it stops—

—and then it vibrates again. Rhythmically.

Like from footsteps.
```

BOOM. BOOM. BOOM.

Gennaro's eyes snap open as he feels it too. He looks up at the rearview mirror.

There is a security pass hanging from it that is bouncing slightly, swaying from side to side.

As Gennaro watches, his image bounces too, vibrating in the rearview mirror.

BOOM. BOOM. BOOM.

> GENNARO
> (not entirely convinced)
> M-Maybe it's the power trying to come back on.

Tim jumps into the backseat and puts the night goggles on again. He turns and looks out the side window. He can see the area where the goat is tethered. Or *was* tethered. The chain is still there, but the goat is gone.

BANG!

They all jump, and Lex SCREAMS as something hits the Plexiglas sunroof of the Explorer, hard. They look up.

It's a disembodied goat leg.

> GENNARO
> Oh, Jesus. Jesus.

When Tim whips around to look out the side window again his mouth opens wide but no sound comes out. Through the goggles he sees an animal claw, a huge one, gripping the cables of the "electrified" fence. He whips off his goggles and presses forward, against the window. He looks up, up, then cranes his head back farther, to look out the sunroof. Past the goat's leg, he can see—

Tyrannosaurus rex. It stands maybe twenty-five feet high, forty feet long from nose to tail, with an enormous, boxlike head that must be five feet long by itself. The remains of the goat are

```
hanging out of the rex's mouth. It tilts its head
back and swallows the animal in one big gulp.
```

Well, there it is ... and it's quite impressive. This is the beginning of the action sequence that will carry us through to the end of the film. We literally see the action as it unfolds, step by step, bit by bit. Notice how visual it is, and how short the sentences are, almost staccato in their presentation, and how much "white space" is on the page. This is the way a good action sequence should read.

The reader and the characters experience the same thing at the same time. We are bonded together, "one on one," so we can experience what the characters are experiencing.

There is a definite beginning, middle, and end to the action. Each beat builds the action line, incident to incident.

We open at the beginning, with the cups on the dashboard vibrating. We know something's going on here, we just don't know what. Look at how the writing of the sequence builds upon the fear and terror of the characters. "BOOM. BOOM. BOOM." Relentlessly, each sound expands and heightens the moment, stimulating the antennae of our imaginations. The writing style, besides being visual, uses short, clipped words or phrases. No long, beautifully formed sentences here. And of course, Spielberg is a master at putting this kind of sequence on film. A perfect example is the opening sequence of *Close Encounters of the Third Kind*.

So far everything remains unseen, which heightens the fear and causes us to expect the worst. The goat is another visual aid that amplifies the tension and pacing. Generally, a good action sequence builds slowly, image by image, word by word, setting things up, drawing us into the excitement as the action gets faster and faster. Good pacing allows the tension to build upon itself, no matter whether it's a chase sequence, as in *Speed,* a thriller sequence, as in *Seven,* the killing of Harlan in *Thelma & Louise,* or the tense waiting period for the emergency action message to arrive in *Crimson Tide.*

Notice after the goat has vanished and the chain is swinging freely, suddenly there's a BANG! and we literally jump in our seats. Then we see the "disembodied goat leg." That's when the fear starts rising among the characters, and that's when *our* palms begin sweating and our mouths become dry, waiting for and dreading what we know is coming... *Tyrannosaurus rex.*

It's very good writing. Sometimes writers will try to cover a weakness in character writing by inserting action sequences, thus avoiding having to characterize. Sometimes action sequences are written in such detail that any attempt to create a good reading experience is simply lost in the blanket of excess verbiage.

Other times you may want to weave a narrative line through a sequence that illuminates the character. An excellent example is the "selling the house" sequence in *American Beauty,* in which Carolyn sets out to sell the house she is showing. What's great about the sequence is that it has one single line of narrative action, selling the house, shown through a series of attempts, each driving the action of the sequence forward. Notice the conflict within the scene. As said many times before, all drama is conflict; without conflict you have no action; without action, you have no character; without character, you have no story. And without story, you have no screenplay.

The sequence begins with Carolyn's planting a "For Sale" sign on the front lawn in a middle-class neighborhood. As she unloads her car, she frowns and slams the trunk shut. Inside the house, she unzips to her slip and fiercely starts cleaning, repeating the mantra: "I will sell this house today. I will sell this house today. . . ." She scrubs countertops in the kitchen, strides a stepladder to dust a ceiling fan, cleans glass doors overlooking the backyard pool area, vacuums the carpet, doing whatever needs to be done.

That's the beginning of the sequence. The middle starts as she swings open the front door with a glorious smile welcoming the first visitors of the day. "Welcome," she says, "I'm Carolyn Burnham." She shows a grim-faced couple the fireplace, leads another unsmiling couple into the kitchen, shows a different couple the bedroom, then shows two mannish women in their thirties the outdoor pool area. "The ad said this pool was 'lagoon-like.' There's nothing 'lagoon-like' about it. Except for maybe the bugs," one of the women says. "There's not even any plants out here." "I have an excellent landscape architect," Carolyn replies, but the women aren't even listening. "I mean, I think 'lagoon,' and I think waterfall, I think tropical," the second woman comments sarcastically. "This is just a cement hole." To which Carolyn responds, smiling, "I have some tiki torches in the garage."

Notice how the one line of action, showing the house, from living room to kitchen to bedroom to the outside, is a continuous line of action, but illustrated with four different couples, giving the impression that Carolyn has been showing the house the whole day. This single line of action, showing the house, is the subject of the sequence, the context; and the content changes from room to room, couple to couple. In effect, this could be labeled a "montage," a series of shots strung together to bridge time, place, and action.

The sequence concludes with Carolyn, at the end of the day, shutting the vertical blinds. Then, "standing very still, with the blinds casting shadows across her face, she starts to cry: brief, staccato SOBS that seemingly escape against her will. Suddenly she SLAPS herself, hard. 'Stop it,' she demands to herself. But the tears continue. She SLAPS herself again. 'Weak. Baby. Shut up. Shut up!' She SLAPS herself repeatedly until the crying stops. She stands there, taking deep, even breaths until she has everything under control. Then she finishes pulling the blinds shut, once again all business. She walks out calmly, leaving us alone in the dark, empty room."

Look what we know about her character from this particular sequence. She fails in her intention, "I will sell this house today"; we've seen her working her butt off doing the best job she can, but it's still not good enough. She thinks she has failed, and failure, to her, is a sign of weakness. Then she pulls it all together, wipes the tears away, and strides out as if nothing had happened.

But look at what we, the reader and audience, get to see: a woman with a low sense of self-esteem and little self-love, who takes failure personally and blames herself for what she is not able to accomplish.

It's brilliant. And it all comes from a sequence: a series of scenes connected by one single idea, with a definite beginning, middle, and end.

Action and character, joined together, sharpens the focus of your screenplay and makes it both a better reading and a better viewing experience.

The sequence is a major building block in laying out the story. The next step is building your screenplay.

12

Building the Story Line

GIOVANNI:
"I believe now that I'm no longer capable of
writing. It's not that I don't know what to
write, but *how* to write it. That's what they
call a 'crisis.' But in my case it's something inside me, something which is affecting my whole life."

—*La Notte*
Michelangelo Antonioni

If we define a screenplay as a linear arrangement of related incidents, episodes, and events leading to a dramatic resolution, how do we go about building and constructing our story line? What's the best way of combining all those thoughts and ideas and words and scenes, all those little snippets of dialogue that are running around inside our heads, to build a unified story line into our screenplay?

How do we build our story line?

Let's start at the beginning. Remember, the definition of the verb *structure* is "to build something or put together something," like a building or bridge. The definition of the noun is "the relationship between the parts and the whole." Both apply to the task of building the story line.

Up until now we've discussed the four basic elements that are needed to write a screenplay—ending, beginning, Plot Point I, and Plot Point II. Before you can write the words *Fade In*, before you can put one word of screenplay down on paper, you need to know those four things.

Now what?

Take a look at the *paradigm:*

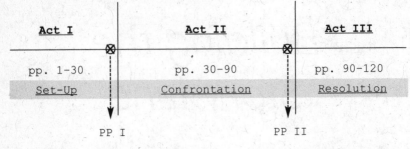

What do you see? Act I, Act II, Act III. Beginning, middle, end. The beginning starts with the opening scene or sequence and goes until the Plot Point at the end of Act I. The middle starts at the end of Plot Point I and goes until Plot Point II. The end begins at the end of Plot Point II and continues to the end of the screenplay. Each act is a *unit,* or *block,* of dramatic action, held together with the dramatic context: Set-Up, Confrontation, Resolution.

Look at Act I:

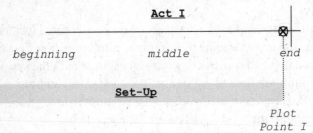

Act I is a unit of dramatic (or comedic) action that goes from the *beginning* of the screenplay to the *Plot Point* at the end of Act I. There is a beginning and an end point. Therefore, it is a whole, complete unto itself, even though Act I is a part of the whole (the screenplay). As a complete unit of action, there is a beginning of the *beginning,* a middle of the *beginning,* and an end of the *beginning.* It is a self-contained *unit,* approximately twenty to twenty-five pages long, depending on the screenplay. The end is *Plot Point I:* the incident, episode, or event that hooks into the action and spins it around in another direction, in this case, Act II. The dramatic *context*, which holds the *content* in place, is the *Set-Up*. In this unit of dramatic action you *set up* your story—introduce the *main character*, establish the *dramatic premise* (what the story is about), and *sketch in the dramatic situation*, either visually or dramatically.

Here's what Act II looks like:

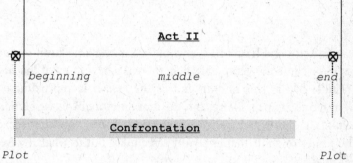

Act II is also a whole, a complete, self-contained unit of dramatic (or comedic) action; it is the *middle* of your screenplay and contains the bulk of the action. It begins at the end of Plot Point I and continues through to the Plot Point at the end of Act II. So we have a beginning of the *middle*, a middle of the *middle*, and an end of the *middle*.

It is approximately sixty pages long, and the Plot Point at the end of Act II occurs approximately between pages 80 and 90 and spins the action around into Act III. The dramatic context is *Confrontation*, and in this unit of dramatic action your character encounters obstacle after obstacle that keeps him/her from achieving his/her dramatic need. Once you determine the dramatic need of your character, what your character wants, you can create obstacles to that need, and then your story becomes your character's overcoming obstacle after obstacle to achieve his or her dramatic need.

Act III is the end, or *Resolution*, of your screenplay.

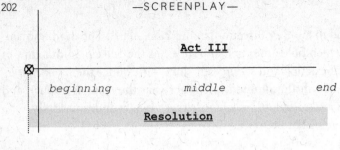

Act III

beginning　　　　　middle　　　　　end

Resolution

Plot
Point II

Like Acts I and II, Act III is a whole, a self-contained unit of dramatic (or comedic) action. As such, there is a beginning of the *end,* a middle of the *end,* and an end of the *end.* It is approximately twenty to thirty pages long, and the dramatic *context* is *Resolution.* Resolution, remember, means "solution," and refers not to the specific scenes or shots that end your screenplay, but to what resolves the story line.

In each act, you start from the beginning of the act and move toward the Plot Point at the end of the act. That means each act has a *direction,* a line of development that begins at the beginning and ends at the Plot Point. The Plot Points at the end of Acts I and II are your destination points; that's where you're going as you're building or constructing your screenplay.

You build your screenplay in terms of individual units of action—Act I, II, III.

How do you build your storyline?

By using 3 × 5 cards.

Take a pack of 3 × 5 cards. Write the idea of each scene or sequence on a single card, and a few brief words of description (no more than five or six) to aid you while you're writing. You need fourteen cards per thirty pages of screenplay. More than fourteen means you probably have too much material for Act I; less than fourteen means you may be too thin and need to add a few more scenes to fill out the *Set-Up.*

For example, if we wanted to structure Act I of *Thelma & Louise,* here's what it would look like on the cards. *Card 1,* Louise is at work; *Card 2,* Louise calls Thelma; *Card 3,* Thelma is with Darryl, doesn't ask him about his trip; *Card 4,* Thelma and Louise pack; *Card 5,*

Louise picks up Thelma; *Card 6,* they drive to the mountains; *Card 7,* Thelma wants to stop; *Card 8,* they're at the Silver Bullet for drinks and eats; *Card 9,* Harlan hustles Thelma; *Card 10,* they drink, talk; *Card 11,* Harlan and Thelma dance, she feels sick; *Card 12,* Harlan takes Thelma outside; *Card 13,* Harlan attempts to rape Thelma; *Card 14,* Louise kills Harlan.

This is a simple summary of the action, and not the way the screenplay will look, but it is a process that lays out the story line; it is an effective way in which you can build, or put together, your story.

Understand that building the screenplay is different from *writing* the screenplay. They are two different processes. That's why I say that one card equals one scene, even though it's a contradiction when you're writing the screenplay.

For example, look at the sequence during which Max visits his mother in the hospital in *Collateral.* When you're building your story line on the cards you may write, "Max visits mother in hospital." Yet, though we write it on one card, in truth, when we write the screenplay, it might be an entire sequence, a series of scenes connected by one single idea. If you look at the film, "Max visiting his mother" is written as a sequence: *Max and Vincent arrive at the hospital; Max visits with his mother, Vincent sweet-talks his mother; Max escapes with Vincent's bag; Vincent chases him; Vincent confronts him; Max, defiant, throws the bag over the freeway.* That's approximately seven scenes (it's longer in the movie), and it all comes from "Max visiting his mother."

Suppose your character is feeling chest pains, and the story leads him/her to the hospital. On one card you write "Goes to the hospital." But when you're actually writing this card for the screenplay, it may become an entire sequence, as in *Collateral:* Your character would arrive at the hospital; the doctors examine him; the lab work is done; various medical tests, like X-rays, an EKG, or an EEG, are conducted; a family member or friend is with him. He may be put in a room, or ward, and he may dislike the admitting physician; the doctors might discuss the case with relatives; your character might be even be placed in the intensive care unit. All this can be specified in a few words on the card: "Goes to the hospital."

One scene per card, even though that will probably be a contradiction when you're writing the screenplay. As my mentor, Jean Renoir, used to say: "Do I contradict myself? Then I contradict myself." It's very important to remember that when you're doing the cards, you're doing the cards. When you're writing the screenplay, you're writing the screenplay. One's an apple, the other's an orange.

Building the story line can be done easily and effectively with cards. You can use as many cards as you like: Edward Anhalt, who adapted *The Young Lions* and *Becket,* used fifty-two cards to build his screenplays. Why fifty-two? Because that's how many cards there were in one package. Tina Fey used fifty-six cards when she wrote *Mean Girls;* Ernest Lehman, who wrote *North by Northwest, The Sound of Music,* and *Family Plot,* used anywhere from fifty to a hundred cards; Frank Pierson wrote *Dog Day Afternoon* in twelve cards—he simply wove the story around twelve basic sequences.

I suggest using fourteen cards per approximately thirty pages of screenplay. That means fourteen cards for Act I, fourteen cards for the First Half of Act II, fourteen cards for the Second Half of Act II, and fourteen cards for Act III. Why fourteen? Because it works. Over the years, teaching thousands of students, both here and abroad, I have found I can tell whether a writer has too much material for Act I based on how many cards he/she lays out—strange, but true. If a writer has fifteen or sixteen cards, I can tell immediately that it's top-heavy; there's too much material for the act. If there are twelve or thirteen cards, I can tell the material is thin, and the writer needs a few more scenes to flesh it out in terms of character and plot, depth and dimension. Sometimes writers will use eleven or twelve cards and then tell me that they'll add a few more scenes when they're writing the script. Sometimes it works, but most of the time it doesn't.

It's just one of those odd things I've discovered out of my experience of teaching and writing screenplays; the cards really become a sort of "psychic" guide to laying out the scenes and sequences you'll need to build your story line. Sometimes I'll use different-colored cards: blue for Act I, green for Act II, and yellow for Act III.

The cards are an incredible method. You have absolute freedom to change, add, or delete. You can arrange or rearrange them, any way you want, adding some, omitting others. It is simple, easy, and effective and gives you maximum mobility in building your screenplay.

Sometimes people want to write down their scenes in outline form on the computer. You know: 1, 2, 3, 4 . . . This does work, but I personally find it very restricting; it's too hard to move scenes around or rearrange them in a different order if you get a sudden idea. Final Draft screenwriting software, in versions 6 and 7, has created a scene card application that lets you write down a card, then rearrange it any way you want. However, I still like the feel of shuffling the cards around; I find it easier to have the cards in my hands so I can arrange and rearrange them at will. But do whatever works for you.

When you first lay down your story line, I suggest you simply write down all those scenes you know you want included in the script. (There's more about this in *The Screenwriter's Workbook*.) Just scribble a few words that will identify the scene and throw them down in no real order, free-association style. You already know your beginning and Plot Point I: Cards 1 and 14. That means you already have two cards, the beginning point and the end point. All you need are twelve more to lay out the action line of Act I.

Let's do an exercise of building a story line by creating the dramatic *context* of each act and then determining the *content*.

Earlier on I mentioned Newton's Third Law of Motion: "For every action there is an equal and opposite reaction"; such a simple understanding about the physical nature of things, yet it took more than six hundred years to achieve that understanding. The principle also works in building a screenplay. First, you must know the *dramatic need* of your main character. What does your main character want to win, gain, get, or achieve during the course of your screenplay? This can apply to each scene as well. Once you establish your character's dramatic need, then you can create obstacles to that need.

I'll say it once again: All drama is conflict. Without conflict, you have no action. Without action, you have no character; without character, you have no story. And without story, you ain't got no screenplay.

The essence of character is action—action is character. Film is behavior, right; what a person does, and not necessarily what he/she says, is who he/she is.

We live in a world of action-reaction. If you're driving a car (action) and someone cuts you off or cuts in front of you, what do you do (reaction)? Swear, usually. Honk your horn indignantly. Try to cut the other driver off, tailgate him. Shake your fist, mutter to yourself, step on the gas! It's all a *reaction* to the *action* of the other driver's cutting you off. Action-reaction—it's a law of the universe. If your character *acts* in your screenplay, somebody, or something, is going to *react* in such a way that your character then *reacts*—thus creating a *new* action that will create another reaction.

Your character *acts,* and somebody *reacts.* Action-reaction, reaction-action—your story always moves toward that Plot Point at the end of each act.

Many aspiring and inexperienced screenwriters seem to have things happen *to* their characters, and as a result, the characters are always *reacting* to their situations, rather than *acting* in terms of dramatic need. When this happens, the main character seems to disappear off the page. It becomes a major problem in the screen-writing process. The essence of character is *action;* your character must *act,* not merely *react.* Again, what a person does, and not what he/she says, is who he/she is. This needs to be established, immediately, from page one, word one.

A good case in point is *The Bourne Supremacy,* where Jason Bourne (Matt Damon) is constantly reacting to someone's trying to kill him. He doesn't know who or why. He *reacts* to the attacks, then attacks, so he is reactive before he becomes active. The same kind of situation is present in *The Manchurian Candidate* (Daniel Pyne and Dean Georgaris), where Denzel Washington reacts to the inciting incident, the ambush that opens the film. Later, when he starts having a recurrent dream, he is *reacting;* that's what prompts him to go in search of what's happening to him and the others in his squad: his dramatic need. Now he becomes *active.* He's *doing* something. In *Three Days of the Condor* (Lorenzo Semple and David Rayfiel), Joe Turner (Robert Redford) is a reader for a CIA cell in Manhattan. Act I sets up his office routine. On this particular day, it is Turner's turn to get lunch for his fellow coworkers. It's starting to rain, so he ducks out the back door, through the streets and alley, to the restaurant. When he returns from lunch, everyone is dead—murdered. That is the Plot Point at the end of Act I. Turner *reacts:* He calls the CIA; he is told to avoid all the places where he's known, especially home. He finds a coworker who hadn't come in to work dead in bed, and doesn't know where to go or whom to trust. He is *reacting* to the situation. He *acts* when he phones Higgins (Cliff Robertson) and tells him he wants his friend Sam (Walter McGinn) to meet him and bring him into headquarters. The meeting goes awry, and Sam is shot. That failing, Turner *acts* by kidnapping Kathy (Faye Dunaway) at gunpoint and forcing her to take him to her apartment: He's got to rest, collect his thoughts, find out what action to take.

Action is *doing* something; *reacting* is having it happen to them.

In *The Shawshank Redemption,* Andy is convicted of killing his wife and her lover and sent to Shawshank Penitentiary for two life sentences, back to back. When he arrives, he must learn to adapt to the prison hierarchy. On his first night inside the cell, another convict *reacts* to his situation by breaking down and crying, bemoaning his innocence. He is yanked out of his cell and beaten mercilessly by the prison guards. He dies. He has *acted,* and the result is that he loses his life.

A short time later, Andy is in the showers, and a group labeled "the sisters" makes a pass at him. Andy declines their advances. From that moment on, Andy is a target. He is beaten and raped mercilessly and, while he defends himself as best he can, he says nothing; he simply reacts to the situation.

He doesn't do or say anything until Plot Point I. That's when he approaches Red, saying, "I hear you're a man who can get things done." It's the first time he's spoken out—taken action. Based on this conversation, the two form a bond, and a mutual support system is now in place.

Action, reaction—two different sides of the same coin.

A good screenplay is set up from page one, word one. Act I is a unit of action in which the major elements of the story need to be carefully integrated and established; the incidents and events in this unit of action must lead directly to the Plot Point at the end of Act I, which is the true beginning of your story.

If the script is not set up correctly, there is a certain tendency to keep adding characters and events to the story line to make it move faster. I recently read a script where there were fifteen characters introduced within the first ten pages of the screenplay. I didn't know *who* or *what* the story was about. The story seemed to skate on the surface of the action without penetrating its layers of texture and depth, making it seem trite, contrived, and predictable.

Why does this happen? As I've learned through my travels and teaching, it seems many writers approach their screenplays without doing enough preparation; they're so anxious to begin writing the script that they don't take the time to explore and develop the relationships between the actions and characters. So they begin from the smallest kernel of information and then feel their way through Act I. They seem to spend most of their time trying to figure out what their story is *really* about and what happens next, so they throw down as many story points as they can in the first act, hoping the story will manifest itself.

It doesn't work. The seeds may be planted, but they are not cultivated, watered, or nourished. The writer tells his or her story in the first ten pages, then is lost and doesn't know what to do next.

Preparation and research are essential to the screenwriting process. It is the responsibility of the screenwriter to know and clearly define who the *main character* is, what the *dramatic premise* is (what the story is about), and what the *dramatic situation* is (the circumstances surrounding the action). If you don't know your story well enough, if you haven't spent enough time doing the required research, then you run the risk of inserting incidents and events into the story line just to try to make it work, and then the narrative thread of the story usually goes awry; the stuff just isn't working.

Sometimes a problem exists because the story line is too thin, and more plot has to be found, but the solution is not creating more characters or interesting incidents to put into the screenplay. Creating more events, or more obstacles to confront, is not the answer; it doesn't do anything except expand the problem.

The trouble is often traceable to a writer's impulse to get the script off to a fast and provocative start. If you've only got ten pages to grab the attention of the reader or audience, then the tendency is to lump all of the characters, their obstacles, and their relationships with other characters into this ten-page unit of dramatic action.

It's too much, too soon. More is not necessarily better. If you take great screenplays like *The Shawshank Redemption, Lord of the Rings, Seabiscuit, American Beauty, Y Tu Mamá También, Thelma & Louise,* and *The Silence of the Lambs,* all the major ingredients of the story line are set up and either in place or referred to within the first ten-page unit of dramatic action. The dramatic elements are simple and direct. That's why the context of Act I is the Set-Up.

The Shawshank Redemption deals with Andy's life in prison, and in the opening sequence, the inciting incident, we set up the murder of Andy's wife and lover, as well as his trial and verdict, before he enters the prison. We have to know why he's sent there and what *crime* he has committed. The three threads of the story line—murder, trial, and verdict—are brilliantly intercut, so we *see* the events leading to his conviction, even though we never actually see him committing the murders.

Many screenwriters might approach a story like this from the perspective of dialogue; they might begin with Andy entering the prison, and then have him, during his relationship with Red, tell his story in bits and pieces. As Red informs us in voice-over, Andy doesn't seem to belong in the prison population; when he walks "he strolled, like a man in a park without a care or worry." During their first few scenes together, Andy could explain to Red the circumstances surrounding the murder of his wife. In terms of setting up the story, this approach might work, but the tendency might be to *explain* rather than *reveal.*

In *Apollo 13* (William Broyles Jr. and Al Reinert), the first ten pages set up all the narrative threads that are needed to establish the situation. After showing newsreel shots of the fire that killed the three astronauts of *Apollo 1,* the script opens with a friendly party-like gathering where people are watching Neil Armstrong's walk on the moon. In just a few words we learn that these people are astronauts in the current NASA program and that the dream of Jim

Lovell (Tom Hanks) is to land on the moon. In just a few pages we know everything we need to know, including the suspicion that Lovell's wife has some deep fear about his going into space again.

The inciting incident occurs on page 10, when Lovell returns home and surprises his family with the news that his space mission will take place sooner than originally scheduled. (Originally, a scene had been written showing Lovell with the NASA officials getting the assignment, but it slowed everything down so it was cut.)

Once he gets the assignment, the next ten pages focus on his training and preparation for the mission, so we can see what the real-life astronauts had to go through to prepare for their flight. Plot Point I is the liftoff into space.

Apollo 13 is an excellent example of classic screenwriting that sets up character and story from page one, word one, both through action and dialogue. The script could easily have started with Lovell and his crews being informed their mission was being pushed up, and if it had been written that way, most of the expository information would have to have been established within the first ten-page unit of the dramatic action.

In *Sense and Sensibility* (Emma Thompson), based on Jane Austen's nineteenth-century novel, it would have been very easy to put in too much too soon. In the first few pages we could have set up the backstory, the relationships within the Dashwood family, the death of the father, and how it affects the three sisters, but this normally would be too much information for Act I. Nevertheless, it's got to be there for us to set up the story correctly.

How did Emma Thompson handle this? In voice-over we hear about the family, see the father on his deathbed, and learn that the family fortune is to be automatically inherited by the son. And he promises his dying father that he will take care of his three sisters. But after the funeral, we see that the son's wife has other plans for her husband's inheritance.

That's a lot of information to present in the first ten pages. But it's been set up in both narration and pictures, so we see that the father's widow and his three daughters are literally without a roof over their heads. The rest of Act I deals with how the family is going to cope with this situation, and we see them play it out in scene after scene. The girls have to be married, of course, for in those days women needed husbands to take care of them. When a possible match between Elinor (Emma Thompson) and Edward (Hugh Grant) doesn't happen, the girls give up the house to their brother and move to the country. Plot Point I.

If all this backstory information had been executed through dialogue, there would have been way too much explanation in the story. It would have been too wordy, the characters passive and reactive, the scenes too long and expository, with the result that the narrative action would not move the story forward.

Build the story line in units of dramatic action. Start with Act I. As a complete unit of dramatic action, the story begins with the opening scene or sequence and ends at the Plot Point at the end of Act I. Let's create a story about Colin, who is falsely accused of embezzling more than a million dollars from his Wall Street company through an ingenious computer scam. During the screenplay, he seeks and finds the true culprit and brings him/her to justice.

Take the 3 × 5 cards. Write down a few words or descriptive phrases on each card. On the first card we want to create the inciting incident, so on Card 1 we write "special effects computer sequence." This is where and how the scam is occurring. Next, Card 2, "Colin going to work." Card 3, "Colin arrives at office." Card 4, "Colin at work." Card 5, "big stock deal in the works." Card 6, "Colin meets with client." Card 7, "Colin with wife/girlfriend at play or party." Card 8, "office—embezzlement of $1 million discovered." Card 9, "emergency meeting of top executives." Card 10, "police investigate." Card 11, "the media learns about it." Card 12, "Colin nervous; embezzlement discovered in his account." What happens next? Card 13, "Colin questioned by police." Then what happens? Card 14, Plot Point I, "Colin arrested for embezzlement."

Step by step, scene by scene, build your story from the beginning to the Plot Point at the end of the act: "Colin arrested for embezzlement." It's like putting together a jigsaw puzzle.

In the fourteen cards you've indicated the flow of dramatic action in Act I through the end of Plot Point I. When you've completed the cards for Act I, take a look at what you've got. Go over the cards, scene by scene, like flash cards. Do it several times. Soon you'll pick up a definite flow of action; you'll change a few words here and a few words there to make it read easier. Get used to the story line. Tell yourself the story of the first act, the *Set-Up*.

If you throw down the cards and end up with a few too many, don't worry about it. Rather, see if you can consolidate the action of a few cards into one card; that way, you'll be able to bridge the incidents of the story line into a cohesive whole. Don't be afraid to play around with the cards. You may want to try them in a different order until they feel right. You're not tied to the order; arrange and rearrange them to suit your needs. The cards are for you. Use them to construct your story, so you always know where you're going. Don't worry about the writing—just focus on the organization and flow of the story.

When you've completed the cards for Act I, put them on a bulletin board, on the wall, or on the floor, in sequential order. Tell yourself the story from the beginning to the Plot Point at the end of Act I. Do it over and over again, and pretty soon you'll begin to weave the story into the fabric of the creative process.

Do the same with Act II. Remember that the dramatic *context* of Act II is *Confrontation*. Is your character moving through the story with his/her *dramatic need* firmly established? You must keep the character's obstacles in mind all the time in order to generate dramatic conflict.

When you've finished the cards, repeat the process from Act I; go through the cards from the beginning of Act II to the Plot Point at the end of Act II. Free-associate, let ideas come to you, put them on cards, and go over and over them.

Use fourteen cards to get from the beginning of Act II to a possible Mid-Point of the story. The Mid-Point is a story progression point, an incident, episode, or event, that occurs around page 60. It could be a scene or sequence, a major event, or an understanding or line of dialogue. Its function is to move the story forward (there's more about this in *The Screenwriter's Workbook*). Then do another fourteen cards that take you from the Mid-Point to the Plot Point at the end of Act II. Then you can resolve the story line with fourteen cards in Act III. Let the story line guide you.

Lay the cards out. Study them. Plot your story progression. See how it's working. Don't be afraid to change anything. A film editor I once interviewed provided me with an important creative principle; he said that within the context of the story, "The things you try that *don't work* will always tell you *what does work*."

It's a classic rule in film. Many of the best cinematic moments happen by accident. A scene *tried* that doesn't work when first tried will ultimately tell you what *does* work.

Don't be afraid to make mistakes.

How long should you spend on the cards?

A few days, not more than a week. It takes me a couple of days to lay out the cards. I spend a day or so on Act I, about four hours. I spend a day on Act II and III.

Then I'll put them on the floor or bulletin board and I'm ready to start working. I'll spend several days going over and over the cards, getting to know the story, the progression, the characters, until I feel comfortable. That means about two to four hours a day spent with the cards. I'll go through the story, act by act, scene by scene, shuffling cards around, trying something here, moving a scene from Act I into Act II, a scene from Act II into Act I. The card method is so flexible you can do anything you want, and it works!

The card system allows you maximum mobility in structuring your screenplay. Go over and over the cards until you feel ready to begin writing. How do you know when to start writing? You'll know; it's a feeling you get. When you're ready to start writing, you'll start writing. You'll feel secure with your story; you'll know what you need to do, and you'll start getting visual images of certain scenes.

Is the card system the only way to construct your story?

No. There are several ways to do it. Some writers simply list a series of scenes on the computer, numbering them (1) Bill at the office; (2) Bill with John at bar; (3) Bill sees Jane; (4) Bill leaves for party; (5) Bill meets Jane; (6) Bill and Jane like each other, decide to leave together. As mentioned earlier on, I don't recommend this method, because you have less freedom to arrange and rearrange scenes.

Another way is to write a *treatment*—a *narrative synopsis* of what happens in your story, incorporating a little dialogue. A treatment can be anywhere from four to twenty pages long. An *outline* is also used, especially in television, where you tell your story in scenes in a detailed narrative plot progression. Dialogue is an essential part of the *outline,* which can be anywhere from twenty-eight to sixty pages in length, depending on the show you're writing for, be it a sitcom, an hour episodic series, or a Movie of the Week (a form that has been temporarily shelved, at least at this writing). That may change in the normal cycle of things. Outlines, or treatments, should not be longer than thirty pages. Do you know why?

The producer's lips get tired.

That's an old Hollywood joke, but there's a great deal of truth to it.

No matter what method you use, you are now ready to move from telling the story on cards to writing the story into your screenplay.

You know your story from start to finish. It should move smoothly from beginning to end, with story progressions clearly in mind so all you have to do is look at the cards, close your eyes, and *see* the story unfolding.

Now all you've got to do is write it!

———————

Determine your ending, opening, and Plot Point at the end of Acts I and II. Get some 3 × 5 cards, different colors if you choose, and start with the opening of your screenplay. Free-associate. Whatever comes to mind for a scene, put it down on the cards. Build toward the Plot Point at the end of the act.

Experiment with it. The cards are for you—find your own method to make them work for your story.

Do it.

13

Screenplay Form

> "Sometimes, the laws of Nature are so sim-
> ple, we have to rise above the complexity of
> scientific thought to see them."
>
> —Richard Feynman
> Nobel Prize-winning physicist

Several years ago, I was conducting one of my seven-week screen-writing workshops, and one of the participants was a prominent television news reporter for the *NBC Evening News*. A graduate of NYU, he had an advanced journalism degree from Stanford and had worked his way up the corporate ladder to become skilled and proficient in his chosen career. He had come to me, he said, because he wanted to turn his journalism skills into a screenwriting career. He had many stories, he went on, several of which had already made it onto the national news scene, and he was confident his scripts would be successful and profitable. It seemed like he had it all figured out: He would write the screenplay, use his contacts in the industry to get the script to the "right people" (whoever *they* were), sell it for a lot of money, and... well, I guess we all know the rest. The Hollywood dream.

Everybody wants to be a screenwriter.

During the first few weeks it became very clear to me that he was extremely talented, that he worked hard, and that he was disciplined. And yes, he had a good idea that would make a good screenplay if executed properly.

And there's the rub: "executed properly."

He wanted to write a screenplay, but he wanted to write it on his terms; he wanted to do it *his* way, not the way it's done professionally in the industry today.

Because he was a professional newsperson, he was determined to write in the form he knew best and was most comfortable with. He wanted to write it in "news format," which meant the scene descriptions and commentary would be on the left-hand margin of the page and the visual description and cues on the right. He placed his dialogue on the left-hand margin, the way playwrights do. Obviously, that's not proper screenplay form; it may be right in the news media, but it's not in the film industry.

When he turned in his first pages, I knew he had a major problem. He wasn't capturing the dimension, either visually or emotionally, on the page. The format got in the way. I suggested he should go back to the beginning and put his story in proper screenplay form. He declined, saying it would get in the way of his telling the story the way he wanted to tell it. I didn't say anything, figuring he would learn the lesson for himself. So, he kept writing in news form, and I kept telling him he was going to have a problem translating what he had written into proper screenplay form. I could tell he didn't believe me; there would be no difficulty, he said adamantly, in transferring his pages into the proper screenplay form. I looked at him, he looked at me, and in that instant I knew his dream was going to collide with the realities of Hollywood. So, as an exercise, after he had completed the first act, I asked him to transfer what he had written into proper screenplay form. He had to do it sometime, I told him, so he might as well do it now.

I didn't hear from him for several days, and then I got a call telling me he'd gotten a new assignment that would take him out of town. During our conversation, I asked how he was doing and if he was having any problems, trying to encourage and support him in any way I could. He paused, hesitated, stumbled around, and I knew he had perceived the truth. Screenplays have a specific form, and if you ignore that form, thinking that at some point down the line you're going to change it into the correct form, it's not going to serve you or the story, and especially not the screenplay. After all, screenplay form is screenplay form, just like rocks are hard and water's wet.

I didn't hear from him during the next week, but at the following class session, he showed me his pages. I could see he had some doubts and reservations in letting me read the pages, and after I had looked them over, I could see why. There was no narrative line of action; it was episodic, and his visuals were somewhat dull and boring. It didn't work at all, and he knew it. He knew what he wanted to write, he just didn't know *how* to do it. It was a washout. Screenplay form had gotten in the way of his ability to tell his story the way he wanted to tell it. That was it for him. He never came back, and to this day I don't know if he ever completed that screenplay or not.

So, what's the moral of the story? If you want to do it, do it right. He wanted to write a screenplay, but refused to learn the proper form. Screenplay form is unique and precise. It's so simple it's difficult. Why?

Look at some of the common assumptions that are so prevalent. The first and most common is that when you're writing a screenplay, it is the writer's responsibility (read: "your" responsibility) to write in the camera instructions so the director and others can see how it should be filmed.

Wrong.

The writer's job is to write the screenplay and keep the reader turning pages, not to determine how a scene or sequence *should* be filmed. You don't have to tell the director and cinematographer and film editor how to do their jobs. Your job is to write the screenplay, to give them enough visual information so they can bring those words on the page into life, in full "sound and fury," revealing strong visual and dramatic action, with clarity, insight, and emotion.

Don't give the reader an excuse not to read your screenplay.

That's what the screenplay form is all about—what *is* a professional screenplay, and what *isn't*. As a reader, I'm always looking for an excuse not to read a script. So when I find a screenplay with improper form, I make a determination: An aspiring writer, a novice, wrote this. The first lesson is simple: You can't sell a script in Hollywood without the help of readers; don't give them a reason not to take you seriously.

Everybody, it seems, has his/her own conception about what is, and what is not, screenplay form. Some people say if you're writing a screenplay you're "obligated" to write in camera angles; and if you ask them why, they'll mumble something about "so the director knows what to film!" They'll create an elaborate and meaningless exercise called "writing in camera angles." And soon, an abundance of camera angles—like long shots, close shots, various instructions about zooms, pans, and dollies—pepper the pages, revealing a novice screenwriter who doesn't know what he or she is doing.

There was a time, in the 1920s and '30s, when the director's only job was to direct the actors, and it *was* the writer's job to write in camera angles for the cameraman. That's no longer true. It's not the job of the screenwriter.

F. Scott Fitzgerald is a perfect example. One of the most gifted novelists of the twentieth century, Fitzgerald came to Hollywood to write screenplays. He failed miserably—he tried to "learn" camera angles and the intricate technology of film, and he let that get in the way of his screenwriting. Not one script he worked on was made without extensive rewriting. His only screenwriting achievement is unfinished, a script called *Infidelity* written for Joan Crawford in the 1930s. It's a beautiful script, patterned like a visual fugue, but the third act is incomplete and it lies gathering dust in the studio vaults.

Most people who want to write screenplays have a little of F. Scott Fitzgerald in them. The screenwriter is *not responsible* for writing in the camera angles and detailed shot terminology. It's not the writer's job. The writer's job is to tell the director *what* to shoot, not *how* to shoot it. If you specify how each scene should be shot, the director will probably throw it away. And justifiably so.

The writer's job is to write the script. The director's job is to film the script, to take words on paper and transform them into images on film. The cameraman's function is to light the scene and position the camera so it cinematically captures the story.

Here's the way it works on almost every motion picture set. One day, I visited the set of *Seabiscuit*. Gary Ross, the incredibly gifted director, was rehearsing Tobey Maguire and Jeff Bridges in a scene, while John Schwartzman, the director of photography, was preparing to set up the camera.

Gary Ross was sitting in a corner with Tobey Maguire and Jeff Bridges, going over the context of the scene. John Schwartzman was telling the crew where to put the lights. Ross, Maguire, and Bridges began blocking out the scene—who'd move on this line, who'd enter on this cue, who'd cross to the barn door, and so on. Once the blocking was established, Schwartzman followed them with his "eyepiece," establishing the first camera angle. When Ross finished working with Bridges and Maguire, Schwartzman showed him where he wanted to position the camera. Ross agreed. They set up the camera, the actors walked through the scene, rehearsed it several times, made minor adjustments, and were ready for a take.

Film is a collaborative medium; people work together to create a movie. Don't worry about camera angles! Forget about writing scenes describing the intricate moves of a Panavision camera with a 50mm lens on a Chapman crane!

Your job is to write the script, scene by scene, shot by shot.

What is a shot?

A shot is the cell, the kernel, of the action; a shot, basically, is what the camera sees.

Scenes are made up of shots, either a single shot or a series of shots; how many, or what kind, is insignificant. There are all kinds of shots. You can write a descriptive scene like "the sun rises over the mountains" and the director may use one, three, five, or ten different *shots* to visually get the feeling of "sunrise over the mountains."

A scene is written in a *master shot,* or *specific shots.* A master shot covers a *general area:* a room, a street, a lobby. A *specific shot* focuses on a specific part of the room—a door, say, or in front of a specific store on a specific street. The scenes from *American Beauty* are mostly presented in master shot. The script *Cold Mountain* utilizes both specific shots and master shots. If you want to write a dialogue scene in master shot, all you need to write is INT. RESTAURANT—NIGHT, and simply let your characters speak without any reference to the camera or shot.

You can be as general or specific as you want. A scene can be one shot (a car racing down the street) or a series of shots (a couple arguing on a street corner in front of a few bystanders).

A shot is *what* the camera sees.

Let's take another look at the screenplay form.

(1) EXT. ARIZONA DESERT—DAY

(2) A blazing sun scorches the earth. Everything is flat, barren. In the distance, a cloud of dust rises as a jeep makes its way across the land-scape.

(3) MOVING
A jeep races through sagebrush and cactus.

(4) INT. JEEP—FAVORING JOE CHACO

(5) Joe drives recklessly. ANDI sits next to him, an attractive girl in her mid-twenties.

                    (6) ANDI
                  (7) (shouting)
          (8) How much longer?

                    JOE
          Couple o' hours. You okay?

(9) She smiles wearily.

                    ANDI
          I'll make it.

(10) Suddenly, the motor SPUTTERS. They look at each other, concerned.

                                        (11) CUT TO:

Simple, right?

If you look at the example, you'll see that the first line describes where we are: the desert in Arizona during the day. It could be morning or afternoon. It does not have to be more specific than that. It is called the Scene Heading or slug line, and it's written in capital letters.

We skip a line, then write, single-spaced, from margin to margin, the description, or action, of the scene. The description paragraph should deal only with what *we see*. Many times, the aspiring screen-writer will put various thoughts or feelings of the characters into the stage description, as if we, the reader, need to know what the character is thinking and feeling. If we can't see it through hand or facial gestures, or hear it through the dialogue, don't write it. If it's written right, you don't need to tell the reader what's going on inside your character's head.

The character's name, placed in caps, like JOE or ANDI, is located in the center of the page; if you want to describe some kind of physical or emotional action, use parentheses. The character is yelling, lying, angry, hesitant, happy, sad, resigned—all these terms describe *how* the character is speaking the dialogue, and they can be placed within the parentheses. When I'm writing a screenplay, I use a lot of stage directions wrapped in parentheses, explaining how I would like the character to respond, but when the script is completed, I go through the screenplay and remove all the stage directions. The actors will play things the way they want to play it, not how I want them to play it.

The dialogue is located in the center of the page, single-spaced, and it is what the character says. What's great about writing a screenplay is that the subtext of the scene, what is *not* said, can sometimes be more important than what *is* said. Again, dialogue serves two basic functions in the scene: *Either it moves the story forward or it reveals information about the character.*

This is proper, contemporary, and professional screenplay form. There are very few rules, and these are just the guidelines:

Line 1—Called the *slug line*, or *scene heading* it states the general or specific locale. We are outside, EXT., somewhere in the ARIZONA DESERT; the time is DAY.

Line 2—Double-space, then, the action is single-spaced: your description of people, places, or action, from margin to margin. Descriptions of characters or places should not be longer than a few lines. And descriptive paragraphs, describing the action, should be no longer than four sentences. That's not a hard-and-fast rule, it's only a suggestion. The more "white space" you can have on the page, the better it looks.

Line 3—Double-space; the general term *Moving* specifies a change in camera focus. (It is *not* a camera instruction. It is a "suggestion.")

Line 4—Double-space; there is a change from *outside* the jeep to *inside.* We are focusing on the character, Joe Chaco. He is the subject of the shot.

Line 5—New characters introduced are always capitalized.

Line 6—The character speaking is always capitalized and placed in the center of the page.

Line 7—Stage directions for the actor are written in parentheses under the name of the character speaking, always single-spaced. Don't abuse parentheses; use only when necessary.

Line 8—Dialogue is placed in the center of the page, so the character speaking forms a block in the center of the page, surrounded by description from margin to margin. Several lines of dialogue are always single-spaced.

Line 9—Stage directions also include what characters do within the scene—any kind of reactions, silent and otherwise.

Line 10—*Sound effects,* or *music effects,* are always capitalized. This is an old tradition in the moviemaking process. Usually the last step in the filmmaking process is to give the film to the music and effects editors. The film is "locked"—that is, the picture track cannot be changed or altered. And usually the production schedule is late and the sound effects and music editors don't have enough time to go through each shot and scene to see what might be needed. So the tradition is that the writer capitalizes the needed effects. That way, the editors can skim quickly through the script looking for music and effects cues, and you can help them by putting references to music or sound effects in capitals. Don't overdo effects. Don't ask for specific songs by specific recording artists, but offer suggestions: "WE HEAR something like Norah Jones." Again, you want to *propose the feeling* of the way you think things should look and feel. With a few exceptions, to use the specific song or music you want may be too expensive for the budget, so you simply "suggest" what you think might be appropriate.

Film deals with two systems—the *film,* what we see, and the *sound,* what we hear. The film portion is complete before it goes to sound, and then the two are put together in sync. It is a long and complicated process. At present, with the widespread use of digital technology and the advances of computer graphic imagery, or CGI, there is a much broader use of multimedia effects—flash forwards, flashbacks, memory, bits and pieces of an old event—but the principles of the two systems remain intact, whether filming with film or in digital. To see the difference in style, you may want to look at *Ordinary People* and compare it with *The Bourne Supremacy* or *Memento;* in all three films the characters are trying to recover an incident, a lost memory.

Line 11—If you choose to indicate the end of a scene you may write "CUT TO:" or "DISSOLVE TO:" (a *dissolve* is two images overlapping each other; one fades out as the other fades in) or "FADE OUT," used to indicate a fade to black. It should be noted that optical effects like "fades" or "dissolves" are usually a film decision, made by the director or film editor. It is not the writer's decision, but if it makes you feel more comfortable in terms of *how to read* the screenplay, do it.

That's all there is to basic screenplay form. It's simple—so simple it's difficult, because each screenplay is unique and can be visualized in a myriad of ways. Just don't tell the director what to do and how to do it.

For most aspiring screenwriters, it's a new form, so give yourself time to learn how to write it. Don't be afraid to make mistakes. It takes a while to get used to it, but the more you do it, the easier it gets. Often I have students simply copy ten pages of a screenplay just to get the feel of the form. It doesn't matter what screenplay it is; choose ten pages at random and just copy it on the computer. If you want, get screenwriting software to help remove the doubt and confusion. Final Draft is the best screenwriting software around and is used by professionals like Tom Hanks, Alan Ball, Steven

Bochco, Julie Taymor, James L. Brooks, Anthony Minghella, and others.

As mentioned before, it is not the writer's job to write in camera angles. As a matter of fact, the word "camera" is rarely used in the contemporary screenplay. "But," people say, "if you don't use the word 'camera' and the shot is what the camera sees, how do you write the shot description?"

The rule is: FIND THE SUBJECT OF YOUR SHOT! Then describe it.

What does the camera, the eye in the middle of your forehead, see? What takes place within the frame of each shot?

If Bill walks out of his apartment to his car, what is the subject of the shot?

Bill? The apartment? The car?

Bill, of course. He is the subject of the shot.

If Bill gets into his car and drives down the street, what is the subject of the shot? Bill, the car, or the street?

The car is, unless you want the scene to take place inside the car: INT. CAR—DAY. Moving or not moving. Then you can focus on Bill.

Once you determine the subject of the shot, you're ready to describe the visual action that takes place within the shot or scene.

I've compiled a list of terms to replace the word "camera" in your screenplay. If you're ever in doubt about whether to use the word "camera," *do not use it*; find another term to replace it. These general terms used in shot descriptions will allow you to write your screenplay simply, effectively, and visually.

SCREENPLAY TERMS

(to replace the word CAMERA)

RULE: FIND THE SUBJECT OF YOUR SHOT.

1. ANGLE ON	A person, place, or thing—ANGLE ON Bill (the subject of the shot) leaving his apartment building.
2. FAVORING	Also a person, place, or thing—FAVORING Bill (subject of the shot) as he leaves his apartment.
3. ANOTHER ANGLE	A variation of a SHOT—ANOTHER ANGLE of Bill walking out of his apartment.
4. WIDER ANGLE	A change of focus in a scene—You go from an ANGLE ON Bill to a WIDER ANGLE that now can include Bill and his surroundings.
5. NEW ANGLE	Another variation on a shot, often used to "break up the page" for a more "cinematic look"—A NEW ANGLE of Bill and Jane dancing at a party.
6. POV	A person's POINT OF VIEW, how something looks to him/her—ANGLE ON Bill, dancing with Jane, and from JANE'S POV Bill is smiling, having a good time. This could also be considered the CAMERA'S POV.
7. REVERSE ANGLE	A change in perspective, usually the opposite of the POV shot—for example, Bill's POV as he looks at Jane, and a REVERSE ANGLE of Jane looking at Bill—that is, what *she* sees.
8. OVER THE SHOULDER	Often used for POV and REVERSE shots. Usually the back of a character's head is in the foreground of the *frame* and *what* he is looking at is the background of the frame. The *frame* is the boundary line of what the CAMERA sees—sometimes referred to as the "frame line."
9. MOVING SHOT	Focuses on the movement of a shot—A MOVING SHOT of the jeep racing across the desert. Bill walking Jane to the door. Ted *moves* to answer the phone. All you have to indicate is MOVING SHOT. Forget about trucking shots, pans, tilts, dollies, zooms, or cranes.
10. CLOSE SHOT	What it says—close. Used sparingly, for emphasis. A CLOSE SHOT of Bill as he stares at Jane's roommate. When Jake Gittes, in *Chinatown,* has a knife in his nose, Robert Towne indicates a CLOSE SHOT. It is one of the few times he uses the term in the screenplay.
11. INSERT	A close shot of "something"—a photograph, newspaper story, headline, face of a clock, watch, telephone number ...

Knowing these terms will help you write a screenplay from the position of choice, confidence, and security—so you know what you're doing without the need of specific camera directions.

Take a look at contemporary screenplay form. Here are the first pages, the opening sequence, of the action film *The Run*. It is the story of a man setting out to break the Water Speed Record in a rocket boat. The opening is an action sequence.

Examine the form; look for the subject in each shot, and how each shot presents an individual mosaic within the tapestry of the sequence. (The "first time around" refers to the title of the individual sequence; it is the first attempt at breaking the Water Speed Record.)

(page 1 of screenplay)

"THE RUN"

FADE IN:
"first time around"

EXT. BANKS LAKE, WASHINGTON—JUST BEFORE DAWN

A SERIES OF ANGLES

A few hours before dawn. Some stars and a full moon are pinned to the early-morning sky.

BANKS LAKE is a long sleeve of water nestled against the concrete walls of the Grand Coulee Dam. The water reflects the shimmering reflection of the moon. All is quiet. Peaceful. Hold.

Then, we HEAR the high-pitched ROAR of a truck. And, we:

CUT TO:

HEADLIGHTS—MOVING

A pickup truck moved INTO FRAME. PULL BACK to reveal the truck hauling a large trailer, the puzzling-shaped cargo covered with a tarpaulin. It could be anything—a piece of modern sculpture, a missile, a space capsule. As a matter of fact, it's all three.

A CARAVAN

of seven vehicles winds its way slowly along the
tree-lined highway. A pickup truck and station
wagon lead the group. Another station wagon
is followed by a truck and trailer. Bringing
up the rear are two large camper trailers and a
tool van. They bear the insignia "Saga Men's
Cologne."

INT. LEAD STATION WAGON

Three people are in the wagon. The radio plays
softly, a Country & Western tune.

STRUT BOWMAN drives, a lean and expressive Texan
who happens to be the best sheet-metal man and
mechanical wizard west of the Mississippi.

RYAN WILLS sits next to the window staring mood-
ily into the predawn darkness. Strong-willed and
stubborn, he is considered by many to be a flam-
boyant boat designer, a crackpot genius, or a
daredevil race driver. All three are true.

(2)

ROGER DALTON sits in the backseat. A quiet man,
he wears glasses and looks like the rocket systems analyst he is.

THE VEHICLES

wind their way along the wood-lined highway heading toward the Grand Coulee Dam and the sleeve of
water known as Banks Lake. (Formerly, it was
known as Franklin D. Roosevelt Lake.)

EXT. BANKS LAKE—DAWN

The sky lightens as the caravan moves to the far
side, the vehicles looking like a column of fire-
flies parading before the dawn.

THE BOATHOUSE AREA

The cars pull in and park. The lead truck pulls to
a stop and a few CREW MEMBERS jump out. Others
follow and the activity begins.

A long Quonset hut has been erected near the water. The BOATHOUSE, as it's known, houses the work area and is complete with work benches, lights, and tool area. The two campers park nearby.

A FEW CREWMEN

jump out and begin unloading various equipment, taking it into the work area.

THE STATION WAGON

Strut parks the wagon; Ryan is the first out, followed by Roger. Ryan walks into the boathouse.

A TV CONTROL VAN

From *Sports World,* as well as some local Seattle sportscasters, begin setting up their equipment.

THE OFFICIALS AND TIMERS

all with the initials FIA emblazoned on their shirts, set up electronic timing devices, timing boards, digital consoles, and floating timing buoys. Video images from the TV Control Monitor are assembled into a montage of activity. The "feel" of this sequence should begin slowly, like someone waking up, then gradually build into a rhythm of a tense and exciting rocket-launch sequence.

(3)

INT. CAMPER LIVING QUARTERS—JUST AFTER DAWN

Ryan puts on his asbestos racing suit and Strut helps him lace it up. He steps into his cover suit, the name "Saga Men's Cologne" clearly seen. Strut fixes something on the suit, and the two men exchange a glance.

Over this, we HEAR the voice of the:

> TV ANNOUNCER (VO)
> This is Ryan Wills. Most of you
> already know the story—one of the most
> innovative racing designers of high-
> speed water vehicles, Wills, the son
> of wealthy industrialist Timothy
> Wills, was approached by Saga Men's
> Cologne to build a racing boat that
> would break the Water Speed Record,
> currently 286 miles an hour, held by
> Leigh Taylor. Ryan did that and more:
> He designed and built the world's first
> rocket boat—that's right, rocket
> boat—revolutionary in concept and
> design—

THE BOATHOUSE

Moving out of the boathouse, mounted on two spe-
cially constructed mounts, is the rocket boat,
"Prototype I," a gleaming, missile-like boat that
looks like a Delta-winged aircraft. It is beautifully designed, a piece of sculpture. The crew
members guide the boat onto the launching track,
disappearing into the water. Over this, the TV
announcer continues.

> TV ANNOUNCER (VO, contd.)
> Just how fast it will go is unknown—
> some people claim it won't even work!
> But Wills says this boat can easily
> break the 400-mile-an-hour barrier.
> But the sponsor, Saga Cologne,
> couldn't get anyone to drive this
> amazing rocket boat—it's too radical,
> too unsafe. That's when Ryan, the
> former hydroplane racer, stepped in
> and said, "I'll do it!"

INT. TV CONTROL VAN BOOTH

We SEE a bank of TV monitor screens. MOVE IN to a
screen where the TV ANNOUNCER is interviewing
Ryan Wills at a press conference.

              RYAN (on TV screen)
I built this boat, piece by piece—I
know it like the back of my hand. If I
thought there was the slightest chance
of failure, or that I might possibly
hurt myself, or kill myself—if I
didn't think it was completely safe, I
wouldn't do it! Somebody's got to do
it so it might as well be me! I mean,
that's what this life's all about,
isn't it? Taking risks?

              TV ANNOUNCER (on screen)
Aren't you nervous, scared?

              RYAN (on screen)
Of course—but I'm confident I can do
the job. If I wasn't, I wouldn't be
here. It's my choice. I'm ready to set
a new Water Speed Record and live long
enough to give you a chance to
interview me *after* I do it!

He laughs.

OLIVIA

Ryan's wife, stands nervously on the sidelines,
biting her lip. She's scared and she shows it.

EXT. TV CONTROL VAN—EARLY MORNING

The TV ANNOUNCER from Ryan's interview stands
near the Control Van, the lake in b.g.

              TV ANNOUNCER
Several years ago, Ryan Wills was a
highly successful hydroplane racer.
He gave it up after an accident put
him in the hospital—some of you
remember that—

FLASHBACK—BANKS LAKE, WASHINGTON—DAY

Ryan's hydroplane flips over and over and over until it lands bottom up. Ryan is thrown free and
floats motionless in the water.

BACK TO PRESENT—THE START AREA

A finger-like dock stretches into the water. A
tow-boat is tied to it.

(5)

PROTOTYPE I

sits on top of the water, being fueled; two oxygen tanks connected with long polyethylene tubing
disappear into the engine. Roger supervises the
fueling.

RYAN

Ryan steps out of the camper and walks toward the
rocket boat. Strut is with him.

>   TV ANNOUNCER (VO)
>   So, here we are—at Banks Lake in
>   eastern Washington, right next to the
>   Grand Coulee Dam—where Ryan Wills will
>   attempt to be the first man in history
>   to set a Water Speed Record in a
>   rocket boat.

AT THE START SITE

Ryan walks down the dock and steps into the boat.

AT TIMING CONTROL

A series of digital timing mechanisms race
wildly, end at zero across the board.

INT. TV CONTROL BOARD IN VAN

The DIRECTOR sits in front of the TV Monitor
Console and prepares for the TV broadcast. Eight
screens are banked in front of him, each with a
different image: crew, finish line, lake, timing
buoys, crowd, etc. One screen follows Ryan as he
prepares for the run.

>   TV ANNOUNCER (VO)
>   Working with Ryan are his two
>   coworkers—Strut Bowman, the
>   mechanical engineer—

STRUT

in the tow-boat, walkie-talkie in hand, watching
Ryan carefully.

> TV ANNOUNCER (VO)
> —and Roger Dalton, a rocket systems
> analyst, one of the lead scientists
> from the Jet Propulsion Lab, and
> formerly on the team of the Galileo
> mission.

ROGER

checking fuel gauges and other details. Everything's ready.

                                                      (6)

RYAN

is buckled into the cockpit. Strut is in the tow-
boat, nearby.

INT. ROCKET BOAT COCKPIT

Ryan checks the three gauges on the control panel
in front of him. He flicks a toggle switch marked
"fuel flow"; a needle jumps into position and
holds. He clicks another toggle switch, marked
"water flow," and another needle is activated. A
red button switch lights up and we see the word
"armed." Ryan puts his hand on the steering wheel,
positions one finger next to the "eject" button.

RYAN

He checks the gauges, takes a few deep breaths.
He's ready.

> TV ANNOUNCER (VO)
> Ryan appears ready—

A SERIES OF ANGLES

of the countdown. Crews, timers, and spectators
quiet down; electronic devices hold at zero; the
TV camera crew is focused on Prototype I, poised
like a bird on the edge of flight.

STRUT

watches Ryan, waits for him to give the "thumbs-up" signal.

RYAN

All we see are eyes peering out of a crash helmet. Concentration high, intention high.

THE TIMING COMPLEX

The timers wait, all eyes riveted on the timing mechanisms and the boat on the lake.

THE LAKE

is quiet, the metric-mile course marked out with three timing buoys.

AT THE FINISH LINE—JACK'S POV

Roger and two crewmen stand looking down course, watching the dot that is the boat.

THE TV CREW

waits, the air heavy with tense anticipation.

                                                    (7)

RYAN'S POV

He stares down course, the "armed" button clearly seen in foreground.

STRUT

checks and double-checks final details. Ryan's ready. He checks the timers—they're ready. It's a "go." He gives "thumbs-up" to Ryan and waits for Ryan's signal.

RYAN

returns "thumbs-up."

STRUT

talks into the walkie-talkie.

                    STRUT
      Timing sequence ready—
              (he begins his countdown)
      5, 4, 3, 2, 1, 0—

THE TIMING BUOY

flashes three lights sequentially, red, yellow, then green.

RYAN

flips the "on" switch and suddenly

THE ROCKET BOAT

explodes into motion, the finger-like flame searing the surface of the water as it leaps forward.

THE BOAT

literally flies toward the end of the lake like a missile, hovering several inches above the water as the hydrofoil tines skim along the water at over 300 mi/hr.

THIS INTERCUT

with Strut, Olivia, the timers, Roger at the finish line, the TV Monitor screens in the TV control van.

RYAN'S POV

The periphery landscape is distorted, flattened as the world plunges into silence and high-speed visual images.

THE BOAT

streaks by as the

DIGITAL NUMBERS

of the timing mechanisms race toward infinity.

VARIOUS ANGLES

as the boat hurtles toward the finish line. Crew, timers, spectators watch in breathless wonder.

RYAN

holds on to the steering wheel when suddenly we see his hands twitch slightly as the boat vibrates.

> TV ANNOUNCER (VO)
> It's a solid run—

THE TIMING CONSOLE

The digital numbers spin at a dizzying speed.

RYAN'S POV

The boat SHIMMIES, builds into a pronounced vibration jarring the entire landscape view. Something is terribly wrong.

FROM THE SHORE

We see the rooster tail becoming irregular and choppy.

STRUT AND OLIVIA

watch the boat shaking violently.

A SERIES OF QUICK CUTS

intercut between spectators and boat. Prototype I veers off course, Ryan frozen at the wheel.

> TV ANNOUNCER (VO)
> Wait a minute—something's not—
> something's wrong—the boat's shaking—

PROTOTYPE I

lists to one side.

RYAN

pushes the eject button.

> TV ANNOUNCER (VO)
> *(hysterical)*
> Ryan can't hold it! He's crashing—
> Ryan's crashing—oh, my God—

(9)

THE COCKPIT

ejects, arches high into the air, the parachute
trailing behind it.

THE CAPSULE

heads toward the water.

STRUT, THE CREW, TIMERS, OLIVIA

watch horrified, disbelieving.

THE BOAT

tips over, smashes into the water, careens out of
control, then cartwheels over and over again, until it disintegrates before our very eyes.

> TV ANNOUNCER (VO)
> Ryan's ejected—wait a minute—the
> chute's not opening—oh, Lord, what has
> happened here today...

VARIOUS ANGLES

as the parachute attached to the capsule fails to
open. Ryan, encased in the plastic cockpit, hits
the water at over 300 mi/hr.

The capsule bounces and skips across the water
like a stone on a pond. We can only guess what's
happening to Ryan inside. The capsule speeds
more than a mile before it finally comes to a
stop.

Silence. The world seems frozen in time. And
then:

```
Ambulance SIRENS shatter the silence, and all
hell breaks loose as people move toward the life-
less figure of Ryan Wills floating helplessly in
the water. Hold, then:

                                          CUT TO:
```

Notice how each shot describes the action and how the terms on the list are used to give it a "cinematic" look without resorting to excessive camera instruction.

Read as many screenplays as you can to familiarize yourself with the form. There are many Web sites devoted to the screenplay. You can download scripts free of charge at sites like simplyscripts.com; or Drew's Script-O-Rama.com; or dailyscript.com; or do a Google or Yahoo! search for "screenplays" and see what comes up. There are many, many sites, and many, many screenplays you can download. To get familiar writing in screenplay form, choose any script, open to any page, and copy ten pages of the screenplay. This exercise is to allow you to get used to the form. Look for the "subject" of the shot. The more scripts you read, the more familiar with the form you'll become.

Allow yourself some time to learn how to do it; it will probably be uncomfortable at first, but it gets easier. The more you do, the easier it gets. When you don't have to think about what you're doing in terms of screenplay form, it becomes second nature. Of course, the easiest way to write in screenplay form is to get screenwriting software like Final Draft. Check it out at www.finaldraft.com.

Once you become familiar with the form, you're ready to move on to the next step: the scene.

14

Writing the Screenplay

BAGBY:
"Gentlemen, today you can walk out that door, turn right, hop on a streetcar and in twenty-five minutes end up smack in the Pacific Ocean. Now you can swim in it, you can fish in it, you can sail in it—but you can't drink it, you can't water your lawns with it, you can't irrigate an orange grove with it. Remember—we live next door to the ocean but we also live on the edge of the desert. Los Angeles is a desert community. Beneath this building, beneath every street, there's a desert. Without water the dust will rise up and cover us as though we'd never existed!"

—*Chinatown*
Robert Towne

"Either you bring the water to L.A.—or you bring L.A. to the water." That's the underlying foundation of *Chinatown*. To weave this theme through the screenplay, dramatizing it through action and character, is just great screenwriting. Speaking to Robert Towne about the amazing journey of writing *Chinatown*, however, uncovers a story of doubt, confusion, and uncertainty. Writing a screenplay is an amazing, mysterious phenomenon filled with joy, frustration, sometimes even sorrow. One day you're totally on top of things, the next day you're down, lost in a maze of confusion and uncertainty. One day it works, the next day it doesn't; who knows how or why. It is the creative process; it defies analysis, except to say it is magic and it is wonder.

The hardest thing about writing is knowing what to write. Take a look back and see where we've come from. Here is the *paradigm*:

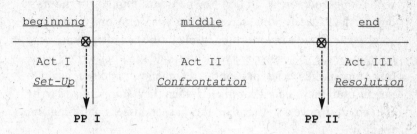

In the beginning, we talked about creating a *subject,* like three guys stealing moon rocks from Houston's NASA facility. We broke it down into an *action* and *character.* We talked about choosing a *main* character and one or two *major* characters, and channeling their action into stealing the moon rocks. We talked about determining our *ending,* our *beginning,* the *Plot Points* at the end of Acts I and II. Then we discussed *building the story line* with 3 × 5 cards, focusing on the *direction,* the line of development, we wish to follow.

Look at the paradigm: **WE KNOW WHAT TO WRITE!**

We've completed a form of preparation applicable to all writing in general, and the screenplay in particular; it is form, structure, and character. You are now able to select the elements of your story that fall inside the *paradigm* of screenplay form and begin the journey of writing it from beginning to end. In other words, you know what to write; now all you've got to do is *write it.*

Whatever has been said or written about the experience of writing, or the creative process, it still boils down to one thing—writing is your own, personal experience. Nobody else's.

There are a lot of people who contribute to the making of a movie, but the writer is the only person who sits down and faces the blank sheet of paper.

Writing is hard work, a day-by-day job, sitting in front of your computer or notepad day in, day out, getting the words down on paper. You've got to put in the time. And some days are better than others.

Before you begin writing, you've got to *find the time* to write.

How many hours a day do you need to spend writing?

That depends on you. I work about four hours a day, six days a week. Stuart Beattie writes eight hours a day, from 9 A.M. to 6 P.M. with a one-hour break. Robert Towne writes four to five hours a day, six days a week. Some screenwriters work only one hour a day; some write in the early morning, some in the late afternoon, some at night. Some writers write twelve hours a day. Other writers work on a story in their head for months, telling it over and over again to people until they *know* it completely; then they "jump in" and write it in about two weeks. After that, they'll spend weeks polishing and fixing it.

Most people need about two to three hours a day to write a screenplay. That's ideal, but sometimes not very practical. In many of my screenwriting classes, I tell my students that if they're working full-time and cannot spend an hour or two a day writing before they go to work, or when they get home, they need to keep the idea current in their minds. They constantly need to think about the story line, the characters, and "what happens next." Sometimes I tell them to carry the cards with them, so they can go over the material when they're standing in line or riding on the subway, bus, or train. Keeping a tape recorder with you when you're driving to work, on lunch or coffee break, or on your way home, helps you to focus on your thoughts and ideas so you can remember them. Then, before you fall asleep at night, listen to your ideas or lines of dialogue and you'll be able to keep the material fresh in your memory. When the weekend rolls around, you can spend around two or three quality hours on Saturday and/or Sunday working on the script.

What's the best time for you to write? Look at your daily schedule. Examine your time. If you're working full-time, or caring for home and family, your time is limited. You're going to have to find the best time for you to write. Are you the kind of person who works best in the morning? Or does it take you until early afternoon to be wide awake and alert? Late at night may be a good time. You're going to have to experiment. Find out.

You may get up and write a few hours before you go to work; or you might come home from work, unwind, and then write a few hours. You may want to work at night, say about 10 or 11 P.M., or you may go to bed early and wake up about 4 or 5 A.M. to write. One of my students, a major studio executive, gets up at 5 each morning, works for an hour or two, has breakfast with his family, and leaves for work. It's hard, but you can do it. If you're a housewife and have a family, you may want to write when everyone's gone for the day, either midmorning or midafternoon. You be the judge of what time, day or night, you can get two to three hours alone.

And a few hours alone means a few hours alone. No telephone, no friends for coffee, no idle chatter, no chores, no demands made on you by husbands, wives, lovers, or children. You need two to three hours alone, without interruption.

Writing is a day-by-day job—shot by shot, scene by scene, page by page, day by day. Set goals for yourself. Three pages a day is reasonable and realistic. If a screenplay is approximately 120 pages long, and you write three pages a day, five days a week, how long will it take you to write a first draft?

About forty working days. If you work five days a week, that means you can get a first draft done in about six weeks. Once you start the writing process, you'll have days when you write ten pages, days when you do three, and so on. Just make sure you try for three pages a day. Or more.

If you're married, or in a relationship, it's going to be difficult—you need some space and private time, as well as support and encouragement.

Women with families can have a more difficult time than others. Husbands and children are not always very understanding or supportive. No matter how many times you explain that you're "going to be writing," it doesn't help. Demands are made that are difficult to ignore. I've had married women tell me their husbands threaten to leave them unless they stop writing, and their children turn into monsters; the domestic routine is being interfered with, and none of them like it. It's tough to handle; emotions of guilt, anger, or frustration get in the way of your need for the time, space, and freedom to write, and if you don't watch out you can easily become a victim of your emotions.

When you're in the writing experience, you're near your loved ones in body, but your mind and concentration are a thousand miles away. *Your family* doesn't care or understand that your characters are in a highly charged situation; *you* can't break your concentration to deal with the snacks, meals, medication, doctors' appointments, laundry, and shopping that you normally do.

Don't expect to. If you're in a relationship, your loved ones will *tell* you they understand and support you, but they won't—not really. Not because they don't want to, but because they don't understand the writing experience.

Don't feel guilty about taking the time *you need* to write your screenplay. If you *expect* your wife, husband, or lover to "get upset" or "not understand" when you're writing, it won't bother you when it happens. *If* it does. You have to be "at choice" when you're writing; expect a tough time and it won't bother you if it happens.

A note to all husbands, wives, lovers, friends, and children: If your wife, husband, lover, friend, or parent is writing a screenplay, they need your love and support.

Give them the opportunity to explore their desire to write a screenplay. During the time they're writing, anywhere from three to six months, they're often going to be moody, explosive, easily upset, preoccupied, and distant. Your daily routine is going to be interfered with, and you're not going to like it. It might become uncomfortable.

Are you willing to give them the space and opportunity to write what they want to write? Do you love them enough to support them in their efforts even if it interferes with your life?

If the answer is no, talk about it. Work out a way so that both sides can win, and then support each other in your communication. Writing is a lonely, solitary job. For a person in a relationship, it becomes a joint experience.

Establish a writing schedule: 10:30 to noon; or 8 to 10 P.M.; or 9 P.M. to midnight. With a schedule, the "problem" of discipline becomes easier to handle.

Decide *how many* days you're going to be writing. If you're working full-time, in school, or involved in a marriage or relationship, with the proper preparation you can expect to work one or two days a week. Just keep your focus—otherwise creative energy is lost. You've got to concentrate clearly on the script you're writing.

With your writing schedule set up, you can get down to work; and one fine day you will sit down to write.

What's the first thing that's going to happen?

Resistance, that's what.

After you write FADE IN: EXT. STREET—DAY you'll suddenly be seized with an incredible urge to sharpen your pencils or clean your work area. You'll find a reason or an excuse not to write. That's resistance.

Writing is an experiential process, a learning process involving the acquisition of skill and coordination, like riding a bicycle, swimming, dancing, or playing tennis.

Nobody learns to swim by being thrown into the water. You learn to swim by perfecting your form, and you can only do that by actually swimming; the more you do, the better you get.

It's the same with writing. You're going to experience some form of resistance. It shows itself in many ways, and most of the time we aren't even aware it's happening.

For example: When you first sit down to start writing, you may suddenly get the urge to clean the refrigerator. Or to wash the kitchen floor. You may want to go to the gym, change the sheets, take a drive, eat, watch television, take a yoga class, or have sex. Some people go out and buy a thousand dollars' worth of clothes they don't need or want! You may get angry, impatient, and yell at everybody and anybody for nothing in particular.

They're all forms of resistance.

One of my favorite forms of resistance is sitting down to write and suddenly getting an idea for *another* screenplay—a *much better* idea, an idea so unique, so original, so exciting, you wonder what you're doing writing *this* screenplay. You really think about it.

You may even get two or three "better" ideas. It happens quite often; it may be a great idea, but it's still a form of resistance! If it's really a good idea, it will keep. Simply write it up in a page or two, put it in a file marked "New Projects," and file it away. If you decide to pursue this new idea and abandon the original project, you'll discover the same thing happening; When you sit down to write, you'll get *another new idea,* and so on and so on. It's a form of resistance; a mind trip, a way of avoiding writing.

We all do it. We're masters at creating reasons and excuses not to write; it's simply a barrier to the creative process.

So, how do you deal with it?

Simple. If you know it's going to happen, simply acknowledge it when it does. When you're cleaning the refrigerator, sharpening pencils, or eating, just know that's what you're doing: experiencing resistance! It's no big thing. Don't put yourself down, feel guilty, feel worthless, or punish yourself in any way. Just acknowledge the resistance—then move right through to the other side. Just don't *pretend it's not happening.* It is! Once you deal with your resistance, you're ready to start writing.

The first ten pages are the most difficult. Your writing is going to be awkward, stilted, and probably not very good. It's okay. Some people won't be able to deal with that; they'll make a decision that what they're writing is no good. They'll stop, righteous and justified because they "knew they couldn't do it." "Who am I kidding?" is the usual refrain.

Writing is a learned coordination; the more you do the easier it gets.

At first, your dialogue's probably not going to be very good.

Remember that dialogue is a function of character. Let's review the purpose of dialogue. Dialogue:

- moves the story forward;
- reveals information about the characters—after all, they do have a history;
- communicates necessary facts and information to the reader;
- establishes character relationships, making them real, natural, and spontaneous;
- gives your characters depth, insight, and purpose;
- reveals the conflicts of the story and characters;
- reveals the emotional states of your characters; and
- comments on the action.

Your first attempts at writing dialogue will probably be unnatural, clichéd, fragmented, and strained. Writing dialogue is like learning to swim: You're going to flounder around at first, but the more you do the easier it gets.

It takes anywhere from forty to fifty pages before your characters start talking to you. And they *do* start talking to you. Let yourself write shitty pages, with stilted, direct, dumb, and obvious dialogue. Don't worry about it. Just keep writing. Dialogue can always be cleaned up during the rewrite. "Writing is rewriting" is the ancient adage.

Those of you who are looking for "inspiration" to guide you won't find it. Inspiration is measured in moments, a few minutes or hours; a screenplay depends on diligence, and is measured in weeks and months. If it takes you a hundred days to write a screenplay, and you're "on" for ten of those days, consider yourself lucky. Being "on" for a hundred days, or even twenty-five days, just doesn't happen. You may hear that it does, but in truth it's the pot at the end of the rainbow—you're chasing a dream.

"But—" you say.

But what?

Writing is a day-by-day job, two to three hours a day, five days a week, either during the day or on weekends, three or more pages a day, ten pages a week. Shot by shot, scene by scene, sequence by sequence, page by page, act by act. And some days are better than others.

When you're *in* the *paradigm*, you can't *see* the *paradigm*.

The card system is your map and your guide; the Plot Points your checkpoints along the way, the "last-chance" gas station before you hit the high desert; the ending, your destination. What's nice about the card system is that you can forget it. The cards have served their purpose.

I said in Chapter 12 that one card equals one scene, but when you're writing the screenplay, that will be contradictory. You'll suddenly "discover" a new scene that works better or that you hadn't thought of. Use it. It will lead you to veer off the path of the cards into a few new scenes or sequences that you hadn't even considered. I think that's great. Do it. You'll be able to tell within a few pages whether it's working or not. Usually you'll finish the pages, then won't know what to do, or where to go. Look at the next card. You'll find you have a perfect lead-in to the next scene on the cards. If it doesn't work, all you've lost is a couple of days, but you've maintained your creative energy. You haven't really lost anything.

It doesn't matter if you want to drop scenes or add new ones; just do it. Your creative mind has assimilated the cards so you can throw out a few scenes and still be following the *direction* of your story.

When you're doing the cards, you're doing the cards. When you're writing the screenplay, you're writing the screenplay. Forget a rigid adherence to the cards. Let them guide you, but don't be a slave to them. If you feel a spontaneous moment that gives you a better, more fluid story, write it.

So, what are some qualities that make up good screenwriting? Several things, perhaps the most important of which is to understand that the foundation of all good dramatic writing is *conflict*. Stating it once again, all drama is conflict; without conflict, you have no action; without action you have no character; without character, you have no story. And without story, you have no screenplay.

Dramatic conflict can be either internal or external; stories like *The Hours, Chinatown, The Manchurian Candidate, A Place in the Sun* (Michael Wilson and Harry Brown), *Cold Mountain*, and *American Beauty* have both internal and external conflict. External conflict is where the conflict is outside the characters and they face physical (and of course, emotional) obstacles, such as in *Cold Mountain, Collateral, Apollo 13*, or *Jurassic Park*. Creating conflict within the story, through the characters and events, is one of those simple, basic "truths" of all writing, whether it be novel, play, or screenplay.

So what is *conflict*? If you look up the word, you'll see it involves "opposition"; and the hub of any dramatic scene is having the character or characters be in opposition to some*one* or some*thing*. Conflict can be anything: a struggle, a quarrel, a battle, or a chase scene; fear of life, or fear of failure or success; internal or external— any kind of confrontation or obstacle, and it really doesn't matter whether it's emotional, physical, or mental.

Conflict must be at the very hub of your story, because it is the core of strong action and strong character. If you do not have enough conflict, the foundation to your writing, you'll find yourself more often than not caught in a quagmire of dull writing.

Keep writing, day by day, page by page. And during the writing process you're going to discover things about yourself you never knew. For example, if you're writing about something that happened to you, you may reexperience some old feelings and emotions. You may get "wacky" and irritable and live each day as if you were on an emotional roller coaster. Don't worry. Just keep writing.

You're going to move through three stages of your first-draft screenplay.

The first stage is the "words on paper" stage. That's when you put it all down—everything. During this stage, if you're in doubt about writing a scene or not writing it, write it. *If in doubt, write.* That's the rule. If you start censoring yourself, you might wind up with an eighty-page screenplay, and that's too short. (Comedies, however, are usually about eighty-five to ninety pages.) You'll have to add scenes to what is with any luck an already tight structure to fill it out and bring it to length, and that's extremely difficult to do. It's easier to cut scenes than add them to an already structured screenplay.

Keep moving forward in your story. If you write a scene and go back to clean it up, polish it, and "make it right," you'll find you've dried up at about page 60, lost all your creative spark, and you might even shelve the project. Many writers I know who've tried to write a draft this way have failed to complete it. Any major changes you need to make, do in the second draft.

There will be moments when you don't know how to begin a scene, or what to do next. You know what happens on the cards, but not how to get into it visually. If this happens, break down the action of your scene into a beginning, middle, and end. What's the purpose of the scene? Where does your character come from? What is his/her purpose in the scene?

Ask yourself "What happens next?" and you'll get an answer. It's usually the *first* thought skittering across the back of your mind. Grab it, and throw it down on paper. It's what I call the "creative grab," because you've got to be quick enough to "catch it" and put it down.

Many times you'll try to improve that first idea to "make it better." If your first thought is to place the scene in a car driving down the highway, and you decide to make it a walk in the country or a walk on the beach, you'll lose a certain creative energy. Do it too many times and your script will reflect a contrived, deliberate quality. It won't work.

There's only one rule that governs your writing—not whether it's "good" or "bad," but does it work? Does your scene or sequence work? If it does, keep it in, no matter what anybody says.

If it works, use it. If it doesn't, don't.

If you don't know how to get in or out of a scene, free-associate. Let your mind wander; ask yourself the best way to get into the scene. Trust yourself and you'll find the answer.

If you created the problem, you'll be able to find a solution to it. All you have to do is look for it.

Problems in a screenplay can always be solved. Just know that if you've created the problem, whatever it is, you can solve it. If you get stuck, go back to your characters; go into your character biography and ask him/her what he or she would do in that situation. You'll get an answer. It may take a minute, an hour, a day, several days, a week, but you'll get the answer—probably when you least expect it, and in the most unusual place. Just keep asking yourself the question "What do I need to do to solve this problem?" Run it through your head constantly, especially before you go to sleep. If I have a problem like this I give myself a dream assignment: "Please reveal the answer to the problem during my dream state." It can be a very powerful tool. Give yourself time for the answer to reveal itself to you, but trust in the process.

Writing is the ability to ask yourself questions and get the answers.

Sometimes you'll get into a scene and not know where you're going, or what you're looking for to make it work. You know the *context*, not the *content*. So you'll write the same scene five different times, from five different points of view, and out of all these attempts you may find one line that gives you the key to what you're looking for.

You'll rewrite the scene using that one line as your anchor thought and eventually be able to create something dynamic and spontaneous. You just have to find your way.

And trust yourself.

Around page 80 or 90, the resolution is forming and you'll discover the screenplay is literally writing itself. You're just the medium, putting in time to finish the script. You don't have to do anything; if you let it come through you, it writes itself.

Writing a screenplay is writing a screenplay. There are no shortcuts.

It may take you six to eight weeks to complete your first "words on paper" draft. Then you're ready to move into the second stage of your first draft: taking a cold, hard, objective look at what you've written.

This is the most mechanical and uninspiring stage of writing a screenplay. You'll take what is perhaps a 180- to 200-page draft of your script and reduce it to 130 or 140 pages. You'll cut out some scenes, add new ones, rewrite others, make any changes you need to, to get it into a workable form. It might take you about three weeks to do this. When you've finished, you're ready to approach the third stage of your first-draft script. This is where you see what you've got, where the story really gets written. You'll polish it, accent it, hone and rewrite it, trim it to length, and make it all come to life. You're out of the *paradigm* now, so you can see what you've got to do to make it better. In this stage you may rewrite a scene as many as ten times before you get it right.

There will always be one or two scenes that don't work the way you want them to, no matter how many times you rewrite them. You know these scenes don't work, but the reader will never know. He/she reads for story and execution, not content. It usually takes me about an hour to read a script, seeing it in my head rather than reading it for prose style or content. Don't worry about the few scenes you know don't work. Let them be.

You'll discover that the scenes you like the *most*, those clever, witty, and sparkling moments of action and dialogue, might have to be cut when you reduce the script to workable length. You'll *try* to keep them in—after all, it *is* your *best* writing—but in the long run you've got to do what's best for your screenplay. I have a "best scene" file where I put the "best" things I've ever written, things I had to cut out to tighten the script.

You have to be ruthless in writing a screenplay. If it doesn't work, it doesn't work. If your scenes stand out and draw attention to themselves, they might impede the flow of action. Scenes that stand out *and* work are the scenes that will be remembered. Every good film has one or possibly two scenes that people always remember. These scenes work within the dramatic context of the story. They are also the trademark scenes that later become immediately recognizable.

If you don't know whether your "choice" scenes work, they probably don't. If you have to think about it, or question it, it probably means it's not working. You'll know when a scene's working. Trust yourself.

There may be times during the screenwriting process when you experience a sinking sensation in the pit of your stomach, when suddenly there is a cloud of negativity and confusion sprinkled on the waters of your creativity. And it seems to come out of nowhere.

Most writers, including myself, try to ignore the feeling, to push it away, hide it under the carpet; yet the more we try to dispel it, to pretend it's not there, to hover behind a false bravado, the more we realize we're stuck, lost somewhere within a maze of our own creation.

That's when we hit "the wall." Almost all writers, at some time or other, experience this wall, or block, and try to force their way through it. Sometimes it works, and sometimes it doesn't.

Most of the time it doesn't. And no matter where you are in the screenwriting process, the first "words on paper" draft or the rewrite, it doesn't take much to be overwhelmed by the writing process. We handle this kind of problem in many different ways, of course, like suddenly finding more "important" things to do, like cleaning the kitchen, going to the market, washing the dishes, or going to the movies. Whatever.

After all, some parts of the story are more difficult than others. And some scenes need more work than others. After a few days of struggling with these particular pages, struggling with some of these thoughts and feelings, you may notice doubts about your abilities as a writer beginning to surface. You may find yourself thinking too much, asking yourself questions like: What am I going to do? How am I going to get back on track? You'll question yourself, your talent, your ability to get the job done.

Then one morning you'll wake up and suddenly recognize that a heavy haze of uncertainty is hanging around your neck, and the feeling that's been tugging at you for the last few days finally erupts like a volcano and you *know* you really don't know what you are doing. You finally admit that you don't know how to help yourself or where to go or what to do; the only thing that makes any sense at all is surrendering to the state you are in—dazed, lost, and confused.

Welcome to the world of screenwriting.

If you are writing a story and do not know what emotional forces are working on your character, it is very easy to "run up against the wall" and keep "going around in circles," ultimately falling into that well known as *writer's block*.

Here's the way it usually works: You're totally immersed in the day-to-day process of screenwriting, but there may be one scene or sequence that does not work as well as it should, and you might begin to wonder why it's not working. Still, it's just a random thought and you probably don't pay much attention to it. But you might become aware of a subtle shift occurring within yourself, maybe some doubts about why this scene or sequence is failing to come together. Then you might find that you're talking to yourself, having a little conversation about "the Problem." The first thing that usually happens is you start questioning yourself. "If I weren't so stupid, I could do this," you might think, and the more you wrestle with the problem, the more your image as a screenwriter begins to erode, and then you start making disparaging comments about yourself and your ability. That's when you begin sliding into "the pit," and soon the entire litany of negative judgments descends upon you.

"I knew I should have stayed away from this subject," you might think, or "I'm no good at writing." Soon you'll begin to expand and enlarge on your insecurities, thinking, "I don't know whether I should be writing this script," or "Maybe I just don't have the talent to do this," or "Maybe I should just find a partner and write it with someone else." It goes on and on.

But underneath all these thoughts, comments, or judgments you're making is the common thread that somehow it's all "your fault." If you could do it, you would, and if you can't, it's because you don't have the talent or ability to do it. In short, we turn it inside and blame ourselves.

No wonder it's called *writer's block.*

If you're in this dilemma, and this veil of doubt and negativity is smothering your creative voice, then it's time to *give the critic a voice.* That means giving that judgmental, critical, and negative voice that's roaming around inside your head the opportunity to speak his or her mind.

Remember that this is one of those common problems that strike fear in the hearts of screenwriters everywhere. I recall a screenwriting student coming into class one night with a strange and somewhat tortured look on her face. When I asked her what was wrong, her eyes welled up with tears and she became very serious, and said, "I don't know where I'm going. I'm totally lost, I'm confused, and my pages stink. All that's happening is talk, talk, talk. I keep going around in circles, and I don't know what to do. I'm so upset I could cry."

It's a universal problem. How you get out of it varies from person to person, script to script, but the first thing to do is to admit *you have a problem* and that it's not going to go away until you deal with it, confront it head-on. That's just one of the truths of life.

In my student's case she was so close to the material she couldn't see it anymore, so the first thing I wanted her to do was just stop writing. When you reach this kind of crisis point, you're so overwhelmed and frustrated that you have to regroup. Just stop writing. Put down your pen and paper, shut off your computer or tape recorder, however you're working, and spend some time contemplating your story: What is the story about? What is the dramatic need of your main character? How are you going to resolve the story line? The answers to these questions are the key to getting back on track.

First, go to your screenplay pages and take out a separate piece of paper and label it *The Critic's Page*. As you start writing the script, every time you become aware of a negative comment, thought, or judgment, just write it down on *The Critic's Page*. Number the comments, label them, just as if you were keeping a journal or making a shopping list. You might become aware of such comments as "These pages are terrible," or "I don't really know what I'm doing," or "This isn't working," or "Maybe somebody else should finish it for me"; maybe "These characters all sound the same" and it's apparent that "I've lost my vision," and so on. Whatever your thoughts and comments are about your pages, just write them down on *The Critic's Page*.

The first day you're doing *The Critic's Page*, you may write two pages of screenplay and four pages of critical comments. On the second day maybe you'll write three pages of screenplay and two or more pages on *The Critic's Page*. The third day maybe you'll do four or five pages of screenplay and a couple of pages of the critic.

At this point, stop writing. The next day, take the critic's pages, put them in order, and read them: all your negative comments for day one, day two, day three. As you think about these comments, mull them over in your mind. As you look these pages over, you'll discover something very interesting: The critic *always says the same thing*. It doesn't matter what kind of scene it is, or who the characters are, or what you write; whether it's the pages from day one, two, or three, whether it's a dialogue scene or an action scene, the critic always says the same thing—uses the same words, the same phrases, the same expressions. It's all the same. Your pages are no good; they stink. No matter *what* you write, this is what your critic is telling you: The pages are no good; you should be doing something else.

That's the nature of the mind: to judge, to criticize, to evaluate. The mind can be either our best friend or our worst enemy. It's so easy to get plugged into our judgments and evaluations of what's right or wrong, good or bad.

Now, it could be that what the critic says is accurate. Maybe the pages *are* terrible, the characters *are* thin and one-dimensional, and you *are* going around in circles. So what? *Confusion is the first step toward clarity.* What you try that doesn't work will always show you what does work. As you struggle through your problem area, just get something down on paper; just write lousy pages. You'll always be able to go back and make them better. That's the process all writers go through. So what if you've "hit a wall" and are going around in circles, dazed, lost, and confused.

Give the critic a voice. If you don't give the critic a voice, it'll turn inside and begin to fester, getting worse and worse until it bursts. It's easy to let yourself become your own victim.

Until you become aware of the critic's voice running around in the back of your mind, you're going to become a victim of that voice. Recognizing and acknowledging that voice is the first step through the block; it's not necessary to act upon, or make a decision about, the judgments and evaluations the critic makes, or to determine whether the critic is right or not. No matter what stage you are at in the writing process, don't get too serious about what the critic tells you. One of the things we have to accept is that we always get lost within the maze of our own creations. And we are our own worst critics.

Writer's block is a powerful enemy and can hammer you into submission; the mere thought of writing will turn you off, and because you're not writing you'll feel guilty, so whenever you sit down to write you'll suddenly feel this blanket of heaviness settle over your head, causing you to lose all objectivity and fall into despair.

Writer's block. It happens all the time. To everybody.

The difference is how you deal with it. How you see it.

There are two different ways to look at this "problem." One is to see your dilemma as a real problem, a real block, something to "overcome" or "break through," a physical and emotional obstacle that is locking you into a creative straitjacket.

That's one way of looking at it.

But there's another way. And that is to see the ordeal as *part of the writer's experience*. After all, it's universal, everybody goes through it; it's nothing new or unusual. If you recognize and acknowledge that, you've reached a creative crossroads. The realization becomes a creative guide to another level of your screenwriting craft. If you can look at it as an opportunity, you will find a way to strengthen and broaden your ability to create characters and story.

You'll see that maybe you need to go deeper into your story and strive for another level of richness, full of texture and dimension.

"A man's reach should exceed his grasp," the poet Robert Browning wrote.

If you understand that being challenged by writer's block, being dazed, lost, and confused, is only a *symptom,* this "problem" becomes an opportunity to test yourself. And isn't that what life is all about—putting yourself on the line in a situation where you test yourself to rise to another level? It's simply an evolutionary step along the path of the screenwriting process.

If you accept this point of view, it means you're going to have to dig deeper into your material; you're going to have to stop writing, go back into your character's life and action, and define and clarify different elements of your character's life. You're going to have to go back and do new character biographies; to define or redefine the characters and their relationships to each other, which are, after all, the hub of your story line.

If you're working on a particular scene, for example, you may need to rewrite it, or change the points of view of your characters; you may need to change locations, or create new actions, episodes, or events for your character. Sometimes you may have to restructure the action in a particular scene or sequence by restructuring the entire act!

Keep writing, day by day, page by page. The more you do the easier it gets. When you're almost finished, perhaps ten or fifteen pages from the end, you might find you're "holding on." You might spend four days writing one scene or one page, and you'll feel tired and listless. It's a natural phenomenon; you simply don't want to finish it, to complete it.

Let it go. Just be aware that you're holding on, then let it go. One day you'll write "Fade Out," or "The End"—and you'll be done. *It* will be done.

The art of screenwriting is finding places where silence works better than words. Recently, one of my students told me that after he had completed writing a scene, the thought occurred to him to go back and take another look at it. Something was bothering him about it and he didn't know what it was. So he read and reread the scene, and suddenly understood how he could make it work more effectively with just *two lines of dialogue!* That's good screenwriting. You don't need pages and pages of dialogue to set up, explain, or move your story forward; just a few lines will do, if you enter the scene at the right point.

And when you've completed the draft, it's a time of celebration and relief. When it's over, you're going to experience all kinds of emotional reactions. First, there's satisfaction and relief. A few days later, you'll be down, depressed, and won't know what to do with your time. You may sleep a lot. You've got no energy. This is what I call the "postpartum blues" period. It's like giving birth to a baby: You've been working on something for a substantial period of time. It's been a part of you. It's gotten you up in the morning and kept you awake at night. Now it's over. It's natural to be down and depressed. The end of one thing is always the beginning of something else. Endings and beginnings, right?

It's all part of the experience of writing the screenplay.

15

Adaptation

NARRATOR:
"The first time he saw Seabiscuit, the colt
was walking through the fog at five in the
morning. Smith would say later that the
horse looked right through him: as if to say
'What the hell are you looking at? Who do
you think you are?' ...He was a small horse
[so] they made him a training partner to
'better' horses, forcing him to lose head to
head duels to boost the confidence of the
other animal...When they finally did race
him, he did just what they had trained him
to do...He lost."

—*Seabiscuit*
Gary Ross

The story of Seabiscuit is a unique and inspirational one, not only
for what the horse accomplished but for the way in which he accomplished it. During the second half of the 1930s, Seabiscuit became a cultural icon throughout the length and breath of the land.
He was universally praised, his exploits and appeal so legendary that
the very name "Seabiscuit" seemed to transcend the sport itself.

But this was more than just a story of a physically and spiritually
broken horse. With his extraordinary rise to fame, he became a
symbol of hope; here was a story of three men and a horse striving
for some kind of belief and faith to hold on to in the midst of
the Great Depression. Seabiscuit became the object of the nation's
faith, someone to root for, something we could believe in. As a
horse, he was not much to look at—he was small and had short
legs—but he was blessed with an indomitable will that remained

intact even after he spent two entire seasons floundering in the lowest ranks of horse racing.

That all changed when the horse came under the forcefully gentle and patient leadership of Tom Smith, a man who personified the freedom of the frontier and preferred the company of horses to that of men. Red Pollard, Seabiscuit's jockey, had been abandoned by his parents as a boy, and for years was a failing jockey who barely survived. Charles Howard was a self-made millionaire who lost the only thing he really loved and lived for, his young son.

Taken together, these three men and a horse were emotionally shattered in their search for unity and wholeness. When they joined together, they fulfilled a need in one another: Charles Howard became the father figure, Tom Smith the teacher, Red Pollard the jockey, the son, the doer; they became a team, a family, sharing their skills to forge the legend known the world over as Seabiscuit. As Red says at the end of the movie: "You know, everybody thinks we found this broken-down horse and fixed him, but we didn't.... He fixed us. Every one one of us. And, I guess in a way, we kind of fixed each other too."

Gary Ross adapted *Seabiscuit* from a best-selling book by Laura Hillenbrand and turned it into an original screenplay based on the life and exploits of the legendary racehorse. As a screenplay adapted from a book, it honored the original source material both in terms of spirit and integrity. It is a moving, inspirational cinematic experience that captures the essence of the legendary horse. When I first read the book I loved it—it was an exciting, informative experience—and I wondered if Gary Ross, the writer-director, would be able to take such broad, sweeping historical events and fuse them into a poignant, gripping story line.

What makes this adapted screenplay so good? And what's the best way to go about adapting a novel, play, magazine article, or newspaper story into a screenplay?

There are many ways, of course. When you adapt a novel or any source material into a screenplay, you must consider your work an *original* screenplay *based* on other material. You can't adapt a novel literally and have it work, as Francis Ford Coppola learned when he adapted F. Scott Fitzgerald's *The Great Gatsby*. Coppola—the noted filmmaker of *The Conversation, The Godfather,* and *Apocalypse Now,* among many other great works—is one of the most arresting and dynamic writer-directors in Hollywood. In adapting *The Great Gatsby* he wrote a screenplay that is absolutely faithful to the novel. The result is a visually magnificent failure; dramatically, it didn't work at all.

Adaptation is both a skill and a challenge. The verb *to adapt* means "to transpose from one medium to another." *Adaptation* is defined as the ability "to make fit or suitable by changing, or adjusting"—modifying something to create a change in structure, function, and form. It only *starts* with the novel, book, play, article, or song. That is the *source* material, the starting point—nothing more. It is a singular art. Adapting an existing work, whether a novel, play, magazine article, newspaper story, or biography into a medium such as a screenplay is difficult, to say the least. Just ask Charlie Kaufman, who wrote *Adaptation,* a film that chronicles the struggle of a screenwriter trying to adapt a novel about orchids into some kind of cinematic experience. Not many can do adaptations well. Each form is so different from any other that any adaptation has to be approached as an original screenplay.

As mentioned earlier, in a novel the dramatic action of the story, the narrative line, is usually told through the eyes of the main character; the reader knows his/her thoughts, feelings, memories, hopes, and fears. There may be chapters written from other characters' points of view, but the dramatic action usually occurs inside the main character's head, within the *mindscape* of dramatic action.

The screenplay, of course, is different; it is *a story told with pictures,* in dialogue and description, and placed within the context of dramatic structure. Film, when you get right down to it, is behavior.

Words and pictures; apples and oranges.

Every screenwriter approaches the craft of adaptation differently. Alvin Sargent, the Academy Award–winning screenwriter of *Ordinary People, Spider-Man 2,* and *Julia,* among other films, reads the source material as many times as it takes to "make it his own," until it's *his* story. Then he writes individual scenes in a random fashion, lays them all together on the floor, and shapes a story line out of those individual scenes.

Ted Tally, the Academy Award–winning screenwriter of *The Silence of the Lambs* and *The Juror,* says he "breaks down the book scene by scene. I try to establish the structural line of events; this event happens, then this event, then this and this happens. What's important from the book is what sticks in your mind. So I put those scenes on cards, one by one, just getting the story down, concentrating on the main needs of the adaptation."

The first thing Tally does is determine who the story is about, and anything that does not serve the main character needs to be cut. When you're adapting a book that may be 350 or more pages into a screenplay that's only 120 pages, you have to be ruthless, yet maintain the integrity of the source material. Which is what Gary Ross did in *Seabiscuit.* Not only did he have to capture the tone and temper of the times, but he wove action that occurred over many years into a two-hour-plus movie, yet still remained true to the source material. And within the historical context of the times, he had to set up the lives of three men, as well as that of Seabiscuit, then structure their journey as they overcame obstacle after obstacle to achieve their success on both a personal and professional level.

It's a general rule that if you're adapting a book or an article to fit the needs of a screenplay, you may have to shift, omit, or add scenes in order to follow the main story line.

"The last thing you're concerned with," Tally says, "is invention for its own sake. If it ain't broke, don't fix it." Meaning that if scenes work within the context of the screenplay, don't change them. If you can't use scenes in the book, you may have to create new ones to make the film work on a visual level, not a literary one. Remember that when you're deliberately breaking a book apart in order to make it into a screenplay, you're going to have to invent new scenes, or invent a way to meld two or three scenes from the novel into one scene in the screenplay. And that means you're going to have to invent transitions to keep the action moving forward. And then you're going to have to invent dialogue for those transitions because you've sacrificed so much information, the story could be confusing.

"You can't be a slave to the book," Tally continues. What he means is that you want the narrative flow in your head, but you don't want it oppressing you. Often during the writing process you'll reference your own story outline more than the novel. And once you complete your first draft, you'll have no reference to the published novel at all. The screenplay becomes only about itself. An adaptation starts to develop its own logic and meaning once you're writing the screenplay.

The hub of adaptation is finding a balance between the characters and the situation, yet keeping the integrity of the story. If you want to see a great adaptation, read *Seabiscuit,* then watch the movie, and notice the skill with which Gary Ross captured the integrity and inspiration of the source material.

Brian Helgeland adapted Dennis Lehane's novel *Mystic River* for Clint Eastwood, and he talks about some of the challenges he had adapting the book into a screenplay. He read the book first: "Once. To get a sense of it. Then I read it another two or three times. I make all the notes in the book itself. Highlight things. Write in the margins. Cross pages out that I don't need. Finally, I start sticking pieces of paper in there and break it down. Once I have the essence of what it's all about, I type an outline. That's when I'll start to add scenes or combine them. Move things around.

"Part of the trick of adaptation is trying to find a workable way of externalizing the book's interior monologues. Sometimes it came down to taking the thoughts and turning them into dialogue."

This is one of the common challenges writers have when they approach an adaptation. I talked with Stuart Beattie, the gifted young writer of *Collateral,* after he had just completed adapting a novel into a screenplay.

I asked how he approached the adaptation. The film, adapted from the novel *Derailed* by James Siegel, is "a thriller novel," he began, "about an ordinary guy who has an affair and his wife gets incredibly derailed as a result of this one moment of weakness. So, there's a morality aspect to it, very much a Hitchcockian kind of everyday man who is put into an extraordinary circumstance. The character keeps trying to get out of it, but just gets deeper and deeper into the situation.

"When I first read the book I was literally on the edge of my seat," he continued. "It was a four-hundred-page book and about three hundred pages into it I knew it would make a great film. Then this incredible hundred-eighty-degree plot twist occurs. You know, it's one of those 'don't do' rules of screenwriting. You just 'don't do' things like putting in an unexpected plot twist at the end.

"Even though I had to get rid of the last third of the book," he said, "the drama is in the family. The girl has type one diabetes. The mother and father are saving up for this new drug that's coming out which would basically save her life. She has a dialysis machine every night that's strung out in the second mortgage payments. They're all in stress. Not connecting anymore. Wrapped up in the pain of the dilemma. That kind of hellhole. So it sets up the situation of him walking out of the marriage. That's basically the set-up. It starts out like it's going to be a family drama, then twists around violently at the end of the Act I, then twists around again and again."

I asked how many times he read the material before he began writing the screenplay. "Two or three times," he told me. "The first time through is the most important, because that's the time you're getting it. I'll write 'good scene, good line, good moment, or something like this could be an opening scene,' that kind of stuff, not knowing where everything's going. Then you've got to let it go and make the movie out of it. And then, a few weeks before shooting, we go back to the book and see if there's anything that's been dropped along the way: a line, a moment, something like that.

"I don't do a very detailed outline after I read the book two or three times. I do a beat sheet. Around a two- or three-page beat sheet. Like, 'the scene in the car, the scene in the elevator, the scene in the house, the scene at the doctor's, and so on.' In a screenplay, I'll normally do a ten-page outline. And usually I try to get that down to a five-page outline. Getting it down to five pages, I've got Act I on page one, Act III on page five ... that just works for me."

When you approach a historical adaptation, like *Cold Mountain*, Charles Frazier's National Book Award–winning novel about the physical and spiritual survival of two lovers at the end of the Civil War, there are other challenges. Anthony Minghella approached the adaptation with the underlying motif of a journey home. It has the main characters, a dramatic and emotional journey, a dramatic purpose, a series of obstacles, a woman waiting with hope and patience, and a place that resides in Inman's heart that represents Cold Mountain. In a time when brothers were fighting brothers and lovers were torn from each other's arms, Cold Mountain becomes a symbol of love, a spiritual place that resides within the heart. It represents not only the physical journey that Inman, the Rebel soldier, endures to return home, but his spiritual journey as well. Survival is uncertain, the wages of war affecting all who walk its path. The entire story is about the return from war and the effects of war's brutality and chaos on the world away from the battlefield.

Minghella departed from the novel, shortening and condensing it, yet kept the obstacles of the journey intact. In the novel, Inman, after enduring test after test of valor, courage, and loyalty, returns home to Cold Mountain and finds his love. And a single night becomes all the time they have together.

There may be times in your adaptation that you have to add new characters, drop others, create new incidents or events, perhaps alter the entire structure of the book. In *Julia,* Alvin Sargent created an entire movie out of an episode from *Pentimento* by Lillian Hellman. In *The English Patient,* the entire movie was conceived from what seems to be only a few paragraphs in the novel. And then Anthony Minghella did some twenty-seven rewrites of the material on paper and in the editing room, shaping it into what became the final film.

The source material and the screenplay are usually two different narrative forms; think apples and oranges. When you *adapt* a novel, play, article, or even a song into a screenplay, you are changing one form into another. You are writing a screenplay *based on other material.* In essence, however, you are writing an original screenplay. And you have to approach it that way.

This is what Peter Jackson, Fran Walsh, and Philippa Boyens had to deal with in *Lord of the Rings: The Two Towers.* The source material for *The Two Towers* is Volume Two of the Trilogy. Books III and IV comprise *The Two Towers.*

The Two Towers novel opens with Book III, the death of Boromir, which was the dramatic climax at the end of the first film, *The Fellowship of the Ring.* In the next few chapters, we read how Aragorn and the others ride to Rohan, then follow the adventures of

Merry and Pippin, who manage to escape the Orcs, leading to their fateful meeting with Treebeard. Then Gandalf returns as Gandalf the White. Then we move to Rohan, where Aragorn and the Fellowship convince King Théoden to retreat to Helms Deep, and it's there, in Chapter 7 of Book III of *The Two Towers,* halfway through the book, that the battle rages between the Orcs and the Fellowhip at Helms Deep. The next four chapters deal with the continuation of the journey. At the end of Book III, Gandalf and Pippin race to Minas Tirith.

Chapter I of Book IV begins as we pick up the action of Frodo, Sam, and Gollum on their journey to Mordor, and then each new chapter follows them through their obstacles and adventures on their way to Mount Doom.

In approaching this book, it would not be very effective, at least dramatically, to structure the screenplay based on the progression of events as they occur in Books III and IV. You would have two different films: one about the Fellowship, the other about Frodo, Sam, and Gollum. In film, you have to keep the story moving forward, and the best way to do that is by intercutting the events between the main characters, then weaving the narrative line of action through the story, like weaving a particular thread through the canvas of a tapestry; the story line always has to keep moving.

"We had the event story, which we grappled with," Philippa Boyens said, "and the ongoing process of whose story we were following at any one time, and the emotional through line of the story, of characters and how they were woven together and connected to the whole—all of the things that every screenwriter grapples with."

"The ring is a metaphor for the machine, for the way that a piece of metal controls and dictates what you do," Peter Jackson says. "A lot of *Lord of the Rings* is about protecting your freedom and the fight against enslavement.... Our first and foremost responsibility was as filmmakers, so we didn't set out with a feeling that we had to be faithful to everything that Tolkien wrote.... The central story line is obviously the story of a hobbit who comes into possession of this very dangerous ring, which he learns has to be destroyed, so he has to go on this journey to destroy it. That's the spine of *The Lord of the Rings,* and we were fairly ruthless right at the beginning with any characters or any events that didn't either directly or indirectly serve that spine."

When the writers approached the material to adapt *The Two Towers* into the screenplay, they took the events as they occurred in the novel and crafted them into a cohesive story line, intercutting Frodo, Sam, and the Gollum's story with Aragorn, the Fellowship, and Merry and Pippin's journey with Treebeard. Then they took the battle at Helms Deep that occurs in Chapter 7 of Book III, and used this as the exciting and rousing climax to end the film. In many ways I think adapting this book into the screenplay of *Two Towers* was a major feat in creative storytelling.

There are times, however, when an adaptation takes on its own life. Perhaps the most unique example of this is the script written by John Huston for *The Maltese Falcon.* Huston had recently finished adapting the script of *High Sierra,* with Humphrey Bogart and Ida Lupino, from the book by W. R. Burnett. The film was very successful, and Huston was given the opportunity to write and direct his first feature. He decided to remake *The Maltese Falcon,* by Dashiell Hammett. The Sam Spade detective story had been filmed twice before by Warner Bros., once as a comedy in 1931 with Ricardo Cortez and Bebe Daniels, and again in 1936 as *Satan Met a Lady,* with Warren William and Bette Davis. Both films failed.

Huston liked the feel of the book. He thought he could capture its integrity on film, making it a hard-boiled, gritty detective story in tune with Hammett's style. Just before he left on a vacation, he gave the book to his secretary and told her to go through it, breaking down the written narrative into screenplay form, labeling each scene as either interior or exterior, and describing the basic action using dialogue from the book. Then he left for Mexico.

While he was away, the secretary's notes somehow found their way into the hands of Jack L. Warner. "I love it. You've really captured the flavor of this book," he told the startled writer/director. "Shoot it just as it is—with my blessing!"

Huston did just that, and the result is an American film classic.

If you're adapting historical events into a screenplay, the term "based on a true story" invokes its own series of challenges.

In *All the President's Men,* adapted by William Goldman from the book by Carl Bernstein and Bob Woodward (about Watergate, lest we forget), there were several dramatic choices that had to be made immediately. In an interview, Goldman says it was a difficult adaptation. Why? Because "I had to approach very complicated material in a simple way without making it seem simple-minded. I had to make a story where there wasn't one. It was always a question of trying to figure out what the legitimate story was.

"For example, the movie ends halfway through the book. We made a decision to end it there, on the Haldeman mistake, rather than show Woodward and Bernstein going on to their greater glory. The audience already knew they had been proven right and gone on and gotten rich and famous and were the media darlings. To try and end *All the President's Men* on an upbeat note would have been a mistake. So we ended it there, on the Haldeman mistake, a little more than halfway through the book. The most important thing about the screenplay was setting up the structure. I had to make sure we found out what we wanted to find out when we wanted to find it out. If the audience is confused, we've lost them."

Goldman opens with the break-in at the Watergate Complex, a taut, suspenseful sequence, and after the capture of the men responsible, he introduces Woodward (Robert Redford) at the preliminary hearing. He *sees* the high-class attorney in the courtroom, becomes suspicious, then involved. When Bernstein (Dustin Hoffman) joins him on the story (Plot Point 1), they succeed in unraveling the thread of mystery and intrigue that leads to the downfall of the President of the United States.

When he wrote *Butch Cassidy and the Sundance Kid,* Goldman stated, "Western research is dull, because most of it's inaccurate. The writers that write Westerns are in the business of perpetuating myths that are false to begin with. It's hard to find out what really happened."

Goldman spent eight years researching Butch Cassidy, and occasionally he would find "a book or some articles or a piece about Butch. There was nothing about Sundance; he was an unknown figure until he went to South America with Butch."

Goldman found it necessary to distort history to get Butch and Sundance to leave the country and go to South America. These two outlaws were the last of their breed. Times were changing, and the Western outlaw could no longer pull the same kind of jobs he'd been doing since the end of the Civil War.

"In the movie," Goldman says, "Butch and Sundance rob some trains, then a superposse forms and chases them relentlessly. They jump off a cliff when they find out they can't lose them, and go to South America. But in real life, when Butch Cassidy heard about the superposse, he took off. He just left. He knew it was the end; he couldn't beat them . . .

"I felt I had to justify why my hero leaves and runs away, so I tried to make the superposse as implacable as I could so the audience would be rooting for them to get the hell out of there.

"Most of the movie was made up. I used certain facts. They *did* rob a couple of trains, they *did* take too much dynamite and blow the car to pieces, the same guy Woodcock *was* on both trains, they *did* go to New York, they *did* go to South America, they *did* die in a shoot-out in Bolivia. Other than that, it's all bits and pieces, all made up."

"History," as T. S. Eliot once observed, "is but a contrived corridor." If you are writing a historical screenplay, you do not have to be accurate about the decisions or emotions of the people involved; but you do have to honor the historical events and the results of those events.

Adapting a sequel poses another kind of creative challenge. "If it works well," the old Hollywood adage goes, "do it again." Films like the *Rocky* series, *Lethal Weapon, Die Hard, Aliens, Shrek,* and the *Terminator* films all pose individual problems.

For my book *Four Screenplays,* I had the opportunity of talking with James Cameron about *Terminator 2: Judgment Day* and the challenge of writing a sequel to the very popular *Terminator.* Cameron went on to do *True Lies* and *Titanic,* the most successful film of all time, and is now exploring the vast terrain of documentaries as well as new feature projects. When I asked him how he approached writing the *Terminator* sequel, he told me it had to be conceived as an original screenplay based on other material. "From a writing standpoint," he said, "the things that interested me the most were the characters. The tricky part was having it all make sense to a member of the audience who didn't remember or hadn't seen the first *Terminator*. Basically, I had a character popping onto the screen in a certain way, and therefore had to create a backstory for that character. I told myself I had to write the script just like there had never been a first film. The sequel had to be a story about someone who encountered something nobody else believes, like the opening scene of *Invasion of the Body Snatchers*, where Kevin McCarthy swears he's seen something shocking, and nobody believes him; then he starts telling the story.

"In *Terminator 2*, the first time we meet Sarah, she's locked up in a mental institution, but the real question is, Is she crazy? Has the past ordeal made her nuts? I wanted to push her character very far.

"I knew the 'bad guy being the hero' could get me into some pretty dangerous territory," he said, "both morally and ethically. I thought there must be a way to deflect this image of bad guy as hero, and use what's great about the character."

The dramatic need of the Terminator is to terminate, to kill anybody or anything that gets in his way. Because he is a cyborg, a computer, he cannot change his nature; only a human or another robot can change the program. So to change the bad guy into a good guy requires changing the dramatic situation, the circumstances surrounding the action.

"The key was the kid," Cameron explained. "Because it's never really explained why John Connor has such a strong moral template. For me, John was pushed by the situation when he sees the Terminator almost shoot the guy in the parking lot. I think everybody invents their own moral code for themselves, and it usually happens in your teens based on what you've been taught, what you've seen in the world, what you've read, and your own inherent makeup.

"John Connor intuitively knows what's right but can't articulate it," Cameron continued. "John says, 'You can't go around killing people,' and the Terminator says, 'Why not?' And the kid can't answer the question. He gets into a kind of ethical, philosophical question that could go on and on. But all he says is 'You just can't.'

"What is it that makes us human?" Cameron asks. "Part of what makes us human is our moral code. But what is it that distinguishes us from a hypothetical machine that looks and acts like a human being but is not?"

So Cameron changed the context of the sequel to make an emotional shift; he turned a killing machine into the protector of young John Connor, the future leader of the rebels. Because he's now the "protector," he must obey the boy's command that it's not "right" to kill anybody. Why it's not right is something the Terminator has to figure out on his own. Basically, the Tin Man gets a heart. It works totally within the context of the sequel and is one of the things that make *Terminator 2: Judgment Day* so successful.

What about adapting a play into a screenplay? Same principles. It's a different *form,* but it's got to be approached in the same manner. There is the proscenium arch, where the stage, the background, the sets, are forever fixed within the restrictions of that arch. The audience becomes the "fourth wall," and during the performance we eavesdrop on the characters and their situation. We hear their thoughts, feelings, and emotions; we *hear* the narrative thrust of the story line. But the real action of the play occurs in the *words* the characters speak, through the *language* of dramatic action. Talking heads.

There was a time in Shakespeare's career when he cursed the restrictions of the stage. In *Henry V,* he lamented the stage as "an unworthy scaffold" and "this wooden O." He begged the audience to "eke out the performance with your mind." He knew the stage couldn't begin to capture the vast spectacle of two armies stationed against an empty sky on the rolling plains of England. Only when he completed *Hamlet* did he transcend the limitations of the stage and create great stage art.

In order to adapt a play into a screenplay, you've got to visualize some of the events that are referred to or spoken about. A play deals with language and dramatic dialogue. In *A Streetcar Named Desire* or *Cat on a Hot Tin Roof* by Tennessee Williams, or Arthur Miller's *Death of a Salesman,* or Eugene O'Neill's *Long Day's Journey into Night,* the action takes place onstage, in sets, the actors talking to themselves or each other. Take a look at any play, whether it's a play by Sam Shepard, like *Curse of the Starving Class,* or Edward Albee's *Who's Afraid of Virginia Woolf?* or any one of Ibsen's masterpieces.

Because the action of a play is expressed through the spoken word, you've got to open it up visually. You might have to add scenes or dialogue that are only referred to in the text, then structure, design, and write them in such a way that they lead you into the main scenes that occur on stage. Search the dialogue for ways to expand the action visually.

Arthur Miller's *Death of a Salesman* offers a good example of taking dialogue from a play and using it as an opportunity to *see* an incident as it happens. There is a scene in which Willy Loman approaches his boss, the son of the man he has worked for for nearly thirty-five years. His "American dream" now shattered and in pieces, Willy has come to ask the man if he can give up the road, literally his way of life, and work in the main office. But Willy Loman is a salesman, and he doesn't know anything else.

Willy asks Howard, the son, for a job on the floor. First he asks for $65 a week, then he drops his request to $50 a week, and then, in a final humiliation, he is literally forced to beg for $40 a week. But this "is a business, kid, and everybody's gotta pull his own weight," Willy is told, and Willy Loman's sales figures have not been the best lately. Willy responds by retreating into his memory, telling Howard what drew him to become a salesman. "When I was a boy...eighteen, nineteen," he says, "I was already on the road. And there was a question in my mind as to whether selling had a future for me...."

He pauses for a long moment, then continues. "[That's when] I met a *salesman* in the Parker House....His name was Dave Singleman. And he was eighty-four years old, and he'd drummed merchandise in thirty-one states. And old Dave, he'd go up to his room, y' understand, put on his green velvet slippers—I'll never forget—and pick up his phone and call the buyers, and without ever leaving his room, at the age of eighty-four, he made his living. And when I saw that, I realized that selling was the greatest career a man could want. 'Cause what could be more satisfying than to be able to go, at the age of eighty-four, into twenty or thirty different cities, and pick up a phone, and be remembered and loved and helped by so many different people? Do you know? when he died—and by the way he died the death of a salesman, in his green velvet slippers in the smoker of the New York, New Haven and Hartford, going into Boston—but when he died, hundreds of salesmen and buyers were at his funeral."

That's Willy Loman's dream; that's what drives him to get up every morning and hit the road, and when that dries up, the dream is dead and life is not worth living. That's something we can *see* if we're adapting a play into a film. Remember Andy Dufrense's line in *The Shawshank Redemption*? "Hope is a good thing, maybe the best of things, and no good thing ever dies." But if the dream collides with reality, as it does in the case of Willy Loman, and all hope is lost, then what's left? The death of a salesman.

The play and the film each stands on its own, a tribute to both playwright and filmmaker.

Suppose you're adapting a person's life into a screenplay. Biographical screenplays dealing with people, either alive or dead, must be selective and focused in order to be effective. If you want to write a biographical script, the life of your character is only the beginning. *Amadeus,* for example, written by Peter Shaffer, deals with only a few incidents in the life of Wolfgang Amadeus Mozart and his relationship with Antonio Salieri.

Choose only a few incidents or events from your character's life, then structure them into a dramatic story line. *Gandhi* (John Briley) tells the story of this modern-day saint by focusing on three stages in Gandhi's life: first, when he was a young law student and experienced how the British enslaved India; second, when he began to practice his philosophy of nonviolent protest; and third, when he tried to bring peace between the Muslims and Hindus. *Lawrence of Arabia* (Robert Bolt and Michael Wilson) and *Citizen Kane* are other examples of selecting only a few incidents in a character's life, then structuring them in dramatic fashion.

A few years ago, one of my students obtained the motion picture rights to the life of the first woman editor on a major metropolitan newspaper. She tried to get everything into the story—the early years, "because they were *so* interesting"; her marriage and children, "because she had such an unusual approach"; her early years as a reporter when she covered several major stories, "because they were *so* exciting"; then getting the job of editor, because "that's what she's famous for."

I tried to persuade her to focus on only a few events in the woman's life, but she was too involved with the subject to see anything objectively. So I gave her an exercise. I told her to write her story line in a few pages. She came back with twenty-six pages, and was only halfway through her character's life! She didn't have a story, she had a chronology, and it was boring. I told her it wasn't working, and suggested she focus on one or two of the stories in the editor's career. A week later, she came back saying she had been unable to choose which stories were the right ones. Overwhelmed by indecision, she became despondent and depressed and finally gave up in despair.

She called me a few days later in tears, and I urged her to get back into the material, to choose three of the most interesting events in the woman's life (writing, remember, *is* choice and selection), and if need be to talk to the woman about what *she* thought were the most interesting aspects of her life and career. She did, and managed to create a story line based on the news item the woman covered that led to her appointment as the first woman editor. It became the hook, or basis, of the entire screenplay.

You have only 120 pages to tell your story. Choose your events carefully so that they highlight and illustrate your script with good visual and dramatic components. The screenplay should be based on the dramatic needs of your story. Source material *is*, after all, source material. It is a starting point, not an end in itself.

Journalists seem to have a difficult time turning an article or news story into a screenplay. Perhaps the reason is that the methods of constructing a dramatic story line in film are exactly the opposite of those in journalism.

A journalist approaches his/her assignment by getting facts and gathering information, by doing text research and interviewing people related to the piece. Once journalists have all the facts, they can figure out the story. The more facts a journalist can collect, the more information he has; he can use some, all, or none of it. Once he's collected the facts, he searches for the hook, or angle, of the piece, and then writes the story using only those facts that highlight and support the material.

That's good journalism. But the facts *support* the story in a screenplay; you might even say they create the story. In journalism, you go from the specific to the general; you collect the facts *first*, then find the story. In screenwriting, it's just the opposite: You go from the general to the specific. First you find the story, then you collect the facts you need to make the story work.

A well-known journalist was writing a screenplay based on a controversial article he had written for a national magazine. All the facts were at his disposal, but he found it extremely difficult to let go of these facts and dramatize the elements he needed to make a good screenplay. He got stuck in finding the "right" facts and the "right" details, and then couldn't get beyond the first thirty pages of the screenplay. He got bogged down, went into a panic, then shelved what might have been a very good screenplay.

He couldn't let the article be the article, and the screenplay the screenplay. He wanted to be completely faithful to the source material, and it just didn't work.

Many people want to write a screenplay or teleplay based on a magazine or newspaper article. If you're going to adapt an article into a screenplay, you've got to approach it from a screenwriter's point of view. What's the story about? Who's the main character? What's the ending? Is it about a man who is captured, tried, and then acquitted for murder, only for us to discover after the trial that he really *is* guilty? Is it about a young man who designs, builds, and races cars and becomes a champion? About a doctor finding a cure for diabetes? About incest? *Who* is the story about? *What* is it about? When you answer those questions, you can lay the story out in dramatic structure.

There are legal issues if you want to adapt a screenplay or teleplay from an article or story. First of all, you must obtain permission to write the script: That means getting the rights from the people involved, negotiating with the author, or her agent, or the magazine or newspaper. In most cases, people are willing to cooperate in trying to bring their stories to the screen or TV. An entertainment attorney who specializes in these matters or a literary agent should be consulted if you're serious about it.

You might want to write the script or outline first, even knowing there's no chance of selling it without obtaining the rights. Something attracted you to the material. What is it? Explore it. You might decide to write the script based on the article or story and then see how it turns out. If it's good, you may want to show it to the people involved. If you *don't do it*, you'll never know how it would have turned out.

The one rule for *all* screenwriters, whether they are doing adaptations or starting from scratch, is "Just keep writing," as Stuart Beattie says. "The greatest thing you can do as a writer is to write and write and write. I often tell aspiring screenwriters that one of the most valuable commodities in Hollywood is cheap talent. That's what you are as an aspiring writer. To think that breaking into the industry is impossible is wrong; people get in all the time. And your value as being cheap talent is a worthy one. Read all the great screenplays. Read *Chinatown*. Know it. And don't give up."

Inspiring words, those.

So, what *is* the fine art of adaptation?

NOT being true to the original. A book is a book, a play is a play, an article is an article, a screenplay is a screenplay. An adaptation is always an original screenplay based on other material. They are just different forms.

Like apples and oranges.

———————

Open a novel at random and read a few pages. Notice how the narrative action is described. Does it take place inside the character's head? Is it told with dialogue? What about description? Take a play and do the same thing. Notice how the characters talk about themselves or the action of the play; talking heads. Then read a few pages of a screenplay (any that are excerpted in this text will do) and notice how the screenplay deals with *external* details and events, what the character *sees*.

16

On Collaboration

Col-lab-o-rate (ka lab' a rāt) v.i. 1) to
work, one with another; to cooperate, as on a
literary work: *They collaborated on a novel.*
—*The Random House Dictionary*

Jean Renoir was a man who loved film with a fervent, almost religious passion. He loved to talk about cinema, and there was no topic too large or too small for him. During the year I was under his tutelage, he shared his experience of the theater, art, acting, and literature and expounded upon the world of cinema. He insisted movies had the potential to be literature, but should never be considered a true "art."

When I asked what he meant by that, he replied that in his definition true "art" is the sole vision of one person, which in the scheme of the filmmaking process is not at all the case. He explained that one person can't do everything required to make a movie. One person can write the screenplay, direct the film, star in it, photograph it, edit it, and score it, like Charlie Chaplin did, but, Renoir stated, the filmmaker cannot act all the parts, or record all the sound, or handle all the lighting requirements along with the vast myriad of other technical details required to make a movie. He can shoot the film but he can't develop it; he has to send it to a special film laboratory for that, and sometimes it doesn't come back the way he wants it, or sees it in his artistic vision.

Because of his background and tradition, Renoir felt that film, though a great art, was never really a "true" art in the sense that writing, painting, or music is a "true" art, because too many people are directly involved in its making and outcome.

"Art," Renoir stated, "should offer the viewer the chance of merging with the creator. One person can't do everything.... True art is in the *doing* of it."

Film is a collaborative medium. The filmmaker depends on others to bring his or her vision to the screen. The technical skills required to make a movie are extremely specialized. And the state of the art is constantly improving. Just take a look at where we've come in the last decade in terms of computer graphic technology. Without James Cameron's brilliant contribution to film technology in *Terminator 2: Judgment Day,* we would not have the computer "morphing technology" we have today. If we did not have that, we would not have had *Jurassic Park;* if we didn't have *Jurassic Park,* we would not have had *Forrest Gump;* without *Forrest Gump,* we wouldn't have had *Toy Story,* which then led to *The Matrix, Finding Nemo, Shark Tale, The Polar Express,* and *The Incredibles.*

The revolution of today is the evolution of tomorrow.

Film is both an art and a science. Sometimes a screenwriter's vision forges the way into new scientific breakthroughs, like James Cameron did in *Terminator 2: Judgment Day,* a film that to my mind is as revolutionary an innovation as the introduction of sound was in 1927. In other times and situations, a scientific invention is conceived that stimulates new ways of looking at something. Writer-director Kerry Conran's *Sky Captain and the World of Tomorrow* is a case in point. It will, in the near future, I think, revolutionize the craft of filmmaking. It literally brings filmmaking into the realm of the home computer, and in the not-too-distant future I can see young filmmakers learning their art and craft in the making of short films at home.

There's always a dynamic interchange between science, art, and technology in the evolution of the movies. If we believe in the future of cinema, we're all like Jay Gatsby, chasing the "green light" that beckons us to the future.

If we listen to the wisdom of Renoir, the only thing we can do by ourselves is write a screenplay. You don't need very much: a computer, pen and paper, or a typewriter and a certain amount of time. Sometimes you may want to write alone, by yourself. But there are other times when you wish you could join forces with someone and write a screenplay together, meaning *collaborate* with someone.

It's a choice you make. It has both an upside and a downside.

The upside of writing alone is obvious: There will be no one interfering with *what* you want to write and *how* you want to write it and *when* you want to write it. In other words, it is your vision and yours alone. There's no one else getting in the way—at least at this stage. There's a lot to be said for that.

The downside of doing it on your own is also obvious: You're alone in a room staring at the blank page or an empty computer screen, and there are moments when you don't know what happens next, or what you want to say or how you want to say it. Sometimes, maybe a lot of the time, the dialogue sounds corny, contrived, and predictable; if it's not happening the way you see it in your mind, the tendency is to turn your frustration, depression, and anger onto yourself and berate yourself for doing such a poor job. So you think the writing sucks, that you can't do it, that it's just not working, that you're not good enough, that you don't have the talent to do it, that the story is trite and banal, and who do you think you're kidding anyway?

You know the drill.

Many times writers choose to join forces just to avoid those negative feelings and that uncertainty. Other times, necessity dictates collaboration. For *Lord of the Rings,* Peter Jackson, Fran Walsh, and Philippa Boyens collaborated because "the writing part was related to how much time I had," Peter Jackson said in an interview. "In the beginning, before we started shooting, we very much wrote the scripts together—we would sit in the same room and write scenes. I'd sit at the computer and type it in because I find, as the person who's ultimately going to direct the film, that if I write the descriptive passages, it's my first opportunity to imagine the film in my head. Fran works in longhand and writes the dialogue of the scene. Philippa does the same thing, but on her laptop. Then I sit down, take the dialogue, and write the descriptive passages around the dialogue. I'm thinking as a director, not as a screenwriter. Once I move into shooting, we're revising the script as the film is being shot, but I can participate much less in the actual physical writing process. It becomes Philippa and Fran, and I react to them, or just say, 'Yep, perfect.' My collaboration as a member of the writing team becomes one much more based on feedback and suggesting ideas. Having said that, we did spend a lot of weekends working on script stuff, all the way through the shoot."

Sometimes a producer or production company has an idea and commissions you to develop it into a screenplay, and then you're in collaboration with the producer and director. In *Raiders of the Lost Ark,* for example, Lawrence Kasdan (with only one screenwriting credit at the time, a rewrite of *The Empire Strikes Back*) met with George Lucas and Steven Spielberg. Lucas wanted to use the name of his dog, Indiana Jones, for the hero (Harrison Ford). The other thing he knew was that the last scene of the movie would be set in a vast military basement warehouse filled with thousands of crates of confiscated secrets, much as *Citizen Kane*'s basement was filled with huge crates of art. That's all Lucas knew about *Raiders* at the time. Spielberg wanted to add a mystical dimension. The three men spent two weeks locked in an office, and when they emerged, they had worked out a general story line. Then Lucas and Spielberg left to work on other projects, and Kasdan went into his office and wrote *Raiders of the Lost Ark.*

Writers collaborate for different reasons. There are times, at least on some projects, when screenwriters think it's easier to work with someone else. Most television writers work in teams, and shows like *Saturday Night Live, Desperate Housewives,* or the *CSI: Miami* and *CSI: New York* shows have a staff of anywhere from five to ten writers working on each episode. A comedy writer has to be both gagman and audience—a laugh is a laugh. Only the gifted few like Woody Allen or Neil Simon can sit in a room alone and know what's funny and what isn't.

When you decide to collaborate on a screenplay with someone, it's important to distinguish the three stages of the collaborative process: (1), establishing the ground rules of the collaboration; (2), the preparation required to write the material; and (3), the actual writing itself. All three stages are essential. If you decide to collaborate, you'd better go into it with your eyes open. For example, do you like your potential collaborator? You're going to be working with that person for several hours a day for several months, so you better enjoy being with him or her. Otherwise, you're starting off with problems.

Collaboration is a relationship. It's a fifty-fifty proposition. Two or more people are joining together *to create an end product,* a screenplay or television show or whatever. That's the aim, goal, and purpose of your collaboration, and that's where all your energy should be directed. Collaborators tend to lose sight of that very quickly.

Sometimes we get bogged down in "being right" and in the process engage in various ego struggles, so it's best you ask yourself some questions before you begin. For example, why are *you* collaborating? Why is *your partner* collaborating? What's the reason you're choosing to work with somebody else? Because it's easier? Safer? Not as lonely? Out of insecurity?

What do you think collaborating with someone looks like? That is, what kind of mental picture do you have of the collaboration? Most people have a picture of one person sitting at a desk in front of a computer or typewriter, typing like crazy, while his or her partner paces the room rapidly, snapping out words and phrases like a party planner. You know, a "writing team." A talker and a typist.

Is that the way you see it? It may have been that way at one time, during the '20s and '30s when writing teams like Moss Hart and George S. Kaufman were turning out plays and movies, but it's not that way anymore. Rather, it may be some kind of variation on what Peter Jackson did with his cowriters on *Lord of the Rings.*

Everyone works differently. We each have our own style, our own pace, our own likes and dislikes. One of the best examples of what I think represents an ideal collaboration was the musical collaboration between Elton John and Bernie Taupin back in the '70s. At the height of their musical fame, Bernie Taupin would write a set of lyrics, then fax them to Elton John, wherever he was around the world, who would then lay down the music, arrange it, and finally record it.

But that's the exception, not the rule.

If you want to collaborate, you must be willing to find the right way to work—the right style, the right methods, the right working procedure. I would suggest that you try out different things, make whatever mistakes you need to make, and just go through the collaborative process by trial and error until you find the best and easiest way for you and your partner to work together. After all, "the sequences you try that *don't* work," as my film editor friend said, "are the ones that show you what *does* work."

There are many choices in creating the ground rules of collaboration, how we go about working with each other. There really are no *rules* on how to collaborate; you get to create them and make them up as you go along. Just as in a marriage, you've got to create it, sustain it, and then maintain it. You're dealing with someone else all the time. Collaboration is a fifty-fifty proposition, with an equal division of labor.

There are four basic and equal positions in collaboration: writer, researcher, typist, and editor. No position is *more* important than another.

What does your collaboration look like to *you* and *your partner*? What are your goals? Your expectations? What do you see *yourself* doing in the collaboration? What is your *partner* going to do? If need be, you might sit down with your proposed partner and write a two- or three-page free-association essay about how you both see your collaboration. Then trade pages; you read his and he reads yours, and you both see what you've got.

Open up a dialogue. Who's going to be sitting at the computer? Where are you going to work? When? Who's going to do what? What's the best time of day for the two of you to be working? Are you going to be working alone and then e-mailing the pages to your partner to edit, or vice versa? Or are you going to be in the same room at the same time?

Talk about it. Discuss it.

Lay down the ground rules that are best for both of you. What's the division of labor? You might list the things that have to be done: two or three trips to the library, three or more interviews, etc. Organize and divide the tasks. I like to do this, so I'll do this; you do that, and so on. Do things you like to do. If you like to use the library, do it; if your partner likes to interview people, let him or her do it. Or do it together, with your partner as the lead. It's all part of the writing process. It's how you utilize your resources.

What does your work schedule look like? Do you both have full-time jobs? When are you going to get together? Where? Make sure it's convenient for both of you. If you have a job or a family or are in a relationship, sometimes it can get difficult. Deal with it.

Are you a morning person, an afternoon person, or an evening person? That is, do you work best in the morning, the afternoon, or the evening? If you don't know, try it one way and see what happens. If it's working, stay with it. If not, try it another way. See what works best for both of you. Support each other. You're working for the same thing: the completed screenplay.

You'll need a couple of weeks simply to explore and organize a work schedule that supports both of you. This might be a good time for the two of you to get together and lay out the story line.

Don't be afraid to try something that doesn't work. Just do it! Make mistakes. Create your collaboration by trial and error. And don't plan on doing any serious writing until the ground rules are set.

The last thing you're going to do is write.

Before you do that, you've got to *prepare* the material.

What kind of story are you writing? Is it a contemporary story or a historical story? A period piece? If so, what period? What do you have to do to research it? Spend one or two days or several weeks at the library? Sit in on a legal proceeding? Whatever aspect of the research you do individually, once you enter it into the computer you can e-mail it to your partner. Again, collaboration is a fifty-fifty division of labor. In terms of developing the story, it's best to work on the story together. Verbalize the story line in a few sentences. Create a subject of the screenplay, the action and the characters. Then break it down into genres: What kind of story are you writing? An action-adventure? Thriller? Love story? Drama? Romantic comedy? The first thing you have to be clear on is what kind of a story you're writing. Where does the story begin and where does it end? What's the action line? Who's the main character? What's it about? Is your story about an archeologist who uncovers ancient artifacts on a highway construction project? What is the dramatic need of your character? What kind of conflict are you going to be working with? Internal conflict—fears, emotions, loss of control—or external conflict: physical injury, an attack or war, the natural elements, survival? If you're writing a mystery story, do you know who committed the crime and why? These are the very first things you need to know. Then you can build and construct your story line.

Do you know the ending, the resolution of your story? Do you know the opening? Plot Points I and II? If *you* don't, who does? Both of you have to know where you're going so you can determine the best way of getting there.

Who is your story about? Write character biographies. You may want to talk about each character with your collaborator, and then write one biography while your partner writes another. Or you may write the biographies and your collaborator edits them. Know your characters. Talk about them, about who they are and where they come from. Feed the pot. The more you put in, the more you can take out.

After you do the character work, start building the story line on cards.

Start laying out the story line; when you know the ending, the beginning, and Plot Points I and II, you're ready to expand your story line in a scene progression using 3 × 5 cards. Discuss it. Talk about it. Argue about it. Just make sure you know your story. You may agree or disagree about certain parts of it; you may want it one way, your partner another. If you can't resolve it, write it both ways. See which way works best. Work toward the finished product—the screenplay. Always serve the material.

When you're ready to write, things sometimes get crazy. Be prepared. How are you going to put it down on paper? What are the mechanics involved? Who says what, and why is that particular word better than this particular word? Who says so? It's two sides of the same coin; *I'm* right and *you're* wrong is a point of view. So is the other point of view: *You're* wrong and *I'm* right.

I've collaborated several times in my writing career, and each time it's different. When I work with someone else on a project, I like to create a Mission Statement. What do we want to achieve or accomplish with the screenplay? For example, in my last screenplay, a science fiction epic adventure, my partner and I wanted to create an "engaging, edge-of-the-seat page-turner." Then we made an agreement to "serve the material."

Then we got together and started throwing down cards for sequences. We knew the ending, beginning, and Plot Points I and II. We got together two, sometimes three times a week for a couple of weeks, and tossed out notes, bits of dialogue, ideas for certain moments and various sequences, and different ways of structuring them. After we'd worked on this part, we got together with a bunch of cards and begin writing down ideas for scenes and sequences. We just threw them down on the cards and didn't worry about where they fit into the structure of the story line.

We spent about three to six weeks preparing the material: doing the research, fleshing out the characters, building the story line, and creating the mechanics of the collaboration. It's an interesting experience, because you're creating another kind of relationship—magic at times, hell at others.

Then, after we completed most of the preliminary work on the characters and story line, my partner, Jim, a special effects wizard, got called for a job he couldn't refuse. It was a major Hollywood special effects film, *Spider-Man 2*, and we both knew he would be working ten to twelve hours a day on it. It was great for him, but not so good for our collaboration; we knew it would leave us with little writing time for our project. So we worked very hard organizing and building the story line and structuring the narrative through line so it would be tight before he started his new job.

Once he felt established in his job and felt fairly secure in terms of deadlines and procedures, we checked in by phone at least once a week, and I began preparing some of the material and writing certain sequences based on the research we'd done, which I then e-mailed to him. Each weekend, he would go over the material I had sent, do some editing and revisions, then send it back to me. The rest of the time he spent with his family.

After a few months, we finally started getting together on weekends and going over the material, figuring out how we'd write the first act. I had already written the opening sequence, the inciting incident, and he wanted to write Act I; he did, and when he finished it, he e-mailed it to me. I edited it and returned it to him, and he made whatever changes he wanted to make. In this way, we moved forward through the project. It took us much longer with him working on *Spider-Man 2*, but we kept the story line in our consciousness so that when his job was finished, almost six months later, it took us only about three weeks to complete the first draft of the screenplay. From that point on, we e-mailed pages back and forth, revised, added scenes, discussed suggestions, and so on until we completed our first draft. All in all, it took us over a year to do this first draft. Then we spent another three or four months rewriting.

That was our collaboration. It worked fine once we established our work schedule and determined how we were going to work. But the thing we had to keep foremost in our minds at all times was how we could best serve the material. We didn't let our egos get in the way over a line or a scene.

If there's a key principle in the experience of collaboration it's to serve the material.

Collaboration means working together.

The key to collaboration—or any relationship, for that matter—is communication. You've got to talk to each other. Without communication, there's no collaboration, only misunderstanding, anger, and disagreement. That's nowhere. You are working together to write and complete a screenplay. There will be times when you'll want to chuck it and just walk away. You might think it's not worth it. You may be right, but usually it's just some of your psychological "stuff" coming up—you know, all that "stuff" from the past that we have to contend with on a day-to-day basis: the fears, insecurities, guilt, judgments, and so on. Deal with it! Writing is a process in which you learn more about yourself. Be willing to make mistakes, and to learn from each other about what is working and what isn't.

It's always good to work in thirty-page units of action. You write Act I, and your partner edits it. Your partner writes the first half of Act II, and you edit it. You write Act III, and your partner edits it. This way you see what your partner is writing and you alternate as an editor and writer in the same way that he or she does.

Sometimes you have to criticize your partner's work. How are you going to tell her that what she wrote is not working, that maybe it would be better if she starts over and rethinks the material? You'd better think about what you're going to say. Realize you'll be dealing with your partner's reactions to *your judgments.* "Judge not lest ye be judged." You've got to respect and support the other person, even if it means criticizing her work. It's nothing personal, it just isn't working the way it could be. So, what do you do? First determine *what* you want to say, then decide *how* to say it the best. If you want to say something, say it to yourself first. How would *you* feel if your partner told you what you're going to tell her?

As in marriage, the rules of collaboration are communication and surrender. After all, it's all a learning experience.

Sometimes changes have to be made in Act I before moving on to Act II. The process is exactly the same; writing is writing. Bring the material to a semirough stage, then move on. You can always polish it, so don't worry about making your pages perfect. In other words, since you're probably going to change it anyway, don't worry about how good it is. It may not be very good. So what? Just get it down; then you can work on it to make it better.

When the first act is done, and it's fairly tight and a clean "words on paper" draft, sit down to read and edit it. Is it working? Do we need another scene here? Can I cut this scene? Does the dialogue have to be clarified? Expanded? Sharpened? Is the dramatic premise clearly staged? In both word and picture? Are we setting it up properly? At this point, you may add a few lines, change a few words or a scene here and there, and occasionally sketch in certain visual aspects.

After you complete the first "words on paper" draft, put it in a drawer somewhere for a week or so, then go back and read it. See what you've got. You should be able to see it as a whole and obtain some kind of overview or perspective on the material. You might need to add some new scenes, create a new character, possibly telescope two scenes into one. Whatever you need to do, just do it!

It's all part of the writing process.

If you're married and want to collaborate with your spouse, other factors are involved. When things get difficult, for example, you can't simply walk away from the collaboration. It's part of the marriage. If the marriage is in trouble, your collaboration will only magnify what's not working with it. You can't be an ostrich and pretend a problem isn't there. Deal with it.

For example, some married friends of mine, both professional journalists, decided to write a screenplay together. She was in between assignments and he was in the middle of one, both for major magazines. She had time on her hands, so she decided to get a head start and began to research the story. She went to the library, read books, interviewed people, then entered the material. She didn't mind, figuring "*someone's* got to do it!"

He had completed his assignment by the time the research was done. They took a few days off, then got down to work. The first thing he said was "Let's see what you've got." Then he proceeded to appraise the material as if it were *his* assignment and as if some unknown researcher, not his wife and collaborator, had done the work! She was angry, but said nothing. She had done *all* the work, and now he was going to come in and *save* the project!

That's how it began. It got worse. They hadn't talked about *how* they were going to work together, only that they *would*. No ground rules had been established, no decisions made about who did what or when, and no work schedule had been set up.

As a writer, she works in the morning and writes very fast, throwing words down quickly with lots of blank spaces, then goes back and rewrites the material three or four times until she feels it's right. He, on the other hand, works best at night, writing slowly, crafting each word and phrase with delicate precision; his first draft is almost a final one.

They are both professional writers, but when they made the decision to collaborate and actually began working together, they had no idea about what to expect. She had collaborated only once before, and he had never worked with another writer in this kind of situation. They both had expectations about what the other would do, but they didn't communicate them to each other. After all, in a marriage, sometimes we take things for granted. And the cost, of course, is high.

They adjusted their mind-sets, and after they had laid out the story, they established their schedule. It was decided that she would

write the first act—which was the material she had researched—
and he would write Act II.

So, she got down to work. She was a little insecure, she told me—
after all, it was her *first* screenplay—and she worked hard to
overcome the resistance of the form that she soon encountered. She
wrote the first ten pages and then, looking for some feedback, asked
her husband to read them. She didn't know if she was on the right
track or not. Was she setting up the story correctly? Was it what they
had discussed and talked about? Were the characters real people in
real situations? Her concern was only natural.

He was working on the second scene of Act II when she gave him
the first ten pages. He didn't want to look at them because he was
having his own problems and was just beginning to find his style.
The scene was a difficult one, and he'd been working on it for several days.

He took the pages, then put them aside and went back to work,
saying nothing to his wife. She gave him a few days to read the material. When he didn't, she became angry, so he promised he would
read it that night. That satisfied her, at least for the moment.

She got up early the next morning. He was still sleeping, having
worked late the night before. She made coffee and tried to work for
a while. But it was no use. She wanted to know what her husband,
her "collaborator," thought about the pages she had written. What
was taking him so long?

The more she thought about it, the more impatient she became.
She had to know. Finally, she made a decision; what he didn't know
wouldn't hurt him. Quietly she crept into his office and softly closed
the door behind her.

She went to his desk and started riffling through his papers to
see what comments, if any, he had made on her first ten pages. She
finally found them, but there was nothing on them—no marks, no
comments, no nothing. He hadn't even read them! Angry, she
started to read his pages to see what he was so hung up about.

That's when she heard the noise on the stairs. As she turned
around the door was suddenly flung open and her husband stood
framed in the doorway, yelling, "Get away from that desk!" She tried

to explain, but he didn't listen. He accused her of spying, of meddling, of invading his privacy. She erupted, and all the anger and tension and withheld communication came pouring out. They went at it, fighting tooth and nail, no holds barred. It *all* came out: resentment, frustration, fear, anxiety, insecurity. It was a screaming match; even the dog started barking. At the peak of their "collaboration" he picked her up bodily, dragged her across the floor, and literally threw her out of the office, slamming the door in her face. She took off her shoe and stood there pounding on the door. To this day, her heel marks are etched into his office door.

Now they can laugh about it.

It wasn't funny then. They didn't speak for days.

They learned a great deal from the experience. They learned that fighting doesn't work in collaboration. They learned to work together and communicate on a more personal and professional level. They learned to criticize each other in a positive and supportive way, without fear and restraint. They learned to respect each other. They learned to serve the material. They learned that every person has a right to his or her own writing style and that you can't change it, only support it. She learned to respect the way he styles and fashions his words into polished prose. He learned to admire and respect the way she worked—fast, clean, and accurate, always getting the job done. They learned how to ask for help from each other, something that was difficult for both of them. In other words, they learned from each other, and supported each other in the same way that three men and a horse did in *Seabiscuit*.

When they completed the screenplay, they felt a sense of satisfaction and achievement in what they had accomplished. They had learned to work together not only on a physical level, but on an emotional and spiritual level as well.

Collaboration means "working together."

———————

If you decide to collaborate, design the writing experience into three stages: the ground rules, the preparation, and the mechanics of writing the material.

After It's Written

What do you do with your screenplay after you've completed it?

First, you've got to find out whether it "works" or not; whether you should engrave it in stone or paper the walls with it. You need some kind of feedback to see whether it's working and whether you wrote what you set out to write.

At this moment you may not really be sure whether it works or not. You can't see it; you're too close to it, lost in the maze of subjectivity.

Of course, the first thing you need to do before you send it out to be read by a few close friends is to back up the screenplay, either on disk or hard copy. This may be obvious, but it bears stating the obvious. Keep the backup copy someplace it will be safe. If you only have the original printout version, and have not backed it up, never give that original to anyone. You have to have a copy of the script always available to you.

I was recently retained as an expert witness in a lawsuit where the screenwriter had backed up his work only on his hard drive. He thought he was covered. When he began negotiations with a German production company on a coproduction deal, he printed out one copy and sent it off to Germany. After he sent the original hard copy, he wanted to install a DSL line so that he could e-mail his scripts with more speed and efficiency, so he hired the local phone company to install it. But the installer told him his hard drive was too full to install the line and that he had to clean it up first. Well, you can probably guess what happened. During the installation, the technician erased the entire hard drive and the writer had no backup, and because the German company had passed on the project, he had no hard copy. Basically, the writer had nothing. He had to start over, from page one, word one, and re-create the screenplay from scratch.

Sound far-fetched? Of course, but it's the truth. The moral of the story: Always back up your material.

Now you're ready to give a copy of your script to two friends, close friends, friends you can trust, friends who will tell you the truth, friends who are not afraid to tell you: "I hate it. What you've written is weak and unreal, the characters flat and one-dimensional, the story contrived and predictable." Friends who will not be afraid to hurt your feelings.

You'll find that most people won't really tell you the truth about your script. They'll tell you what *they think* you want to hear: "It's good; I liked it! I really did. You've got some nice things in it." Or "I think it's commercial," whatever that means! People's intentions are good, but they don't realize they're hurting you more by not telling you the truth, not telling you what they really think about it.

Your name is going to be on the title page, so you want it to be the best script you can write. If you feel a suggestion can improve your screenplay, use it. Any changes you make in a rewrite must be made from choice, and you have to be comfortable with those changes. This is your story, and you'll know instinctively whether the changes work or not.

Which brings us to the subject of the rewrite. You know the adage "Writing is rewriting"; well, it's true. The draft you send out into the marketplace is really three different drafts: the first "words on paper" draft; what I call "the mechanical draft"; and the third draft, "the polish." This is the draft where most of the script gets written.

After you complete the first "words on paper" draft, put it aside for a week. Then go back and reread the material from beginning to end in one sitting. Be sure to lock up all pens, pencils, and paper and to keep the computer turned off. You don't want to take any notes as you read. You just want to read. When you go through the first "words on paper" draft, you'll find yourself on the roller coaster of emotion. Some parts you think are terrible: The writing is poor, the story is all told in dialogue, the descriptions are too long, too thick, too cluttered, and what you're reading feels weak, awkward, too direct, and just doesn't work.

Then you'll read other pages that you think work okay. The dialogue is good, the action tight, and overall it seems to work pretty well. Then you'll go back on the roller coaster again, alternating between the emotions of elation and depression.

That's good.

After you've finished reading the script, put it away again. Now write three essays. The first essay, in free association, is to write what first attracted you to the material. Do this in two or three pages, more if you choose. Was it the character, the situation, the idea, or the action line that originally attracted you to the material? Just answer this question: What really attracted you to the material? Throw down your thoughts, words, and ideas. Don't worry about grammar or punctuation. Write in fragments if you want to. When you've completed this first exercise, go on to the next.

The second essay, also in free association, answers this question: What kind of a screenplay did you actually end up writing? You may have started to write a mystery-thriller with a strong love interest and ended up writing a love story with a strong mystery-thriller aspect. Many times, we'll start out writing one kind of story only to end up writing another. For example, one of my students started out to write about the relationship of a day laborer to a woman above his class, and ended up writing about the relationship between the laborer and his brother when the woman comes between them. We want a clean, coherent narrative through line in the screenplay. Write this second essay in two or three pages.

For the third essay: You saw what originally attracted you to the screenplay, and may have veered from this slightly while writing the first "words on paper" draft, so what you started out to do may be slightly different from what you ended up doing. In this third essay, you want to answer this question: What do you have to do *to change* what you *did* write into what you *wanted* to write? In other words, intention must equal result. In my student's case, she had to go back

to the beginning and establish and strengthen the relationship between the two brothers. Sometimes you'll be happy with what you
ended up with. Great! Other times you'll have to make changes.

When you've finished these three essays, think about what you
have to do to strengthen and solidify your story line so your intention equals your result.

Now read the first "words on paper" draft in units of dramatic
action. Read Act I and make notes in the margins. Out of twenty or
so scenes, you'll find you can keep ten of them intact. Of the remaining ten, you may have to change the focus in five or six of them
by rewriting dialogue and possibly adding some action, and you
may see that the remaining five scenes don't work at all. So, you'll
have to write five new scenes. All in all, you may have to change anywhere from 65 to 80 percent of Act I.

Just do it. You've spent several months working on this script, so
you want to do it right. If you sell your material, you're no doubt going to have to make changes anyway, either for the producer, director, or star. Changes are changes; nobody likes them, but we all do
them.

In Hollywood, nobody tells you the truth, what they really think;
they might tell you they like it, then add, "But it's not something we
want to do at the present time"; or "We have something like this in
development," or "We've already done this movie."

That's not going to help you. You want feedback; you want
someone to tell you what he or she really thinks about your script,
so choose the people you give this first draft to carefully.

After they've read it, listen to what they say. Don't defend what
you've written; don't *pretend* to listen to what they say and leave
feeling righteous, indignant, or hurt.

See whether they've caught the "intention" of what you wanted
to write about. Listen to their observations from the point of view
that they *might* be right, not that they *are* right. They'll have observations, criticisms, suggestions, opinions, and judgments. *Are* they
right? Question them; press them on it. Do their suggestions or
ideas make sense? Do they add to your screenplay? Enhance it? Go
over the story with them. Find out what they like and dislike; what
works for them and what doesn't. At this point, you still can't see

your screenplay objectively. If you want another opinion "just in case," be prepared to get confused. If you give it to four people, for example, they'll all disagree. One person will like the holdup of the moon rocks, another won't. One person will say he likes the holdup, but not the *result* of the holdup (the characters either get away or don't); and the other one wonders why you didn't write a love story.

It doesn't work. You want the initial feedback of two people you can trust. When you've incorporated their suggestions, then you can send it out into the market.

Your script must be clean, neat, and professional-looking, meaning it's got to be in correct industry format, with Courier 10 or 12 font. The *form* of your screenplay must be correct. Here's where a software program like Final Draft can be extremely beneficial.

Many people ask if they should number their scenes. I personally counsel them against it, but it's only a personal preference. Some people do, some people don't. Sometimes writers get hung up in the numbering, and that's really not what it's about. It's simply a matter of choice. Just know that it's not the writer's job to number the scenes. Final shooting scripts have numbers running down the left margin. They indicate scene breakdowns compiled by the *production manager,* not the writer. When a script is bought, and the director and cast are signed, a production manager is hired. The production manager and director will go over the script, scene by scene, shot by shot. Once locations are established, the production manager and his assistant will make a production board, a large foldout folio with each scene, interior or exterior, specifically notated on cardboard strips. When the production board is complete and the scenes notated and approved by the director, the production secretary types the numbers of each scene on each page for a shot-by-shot breakdown. These numbers are used to identify each shot, so when the film (maybe 300,000 to 500,000 feet of it) is processed and catalogued, every piece of film will be identified. It is not the writer's job to number the scenes.

A word about the title page. Many new and aspiring screenwriters feel they should include statements, registration or copyright information, various quotes, dates, or whatever on the title page. They want to present "The Title," an original screenplay for an "Epic

Production of a Major Motion Picture for an All-Star Cast," by John Doe, "Registered at the Writers Guild of America."

Don't do it. The title page is the title page. It should be simple and direct: "The Title" should be in the middle of the page, "A Screenplay by John Doe" directly under it, and your address or phone number in the lower-right-hand corner. Several times, as head of the story department, I would receive material from new writers without any information about where I could reach them. Those scripts were held for two months, then dumped into the wastebasket.

You don't need to include any copyright or registration information on the title page. But it is essential for you to protect your material.

There are three legal ways to claim ownership of your screenplay:

1. Copyright your screenplay: To do this, obtain copyright forms from the Library of Congress. Write to:

> Registrar of Copyright
> Library of Congress
> Washington, D.C. 20540

You can also obtain copyright forms from your local Federal Building. There is no charge for this service.

2. Place a copy of your screenplay in an envelope and send it to yourself, special delivery, return receipt requested. Make sure the postmark shows clearly; this will prove the date of authorship and will be helpful in any legal situation that may arise. When you receive the envelope, file it away. DO NOT OPEN IT! This may not stand up in a court of law, but it shows, by the date and stamp, that your screenplay was written by you on such and such a date.

3. The easiest and most effective way to register your material is with the Writers Guild of America, West or East. The Writers Guild provides a registration service that "provides evidence of the writer's prior claim to authorship of the literary material involved and the date of its completion." You may register by sending a clean copy of the script to the WGA, West or East, or by registering the material with them online. At this writing the cost for registration is

$10 for members in good standing and $20 for nonmembers. If you want to register your script by mail at the WGA, send a clean copy of your screenplay with a check for the proper amount to the Registration Office:

For writers west of the Mississippi:
> Writers Guild of America, West:
> 7000 West Third Street
> Los Angeles, CA 90048
> Within Southern California: (323) 951-4000
> Outside Southern California: (800) 548-4532
> Fax: (323) 782-4800
> www.wga.org

For writers east of the Mississippi:
> Writers Guild of America, East
> 555 West 57th Street, Suite 1230
> New York, NY 10019
> Tel: (212) 767-7800
> Fax: (212) 582-1909
> www.wgae.org

To register online, go to www.wga.org and click "register your script online."

If you register by mail, they will take the clean copy of your screenplay, microfilm it, and store it in a safe place for ten years, at which time you can renew the material again. Your receipt is proof that you've written what you say you've written. If someone does plagiarize your material, and you can prove "prior access," your attorney will subpoena the Custodian of Records of the WGA, who will appear in your behalf.

There have been times when a writer has submitted material to a producer or studio and it's been rejected, and sometime later the writer has seen his/her idea in a movie and thinks the concept was ripped off. Sometimes this happens, and sometimes people *think* it happens. Several years ago, the world-famous humorist-journalist Art Buchwald, with Alain Bernheim, wrote a movie treatment for a film called *Coming to America* for Paramount Pictures. A deal was negotiated and they were paid. The studio ultimately passed on the idea and Buchwald continued with his journalistic chores. Later, an Eddie Murphy movie was released by Paramount that seemed to have been taken directly from the treatment that Buchwald and Bernheim had written. Buchwald filed a lawsuit against Paramount Pictures claiming the studio had taken their idea and not paid them for it.

The lawsuit garnered a lot of headlines, and also set a major precedent. In order to prove their case, Buchwald and Bernheim had to reveal studio accounting practices, which was a monumental task, to say the least. Finally, after a long litigation, the court awarded them some $900,000 for copyright infringement. They'd been able to prove "prior access," meaning they proved they had submitted their idea to Paramount.

Many times you'll hear writers worrying about whether to submit a screenplay to a studio or production company because of fears their ideas will be stolen. Well, according to copyright law, you "cannot copyright an idea, only the *expression* of the idea." An idea is three guys stealing moon rocks from Houston's NASA facility. *How* they do it, and *who* the characters *are* who do it, is "the expression of the idea." That's why if you write an unsolicited screenplay and want to submit it to a studio or production company, you will be asked to sign a release forgoing any right to litigate over any claims, either now or in the future, of copyright infringement.

For example, many years ago a friend of mine wrote a script for a movie that was about a competitive skier on the European ski circuit. She sent it to a number of production companies. The companies all returned the material with a "thanks, but no thanks" letter.

A couple of years later she went to see a movie about a skier on the European ski circuit, made by a company she had submitted her script to. She saw a number of similarities to her screenplay. In fact, she thought it was her story.

So, she went to court and filed a lawsuit and ultimately was granted a settlement because she proved prior access—she had registered her script at the WGA, West, and had a copy of the rejection letter from the production company.

Nobody did anything "intentional" in this situation. The production company had refused her idea, for whatever reason, and when later it went looking for a subject for a film, someone "had an idea" about a competitive skier.

There have been other times when a movie is released, and writers who have written a work, usually an unproduced novel or screenplay, claim copyright infringement. They had submitted their material to the company but it was returned, unopened and unread. They had no case. They could not prove prior access, and while the ideas may have been somewhat similar, the "expressions of the idea" were not. I've been called as an expert witness on several of these cases, and not one was legally substantiated.

When you're ready to get your material into the marketplace, you'll need about ten copies. Most story executives don't return material. If you send it to a producer or company, you'll need to keep a record of when you sent it and to whom. If you do send it to a company, someone must know the script is coming, either through e-mail or as hard copy. Otherwise, the material will be deleted, or returned unread, as no release form was signed. (Sending a self-addressed, stamped envelope with your material simply lets the producer or story editor know you're a novice screenwriter. Don't do it. The chances are it won't be returned anyway.) So, make ten copies. You'll register one, either online or as hard copy. That leaves nine. If you're fortunate enough to get an agent to represent you, or hire an entertainment attorney, they'll want five copies immediately. That leaves you with four.

Make sure your screenplay is bound with paper fasteners; do not submit it loose. If you want, you can put a simple cover on it, a cover that bears some connection to the screenplay. Do not use a fancy, embossed leatherette cover. Make sure your script is on 8 ½ × 11 paper, and not 8 ½ × 14, legal size.

You've got one shot with your script, so make it count. One shot means this: When I was head of the story department at Cinemobile, every submission received was logged in a card file and cross-indexed by title and author. The material was read, evaluated, and written up in synopsis form. It's called "coverage." The reader's comments were carefully registered, then filed away.

If you submit your screenplay to a studio or production company, and they read and reject it, and then you decide to rewrite it and resubmit it, chances are it won't be read. The reader will pull up the original synopsis, read the coverage, and pass on the material. If you do make changes, change the title, or use a pseudonym. No one reads the same material twice.

Do not send a synopsis of your script along with your material; it will not be read. No one in Hollywood will read a treatment unless you're an established screenwriter. In Canada, Europe, South America, and perhaps the Far East, a writer can often sell his/her treatment and get money (though not much) from the government-subsidized film industry to develop the story into a screenplay—but that's only on the international film scene. In Hollywood, if you send a synopsis with your material it will be to your disadvantage and like as not, immediately thrown out. Usually, a screenplay has to pass the gauntlet of "The Reader." Decisions about whether or not to seriously consider a particular screenplay are usually based on this reader's comments.

So then how do you get it to people? Since most people in Hollywood don't accept unsolicited material—that is, they don't accept material unless it's submitted through an authorized literary agent, an agent who has signed the Artists-Managers Agreement drawn up by the WGA—the question then becomes: Do I need an agent to sell my script, and if so, how do I get an agent?

I hear that question over and over again. If you're going to sell your script for a cool million or more and have Tom Cruise and Julia Roberts star in it, you'll need a literary agent. So, how do you get an agent?

First, you must have a completed screenplay. An outline, or treatment, doesn't work. Then you can contact the Writers Guild of America, West or East, and ask them, by e-mail, mail, or phone, to send you the list of authorized signatory agents to the Artists-Managers Agreement. They'll send you a list of agents. Those agents who are willing to read unsolicited material from new writers are indicated, usually with an asterisk.

List several of them. Contact them by mail, e-mail, or phone; ask if they would be interested in reading a screenplay by a new writer.

Give your background; sell yourself. Everybody is a buyer and seller in Hollywood.

Most of them will say no. Try some more. They'll say no, too. Try some more. Hollywood is a "no" town; it's easier to say no than yes. But just think what would happen if someone were to say yes to the material.

If the film goes through the line of executives to finally be "green-lit" for production, and the film does get made, and does well at the box office, that's a dream come true for you. On the other hand, if it doesn't do well, the person who brought in the material may be let go. After all, there are millions of dollars riding on his/her decision. The average life span of a film executive in Hollywood is about five years.

Be that as it may, the irony is that executives are always looking for good material. There is a dearth of salable material in Hollywood. Most of the screenplays submitted are derivative of old movies or television series or are takeoffs or satires on films that have already been made. The opportunities for new screenwriters, writing fresh and original ideas, are enormous.

Most of the time when you're seeking representation, you'll talk to the agent's assistant or secretary. Sometimes they'll even be the ones to read your screenplay. If they like it they'll recommend it. Let anyone who wants to read your script read it. A good script does not go unfound. As long as it's legally protected, there's usually not a problem.

Even if an agent likes your screenplay, he/she may not be able to sell it. But he will be able to show it around as a sample of your writing ability. As one agent told me, there's nothing as hot as a script that "almost" gets sold. Sometimes that will lead to a rewriting assignment, or an opportunity to pitch another one of your script ideas. Sometimes, if a producer or story editor likes your work, you may be able to get a "development deal" from a studio or producer to write an original, or to adapt one of their ideas or books into a screenplay. Everybody's looking for writers, no matter what "they" say.

Give the agent three to six weeks to read your material. If you don't receive a reply from him or her within that period of time, you can call.

If you submit your script to a large, well-known agency, like William Morris, ICM, or CAA, the established agents will ignore it. But they have readers and trainee agents there, and they all have an incentive to read it and possibly discover a marketable script.

If you're fortunate, you might even find someone who likes your work and wants to represent you.

Who is the best agent?

The agent who likes *your* work and wants to represent *you*.

If you contact eight agents, you'll be lucky to find one who likes your work. You can submit your script to more than one agent at a time, but not at the same agency.

A literary agent gets a 10 to 15 percent commission on whatever he or she sells. Good material does not get away from the readers in Hollywood; they can spot potential movie material within ten pages. If your script is good and worthy of production, it's going to be found. *How* it's found is another matter.

It's a survival process. Your screenplay is entering the raging current of the Hollywood river, and like salmon swimming upstream to spawn, only a few will make it.

If finding an agent the "normal" way is not working for you, a good way to get your work read and possibly "discovered" is by submitting it in one of the many screenwriting contests that now exist throughout the world. A mention to a production company that your script has been selected as one of the finalists, or winners, in a prominent screenwriting contest like the Nichols Fellowship, Final Draft's Big Break Contest, the Chesterfield Competition, Script-Shark's Annual Screenwriting Competition, the Diane Thomas Award, or any of several other competitions, carries a strong appeal in the exclusive world of Hollywood. Each contest receives from three to five thousand entries each year, and at present there are over a thousand of them; just go online and Google "screenwriting contests." Take a look at the Database of Screenwriting Contests and Competitions (www.filmmakers.com/contests) and you'll find a list of contests and information on financial prizes, entry dates, deadlines, etc. The legitimate contests offer awards of up to $10,000 cash, as well as meetings with top agents and executives in the industry. I've been one of the judges for the Final Draft competition several times now and can tell you that the quality of the work is high. Many of the winners have gone on to find agents and have their screenplays produced. That's a good percentage of success, and a good way to break into the business.

Another way to bring your script to the attention of production executives is called "online posting." For a fee you can send your script to an online literary service like ScriptShark.com, a division of Baseline StudioSystems. ScriptShark is a professional script coverage and story development service specifically designed for the entertainment industry. It works this way: You submit your screenplay to ScriptShark and an industry reader will read and evaluate your material, then give you professional feedback. If the reader likes the material, he/she will post the synopsis of the story on the service's Web site. Most development and creative executives from major production companies check the postings daily because they're always looking for new material; thus it's a good way to get your material seen without going through an agent or attorney. And indeed, ScriptShark has been instrumental in helping more than one writer move forward professionally. Several screenwriters have sold/optioned scripts, and ScriptShark has assisted them in setting up pitch meetings, landing writing assignments, and getting representation.

After you complete your screenplay, you're entering the battlefield. Last year, more than seventy-five thousand screenplays were registered at the Writers Guild of America, West and East. Do you know how many movies the studios and independent production companies made last year? Not that many: between four and five hundred. And while the number of studio productions today is increasing *slightly,* the number of people writing screenplays is *dramatically* increasing. As the number of people writing screenplays is increasing, so is the cost of making movies—it costs several thousand dollars a minute to make a major Hollywood production. That's why even a medium-budget movie in Hollywood today costs somewhere between $60 and $80 million—and the cost of prints and advertising is mind-boggling. A Hollywood production has to gross at least two and a half times its negative cost to break into profit. So, if a film cost $60 million to produce, it has to gross more than $150 million to just to break even. Not many films gross $150 million. And if a film doesn't open in its first or second weekend with good numbers, it will just disappear after a few weeks. But with the ancillary markets, foreign markets, the DVD market, merchandising products, and TV and cable sales, at some point in the future the film might still make some kind of profit.

The only thing that does not change is the story. You may have the greatest special effects in the world, or the most popular actors in the world, but if there is no story that engages the hearts and minds and emotions of the audience, you don't have much of anything. The story is the center, the hub, the dynamic force that holds everything together. *Sideways* is a good example. Adapted from a novel by Rex Pickett, written by Alexander Payne and Jim Taylor, starring four largely unknown actors, it is an exceptional movie. You can make a good movie from a good script; you can make a good movie from a mediocre script; but you can't make a good movie from a bad script. And that's where all your energies should go—into writing the best script you can.

What kind of a deal can you expect to make if someone wants to buy your screenplay? Prices vary, but a good rule of thumb is the Writers Guild of America minimum. The minimum is broken down into two categories: a low-budget movie that costs between $1.2 and $5 million to produce, and a high-budget film that costs more than $5 million. At this writing, the WGA minimum for a low-budget, original screenplay, including a treatment, is $48,738; for a high-budget film, $91,495. These minimums will increase each time a new MBA (Minimum Basic Agreement) is negotiated.

Most screenwriters don't sell their first screenplay, but there are exceptions. One of my former students at the Professional Writing Program at USC wrote her thesis script and started sending it around. An agent's assistant read it, liked it, and gave it to her boss; he read it, liked it, and sent it to a friend of his, a production executive. The executive liked it, told the agent, and the agent promptly sent it out and sold it for about $600,000. Now, the writer didn't get all this money up front. She got a few thousand dollars when she signed the agreement, and if and when the producer gets a production/distribution agreement, she'll get a large chunk; then, on the first day of principal photography, she'll get another chunk, and there may even be a "production bonus."

An "eyeball" price for a screenplay used to be 5 percent of the budget, though that varies substantially. If you sell the script, you'll probably receive a "percentage of the profits," at least on paper. You may get anywhere from 2.5 to 5 percent of the producer's net—whatever you can get. But since hardly any films ever show a profit, at least in the accountants' books, the chances are slim to none that you'll ever receive any of your percentage.

If someone wants to buy your script, he/she will probably *option* it for a year, with an option for a second. With an option, someone pays you for the exclusive right to get a "deal" or to raise financing for a certain period of time, usually a year or two. The option price may be anything, from $1 a year to $100,000 or more—whatever you, or your attorney, can negotiate.

It may take you more than a year after you receive your option money to receive the full amount for the screenplay. This is the standard-type "step deal" in Hollywood. The numbers may vary, but the procedure will not.

If you do get an offer on your script, let someone represent you, either an agent or an attorney. An attorney will either charge by the hour or receive 5 percent of your earnings from the project.

You can obtain an option for a book or novel just like a screenplay. If you want to adapt a book or novel, you must obtain the motion picture and theatrical rights to it. To find out if the material is available, call the publisher of the hardbound edition. Ask, either by mail, e-mail, or phone, for the subsidiary rights department. Inquire if the motion picture and theatrical rights are available. If they are, they'll tell you or refer you to the literary agent who represents the author. Contact the agent, who will tell you whether the rights are available or not.

If you decide to adapt the material without obtaining the motion picture rights, you might find you've wasted your time, that the rights are not available and somebody else owns them. If you can find out who has the rights, that person or company might be willing to read your screenplay. Or might not.

If you want to adapt the material simply as an exercise, do it. Just be sure you know what you're doing so you're not wasting your time.

It costs so much to make a movie today that everyone wants to minimize the risk; that's why money paid to a writer is termed "front money," or "risk money."

No one likes to take a risk. And the motion picture business is one of the biggest crapshoots around. No one knows whether a given film is going to "go through the roof," like *Star Wars, Titanic,* and *Lord of the Rings,* and people are reluctant to put up a lot of front money for an uncertain return. Do you know anyone who spends money easily? Including yourself? Studios, production companies, and independent producers are no exception.

Option money comes out of producers' pockets and they want to minimize the risks. So don't expect a lot of money for your material the first time out: It just doesn't work that way.

There are always exceptions, of course, and these are the ones you always hear about—but they *are* the exceptions, not the rule.

When you really get down to it, you're writing your screenplay for yourself first, for money second.

Only a handful of well-known and established writers in Hollywood get enormous sums of money for their screenplays. There are about 9,500 members of the Writers Guild, West, and only a few are hired to write screenplays. And less than a handful earn six figures a year. And those who do earn every penny of it.

Don't set up unreal expectations for yourself.

Just write your screenplay.

Then worry about how much money you're going to make.

Like the ancient scripture the Bhagavad Gita says: "Don't be attached to the fruits of your actions." You are writing your screenplay because it's something you want to do, not because you want to sell it for a lot of money. It just doesn't work that way.

Keep your dreams and reality separate. They're two distinct worlds.

A Personal Note

"Hope is a good thing, maybe the best of
things, and no good thing ever dies."

—*The Shawshank Redemption*
Frank Darabont

When I first started out as a writer and teacher, I asked myself what I wanted to accomplish in my teaching and books, and the answer was always the same: I wanted screenwriters to write better movies, movies that would serve and inspire audiences around the world to find their common humanity. I knew future technologies would emerge and that there would be new, more advanced ways of telling stories with pictures. But I felt that if people understood what makes a good story, what makes a good screenplay, it would be of value to filmmakers and audience alike. When I uncovered the *paradigm*, I didn't really discover anything new; this concept of storytelling has been around since Aristotle's time. I simply uncovered what was already there, gave it a name, and illustrated how it worked in contemporary movies.

Over the last few years there's been a significant technological evolution going on in the world of film, and understanding the role of dramatic structure in the screenplay has become the focus of intense and international debate. The discussion rages between conventional and unconventional methods of storytelling, between linear and nonlinear means of storytelling, between *Chinatown* and *The Manchurian Candidate; The Lord of the Rings* and *The Bourne Supremacy; Thelma & Louise* and *Pulp Fiction; The Shawshank Redemption* and *The Hours; Y Tu Mamá También* and *Run Lola Run;* and many, many more. Of course, each screenplay, each story, is unique and individual, but I find these debates good because they inspire conversations of discovery, new points of departure in the evolution of the screenplay. The essence of structure does not change; only the form changes, the way in which the story is put together. And if that leads to new ways of telling stories with pictures, then I've accomplished what I set out to do. So while "we may be through with the past," as the Narrator says in *Magnolia*, "the past may not be through with us."

I believe the silver screen is like a mirror, reflecting our thoughts, our hopes, our dreams, our successes, our failures. Writing a screenplay and going to the movies is an ongoing journey, a lifetime adventure; for those images on the page and those dancing shadows of light on the giant screen simply reflect our lives, where the end might be the beginning, and the beginning the end.

As I sit in a darkened theater, I'm sustained by an unbridled hope and optimism. I don't know whether I'm looking for answers to my own questions about life, or whether I'm sitting in the dark silently giving thanks that I'm not up there on that giant screen confronting the struggles and challenges I'm seeing. But I do know that somewhere in those reflected images, I may glean an insight, an awareness, a hope that might embrace the personal meaning of my life.

I think about this as I look back over the footprints of my journey. I see where I began my trek, gaze over the ground I've covered, the trails I've traversed, and understand it's not the destination but the journey itself that is both the goal and the purpose.

Just like writing a screenplay. It's one thing to *say* you're going to do it; it's another to *do* it.

Everybody's a writer.

That's what you'll find out. As you share your enthusiasm about your screenplay, everybody will have a suggestion, a comment, or a better idea about what *they* would have done. Then they'll tell you about the great idea *they* have for a screenplay.

Try not to make any judgments about what you've written. It might take years for you to "see" your script objectively. You may never. Judgments of "good" or "bad" or "right" or "wrong," or comparisons between "this" and "that," are meaningless within the creative experience.

It is what it is.

Hollywood is a "dream factory," a town of talkers. Go to any of the various hangouts around town and you'll hear people talking about the scripts they're going to write, the movies they're going to produce, the deals they're going to make.

It's all talk.

Action is character, right? What a person *does,* and not what he says, is who he *is.*

Everybody's a writer.

There is a tendency in Hollywood to second-guess the writer; the studio, the star, the director, the producer will all make changes in the script that they think will "improve" it. Sometimes they do, and sometimes they don't. Most people in Hollywood assume they're "larger" than the original material. "*They*" know what has to be done to "make it better." Directors do this all the time.

A film director can take a great script and make a great film. Or he can take a great script and make a terrible film. But he can't take a terrible script and make a great film.

No way.

Some film directors know how to improve a screenplay by visually tightening the story line. They can take a wordy dialogue scene of three to four pages and condense it into a tense and dramatic three-minute scene that "works" with five lines of dialogue, three looks, somebody taking a drink, a dog barking, and an insert of a clock on the wall. Michael Mann did this in *Collateral;* he sculpted the original screenplay by Stuart Beattie, visually tightening it into a tension-packed film that captures both the essence and the integrity of the script.

That's the exception, not the rule.

The rule is that most directors and stars in Hollywood have little or no story sense at all. They'll second-guess the writer, making changes in the story line that weaken and distort it, and eventually a lot of money is spent making a lousy film that nobody wants to see. And you're only as good as your last film.

In the long run, of course, everybody loses—the studios lose money, the director adds a "flop" to his "track record," and the writer takes the rap for writing a bad screenplay.

Everybody's a writer.

Some people will complete their screenplays. Others won't. Writing is hard work, a day-by-day job, five or six days a week, three or more hours a day. And some days are better than others. A professional writer is someone who sets out to achieve a goal and then does it. Just like life. Writing is a personal responsibility; either you do it or you don't. And then there's the old "natural law" of survival and evolution.

There are no "overnight success stories" in Hollywood. Like the saying goes, "The overnight success took fifteen years to happen."

Believe it. It's true.

Professional success is measured by persistence and determination. The motto of the McDonald's Corporation is summed up in its poster called "Press On":

> *Nothing in the world can take the place*
> *of persistence.*
> *Talent will not; nothing is more common*
> *than unsuccessful men with talent.*
> *Genius will not; unrewarded genius*
> *is almost a proverb.*
> *Education will not;*
> *the world is full of educated derelicts.*
> *Persistence and determination alone*
> *are omnipotent.*

When you complete your screenplay, you've accomplished a tremendous achievement. You've taken an idea, expanded it into a dramatic or comedic story line, then sat down and spent several weeks or months writing it. Inception through completion. It's a satisfying and rewarding experience. It's been your best friend and your worst enemy. It's kept you up nights and let you sleep like a baby. "True art is in the *doing* of it," Jean Renoir said.

Commitment and sacrifice are two sides of the same coin.

Wear that proudly.

Talent is God's gift. Either you have it or you don't. Don't let selling or not selling your screenplay alter your internal state of mind, your feelings about yourself. Don't let it interfere with the experience of writing. In the long run, you did what you set out to do. You fulfilled your hopes and dreams, fulfilled your goal.

Writing brings its own rewards. Enjoy them.

Pass it on.

Index